BERURIA THE *TANNAIT*

A Theological Reading of a Female Mishnaic Scholar

Dalia Hoshen

University Press of America,® Inc.
Lanham · Boulder · New York · Toronto · Plymouth, UK

Copyright © 2007 by
University Press of America,® Inc.
4501 Forbes Boulevard
Suite 200
Lanham, Maryland 20706
UPA Acquisitions Department (301) 459-3366

Estover Road
Plymouth PL6 7PY
United Kingdom

All rights reserved
Printed in the United States of America
British Library Cataloging in Publication Information Available

Library of Congress Control Number: 2007929173
ISBN-13: 978-0-7618-3810-4 (paperback : alk. paper)
ISBN-10: 0-7618-3810-4 (paperback : alk. paper)

∞™ The paper used in this publication meets the minimum
requirements of American National Standard for Information
Sciences—Permanence of Paper for Printed Library Materials,
ANSI Z39.48—1984

Contents

Preface v

Introduction 1
Methodology 2

1. Introduction to a Talmudic Theory of Status 9

2. Beruria and the Theological Theory of Torah 21

3. The Teachings of Beruria the *Tannait* 31
Halakha 31
Halakha and Aggada 37
Beruria the Halakhist-Aggadist 38
Sins and Repentance 43
The Aggadist: The Fertile Scholar 48
The Engulfing Presence of Torah and the Scholar's Union 51
Sexuality, Existentialism, Torah 54

4. The Post-Talmudic Beruria and Talmudic Culture: "The Beruria Incident" 69
"The Beruria Incident" as a Commentary to the Talmudic Text 70
"The Beruria Incident" as an Independent Talmudic Piece 73
Torah Study and the Deviant Wife 78

Discussion 1: Preference of Torah Over Commandments	81
Discussion 2: On Sex, Transgression, and Teaching	87
Ben Azzai	87
R. Eliezer	88
R. Joshua	90
5. The Talmudic Story of Beruria in Context	**113**
R. Eliezer ben Hyrcanus	115
R. Ḥananya ben Teradion	119
Beruria: The Fire Covenant of Father and Daughter	130
Final Word	132
Abbreviations	**141**
Bibliography	**143**
Index	**149**

Preface

My interest in the character of Beruria began almost two decades ago, when I was a research fellow at the Shalom Hartman Institute in Jerusalem. At a conference dedicated to Women and study of Torah in Judaism, the figure of Beruria arose in the context of the feminist discourse.

In the light of my experience as a young PhD student in Talmud, I was not convinced of the relevance of the criteria of feminist discourse to the comprehension of the Talmudic culture and its basic concepts. I felt that the value of Torah and the function of its study as expressed through its scholars are associated with the theological-philosophical realm of the Talmudic conception of Torah as the divine logos in its relation to Man. I found the Torah better located within that theological sphere than within the sociological or political field, where the Talmudic community utilized the Torah for its needs and in its internal power struggles. Thus, I tended to think that the phenomenon of Beruria in Talmudic literature, as a female scholar, also belongs to the theological sphere of the conception of the Torah, and not to the sociological sphere of her being a woman.

It is not surprising that my non-feminist perspective on Beruria was not popular among traditional Talmudic scholars, nor among my research peers. Therefore, in order to explain my new perception, I had to construct an alternative discourse on social status in the Talmud, with implications for women's status in particular. To this purpose, I wrote a form of introduction to a discussion of women's status in the Talmudic sources, whereas Beruria served as a paradigm for the entire theory.

I taught and presented the findings of that research, initially composed in Hebrew, and later translated into English in various forums. The responses I received regarding the status theory in its application to Beruria were quite varied. The reactions ranged from fascination for how such a theory could be taught by a woman to a feeling that if a woman had not authored the paper, the theory would have been branded chauvinistic.

The huge growth of interest in women's studies in various disciplines beckoned me back to the theory of status and Beruria over the last few years. Beruria's persona has surfaced in research wholly in the feminist context. This trend has driven me to reanalyze the theological Talmudic theory, and to a new comprehensive examination of the Beruria texts. For the first time, the result revealed a unique doctrine of this female scholar, in its general philosophy as well as in various Talmudic branches. Surprisingly, I discovered strong bonds between Beruria's teaching and familiar positions in the Talmudic world, even those which had been thought of for generations as misogynist.

Indeed, the philosophical-theological methodology I applied challenges not only the modern, but also the traditional approaches, which feminized Beruria's persona, and viewed the entire Talmudic culture along the feminine dimension. This cast a dark shadow on the question of continuity between Talmudic and traditionalist cultures.

My study of the character of Beruria has engaged over the years many people, some of whose names I have alas forgotten. Students and members of various audiences have asked invaluable questions, sharpening points for discussion. Colleagues and readers from various disciplines have read this draft, and have expressed their impressions and criticisms. People of sharp thinking and florid language, have each contributed their time and interest to this creation. I would like to thank them all.

I would like to thank those who contributed to the final form of the research. Firstly, I would like to thank the staff of the Jewish National Library in Jerusalem, who ensured I never lacked a book or pamphlet I needed. I would like to thank Dr. Avraham Greenbaum, who was the first editor of the book, accompanied me at its various stages, and ensured it metamorphosed from idea to reality, through endless appreciation and encouragement. I would like to thank Eve Golditch, who read the manuscript and made valuable comments. Thanks to Chana Stein who contributed a great deal of her time in editing the manuscript. Lastly, Moshe, my husband, who was my *hevruta* (friend and colleague) to this study in its various evolutions during the last seventeen years, left his imprint on the book's ideas and form. Thanks beyond words!

Dalia Hoshen
Jerusalem, Israel
October 2006, *Tishre* 5767

Introduction

This study is devoted to second century Beruria,[1] the only female scholar who appears in Talmudic literature.[2] As Judaism passed through cultural changes under the "troubles of the times," the teachings of this character were not studied, nor was the integration of her scholarship integration into the broad scope of the Talmudic teachings. Furthermore, the keys to the conceptual system of the Talmudic world (in its various strata) seem to have been lost during the time of post-Talmudic Judaism, and with them the ability to understand the functioning of religious phenomena in Talmudic culture.

This is true as regards the Talmudic world as a whole—its principles and its scholars. It is even truer in regard to Beruria. The texts attributed to her are few. Most of them are not in the area considered important by the post-Talmudic Rabbis, because they were not in the legal (halakhic) area. In addition, the question of her status as a woman took precedence over interest in her scholarship. Even worse, at some point in history, this question led to scorn for her scholarship and even to its total negation. Thus, we hear in modern scholarship the argument that this female sage never existed, or that the learning attributed to her by the Talmudic literature is of little value. This denuding of Beruria from her scholarship has made her a hollow figure, which, in the opinion of these scholars, serves only as a reflection of the Talmudic literature and culture. These last two are not viewed as part of the world of learning, but rather in the political arena of showing power, and of power struggles, and in the psychoanalytic arena of fears and suppressions—here obviously applied to the inter-sexual realm.

Following the sources (3rd–5th c.) which testify to Beruria's scholarship, this study will attempt to return this figure to that scholarly sphere. By our new conceptual theory, we will show that the scholarship of Beruria, as a female scholar, is in keeping with the relation between scholarship and status as it appears in the Talmudic literature. This relation distinguishes between Commandments, which belong to the socio-biological stratum of Man, and Torah, which belongs to the divine nature of God. Thus, the question of status in general, and women's status in particular, belongs to the theological relations between these two strata.

Applying the theological theory of status to the Talmudic literature pulls the rug from under the claim that such a figure as Beruria the scholar could not have existed in the Talmudic world. Furthermore, when looking in depth at Beruria's texts, and exposing her conception in its particular method and features, we find it well integrated with other known conceptions appearing in the Talmudic literature. Beruria's method concerning Law (Halakha), Thought (Aggada), and Exegesis (Midrash) is found to be very close to that of the first/second century Mishnaic sage, R. Eliezer ben Hyrcanus, whose philosophy is symbolized by fire features.[3] This "fire conception" will be the model according to which Beruria's philosophy is compared with that of R. Eliezer. The affinity to R. Eliezer shows that Beruria's scholarship is rooted in Talmudic soil. Beyond this, the affinity between these two scholars has particular importance, since in post-Talmudic literature R. Eliezer was conceived as the great opponent of women's scholarship, and as the originator of a prohibition to teach them Torah.

This paradoxical point, whereby the analysis of the Talmudic sources gives results contrary to those which are deduced by the post-Talmudic literature, reflects the crisis in Jewish culture over the ages. Hence, we must apply caution when approaching the analysis of the Talmudic literature by itself, not to join the contemporary populist tendency[4] to place all kinds of sources under a single roof using terms like "Judaism," "Our fathers,"[5] "Tradition", and so on. This is true when examining all questions in Jewish culture, but especially when examining the question of status, and of a female scholar such as Beruria.

Methodology

The textual methodology employed in this study distinguishes between the Talmudic and post-Talmudic literature (halakhic or non-halakhic). Even though the latter rests on the former by quotations and traditions, commentary and subject studies, there is not necessarily continuity between the two.[6] The accepted end of the period of the Sages (*HaZaL*, or what is considered to be within the Talmudic literature) is the Arab conquest (7th c.).[7] From both sides of this historical border differences are reflected. The differences between the two periods are not merely linguistic, structural or conceptual, but, as we have argued elsewhere, "texto-cultural."[8] This means, in brief, that the midrashic-exegetical culture is reflected in the Sages' sources, in contrast to the later, non-midrashic texts.[9] Obviously, the post-Talmudic literature is indispensable to a deeper understanding of the Talmudic literature, both because of its proximity in time and because of its preservation of interpretational traditions. But the original Talmudic literature ought also to be examined by itself, independent of the later literature. Even within these two broad periods, sub-divisions[10] can be discerned (Talmudic: tannaitic,[11] amoraic,[12] savoraic[13]; Post-Talmudic: Geonim,[14] Rishonim,[15] Aharonim[16]), based on particularity, discontinuity, or development.[17] However, we argue that it is the deviation from the midrashic process, which creates the main literary dichotomy (Talmudic vs. Post-Talmudic).[18] From the Geonic period onwards, we may observe the process of separating the Halakha (the study of the legal part of Torah) from the Aggada (the study of the non-legal part of Torah).[19] This distinction was part of a general trend to canonize the halakhic part of the Talmud by turning the Talmud into an authoritative ruling book.[20] This trend was articulated in the first Geonic generations[21] by their literary patterns of mutilated *halakhot* and codes, as well as by the great project of the Responsa in the late Geonic generations. Along with the canonization of the halakhic part of the Talmud, we find the secularization of the aggadic part.

R. Sherira Gaon (10th c.) says:

> Regarding the *aggadot*—these things that are deduced from Scripture and are called Midrash and Aggada, they are "assessments" (*omdana*). Therefore, we do not rely on them, as it was said; we do not learn from the *aggadot* . . . and what seems right in them and is rational and supported by Scripture we will accept, and there is no conclusion nor end (*tichla vakez*) to the *aggadot*.[22]

His son R. Hai Gaon (10th–11th c.) says:

> You should know that aggadic sayings are not as Halakha, but everyone learns (*doresh*)[23] what ever occurs to him; namely, they are not clear-cut (*hatukh*). Therefore, we do not rely on them.[24]

The secularization of the Midrash and Aggada means not merely applying a rational criterion to "all these things which are deduced from Scripture," but implies rationalism as a prerequisite for actually accepting or rejecting them. More strictly, it cancels their authority as Torah in the sense of *"hora'a"* (instruction/obligation),[25] which would have required continuing to learn them, even though they were not accepted as laws (*"devarim she'enam halakha"*).[26]

The duality of Halakha and Aggada shaped rabbinical creativity during the next millennium, which was limited increasingly to the realm of Halakha. The latter too was severed from its midrashic root, and was valued only for its final legal nature. The rationalist attitude to the Aggada eventually led to the complete neglect of Midrash and Aggada. As there was neither necessity nor obligation to accept them, there was no intellectual drive for the creative resolution of irrationality and paradoxes, as in the case of Halakha.[27] The divergence of the post-Talmudic literature from the midrashic-aggadic domain is expressed by the neglect of aggadic texts within the Talmudic sources,[28] and also by the cessation of the midrashic process itself in the part of the Halakha, which crystallized the Talmudic text.[29] This led to the isolation of the post-Talmudic literature from the scriptural channels,[30] and consequently the weakening of that cultural attachment.[31] The change of cultural direction in post-Talmudic literature enabled alien influences (Arab, or later Christian) to take root. These influences had an impact on halakhic interpretation and methodologically weakened the original link between the halakhic and aggadic domains.

Hence, when we come to investigate the figure of Beruria we will focus on the Talmudic sources. We will, however, not ignore the relevant post-Talmudic commentary and rulings. Nonetheless, when referring to them as a potential interpretation of the Talmudic sources, we will be aware of the cultural differences between these two types of texts.[32]

But first, in order to understand the phenomenon of the Mishnaic female scholar, we must sketch the epistemological lines along which any discussion of women's status in the Talmudic literature should be examined.

Notes

1. See below p. 22, a discussion concerning the historical question regarding this figure.

2. "Talmudic literature" in its broad meaning includes in addition to the Talmuds, Tosefta and the Midrashim.

3. See D. Hoshen, "The Fire Symbol in Talmudic-Aggadic Exegesis" (PhD diss., Bar-Ilan University, 1989); *id.* "Semiotics as a Religious Question," in *Approaches to Ancient Judaism, New Series*, vol. 5, ed. H. W. Basser and S.

Fishbane (Atlanta: Scholars Press, 1993), 69–77; *id.* "Fire in Revelation and Torah Study," *Le'ela* 52 (2000): 35–42.

4. About this criticism, see E. E. Urbach, *The Sages, Their Concepts and Beliefs* (Jerusalem: The Magnes Press, 1975), 4–5, D. Hoshen, "Agnon's Writing: An Additional Tier in the Talmudic-Aggadic Literature" (PhD diss., Bar-Ilan University, 2000), 35, 56; *id. Agnon: A Saga is (not) a Talmudic Sugia* (Jerusalem, Rubin Mass, 2006), 47-8. For examples regarding our subject (women's status) see S. Ozick, "Women—Notes Towards Finding the Right Question," *Forum* 35 (1979): 37–60, who unites within one category of "Judaism" a variety of sources: beginning with the Bible through *Tsena Urena*, up until contemporary synagogue customs. See also M. Falk, "Towards a Feminist Jewish Reconstruction of Monotheism," *Tikkun* 4, no. 4 (1989): 53–6. Concerning Beruria's character, see R. Adler, "The Virgin in the Brothel and Other Anomalies: Character and Context in the Legend of Beruriah," *Tikkun* 3, no. 6 (1988): 28. There, she sews a quilt made of "stories from many times and many texts . . . rabbinic and post-rabbinic lore." She places all these sources under the roof of "our teachers." For a similar criticism relating to Adler's methodology, see D. Boyarin, *Carnal Israel, Reading Sex in Talmudic Culture* (Berkeley: University of California Press, 1993), 188–9. However, Boyarin applies the chronological criterion mainly to the distinction between the tannaitic and amoraic sources (see below nn. 11, 12). The cultural border between the amoraic (at least part of the cultural "powers" represented within there) and the post-Talmudic sources, tends to be missed by their inclusion within one cultural hegemony.

5. See E. Sarah, "Beruria: A Suitable Case For Mistreatment . . . or Why We Haven't Got the Sayings of Our Mothers," *European Judaism* 26, no. 12 (1993). Sarah coins the term "our mothers" as the silence of the feminine voice of Judaism. In spite of Sarah's recognition of the chronological differences between the sources (Talmudic, post-Talmudic), she seems to consider the sources as part of a single formation and inheritance of Judaism.

6. For an example of this discontinuity, see D. Hoshen, "Sexual Relations Between Husband and Wife, the Rishonim Reinterpretation of the Talmudic Sources," *S'vara, A Journal of Philosophy, Law, and Judaism* 3, no. 1 (1993): 39–45, *id.* "External Structure versus Binary Structure in Sexuality: The approach of the Rishonim and the Talmudic Sources," *Mo'ed, Annual for Jewish Studies* 15, no. 3 (2005): 63-84. The question of innovation and tradition regarding the Talmudic and post-Talmudic periods is frequently discussed in research, although less in terms of discontinuity than in terms of development. See, for instance, I. M. Tashma, *Talmudic Commentary in Europe and North Africa: Literary History* (Jerusalem: The Magnes Press, 1999); *id. Early Franco-German Ritual and Custom* (Jerusalem: The Magnes Press, 1999).

7. For this definition, see Urbach, *Sages*, 1. For other definitions, see for instance, the discussion of R. Brody, *Readings in Geonic Literature* (Tel Aviv: Hakkibutz Hameuhad, 1998), 4–10.

8. See Hoshen, "Agnon's Writing," 64–121, *id. Agnon*, 49-104.

9. The status of the Late Midrash's sources (mainly in Palestine during the Geonic period) is more problematic. The Late Midrash has retained sources of the Early Midrash, but on the other hand it is not just a collection (*Yalkut*). The direct exegesis of Scripture did not cease completely (L. Zunz, *Die Gottesdiesntlichen Vorträge der Juden Historisch Entwickelt*, [Jerusalem: Mosad Bialik, 1974], 176), even though its unique features should be examined separately. Since the field of the Late Midrash is poorly researched, we can only say at this point that it seems to be a hybrid literary product. This hybrid aspect is due to its proximity to the early hermeneutic culture, and its diversion-transition to the later commentary.

10. For the following sub-division, see M. Elon, *Jewish Law, History, Sources, Principles* (Philadelphia, Jerusalem: The Jewish Publication Society, 1994), 1:39–45. There has been considerable research about that division, and the definition of its parts from various perspectives.

11. The period of the Mishnaic sages (Tannaim) is 70–200 CE.

12. The period of the Talmudic sages (Amoraim) is 200–400 CE in the Land of Israel, and 200–500 CE in Babylon. See E. E. Urbach, *Encyclopedia Hebraica*, vol. 1 (Jerusalem and Tel Aviv, 1949), s.v. *aggada*, regarding the continuity between the tannaitic and the amoraic Aggada. Following him, see J. Fraenkel, *Darkei Ha-aggada Vehamidrash* (Givataim: Yad LaTalmud, 1991), 1:5.

13. The period of the post-amoraic sages (Savoraim) is 500–600 CE. See also D. Weiss Halivni, *Midrash, Mishna and Gemara* (Cambridge, Mass.: Harvard University Press, 1986), 76, about the stamaic period between last Amoraim (427 C.E.) and the first Savoraic ones (501/520 CE).

14. The period of the Rabbis, from the Arab conquest, especially in Babylon, between 637–1000 CE.

15. Rishonim—the first Rabbis, the period of the post-Geonic Rabbis, in East and West between 1040–92 CE.

16. Aharonim—the last Rabbis. The period of the post-Rishonim Rabbis from sixteenth century onwards.

17. The question of the development throughout the periods was mainly discussed from the halakhic respect, and the tracing of early Halakha throughout tannaitic and amoraic time was the subject of research in the last third of the 20th c. See E. E. Urbach, *The Halakha: Its Sources and Development* (Givatim: Yad La-Talmud,1984); Y. D. Gilat, *Studies in the Development of the Halakha* (Ramat Gan: Bar-Ilan University Press, 1992). Gilat extends his research to the post-Talmudic literature.

18. See Z. Frankel, *Hodegetik zur Mischna* (Warsaw: M. L. Calingold, 1923) 17, Elon, *Jewish Law,* 39–40, although they do not explain this dichotomy in its traumatic results, as we understand it, namely in terms of cultural break and discontinuity. In contrast, Gilat *(Halakha,* 374) argues that midrashic creativity did not cease absolutely with the sealing of the Talmud, but continued to exist from Geonim to Aharonim, even though he admits that this was not an

independent process but based on the Talmud (see his references from Rishonim and Aḥaronim).

19. About this separation, see Hoshen, "Fire," 11ff., Fraenkel, *Darkei Haggada*, 2:504. See also, Tashma, *Talmudic Commentary*, 2:190, who reviews the paucity of commentary to the Aggada as opposed to its quantity in the Halakha, in the Middle Ages until the middle of the 14th c.

20. L. Ginzberg, *Geonica, Texts and Studies of the Jewish Theological Seminary of America* (New York: The Jewish Theological Seminary of America,1909), 1:72–3, and following him S. Asaf, *The Period of the Geonim and their Literature* (Jerusalem: Mosad Harav Kook, 1955), 147, R. Brody, *The Geonim of Babylonia and the Shaping of the Medieval Jewish Culture* (New Haven: Yale University Press, 1998), 161.

21. J. H. Weiss, *Zur Geschichte der Judischen Tradition* (Wilna: Romm, 1904), 4:21. He considered *Sheiltot*, too, as a kind of codex.

22. *Otzar ha-Geonim, Ḥag. (Otzar ha-Perushim)*, ed. B. M. Lewin (Jerusalem: H. Vagshel, 1931), 4:60 (my translation). Similarly see R. Saadia Gaon (9th c.) in *Otzar ha-Geonim, Ḥag.* 65. More explicitly see R. Samuel ben Hofni Gaon (11th c.) in A. Harkavy, *Studien und Mittheilungen* (Leipzig: G. Haessel, 1880), 3:2–3, n. 34.

23. It seems that R. Hai Gaon refers here to the sage who said the *midrash/aggada*, but it could be understood as referring to the learner, or both.

24. *Otzar ha-Geonim, Ḥag.* 59 (my translation).

25. See E. Ben Yehuda, *A Complete Dictionary, Ancient and Modern Hebrew* (Jerusalem, NY: T. Yosluf, 1959), 16:7699, for the basic meaning of the word as "instruction," which extends to various usages. For the same general hypothesis concerning the post-Talmudic attitude to the Aggada, see below n. 74. Cf. Tashma, *Talmudic Commentary*, 2:193, though Tashma is not satisfied with this reason.

26. R. Hai Gaon used this phrase, see *Otzar ha-Geonim, Ḥag.* 60.

27. See also Tashma, *Talmudic Commentary*, 2:191.

28. The main example is Rif (R. Yitzhak Alfasi, Morocco 11th c.) whose halakhic composition based on the Talmudic text omitted many aggadic passages. For this and other post-Talmudic commentaries, see Tashma, *Talmudic Commentary*, 1:150, 2:191.

29. As the Talmud was canonized as a "sealed book," not open to its scriptural generative channels, even when post-talmudism related to verses, it was without the same quality of commentary, as had been the case with Midrash (see Brody, *Geonim of Babylonia*, 312–14). Regarding the Talmudic *sugia* (the discursive part) as methodological successor of *midrashei halakha*, see Weiss Halivni, *Midrash, Mishna and Gemara*, 91. For an approach that considers Talmudic text (as parts and as a single tapestry) as also generated, content-wise, from the midrashic process, see D. Hoshen, "On the Quality of the Rabbinic Text, The Opening of the Mishna," in *The Mishnah in Contemporary Perspective*, vol. 2, ed. J. Neusner and A. J. Avery-Peck (Leiden: Brill, 2006), 36–80.

30. The limited occupation of the Geonim with Scripture, and the way they related to it, turned 10th-11th c. Spanish Bible studies into a branch of linguistics (see Tashma, *Talmudic Commentary*, 2:34). The later Ashkenazi and Sephardic commentaries did not restore commentary to biblical channels, nor did they revive the Bible. The Bible continued to be a cold dead substrate for applying linguistic (*peshat*) rationalism (Ibn Ezra, Maimonides), or mysticism (Nahmanides, and others).

31. Medieval commentary cannot be considered as Midrash—not only because of the methodological differences (Brody, *Geonim of Babylonia*, 315), but also epistemologically and philosophically (see Hoshen, *Agnon*, 67-72). Regarding foreignness/authenticity in generating post-Talmudic commentary (in Ashkenaz), see Tashma, *Talmudic Commentary*, vol.1, chap. 3.

32. However, a separate study of the post-Talmudic sources, from an independent perspective, will not be carried out here.

Chapter One

Introduction to a Talmudic Theory of Status

The problem in assessing women's status in rabbinical society depends on one's criteria. If status is a matter of rights and duties, the fact that women are exempt from most temporal actions[33] and some non-temporal commandments,[34] in a society in which scriptural commandments are the only scale of evaluation of human worth,[35] seems to lead to the conclusion that the female is inferior.

This appears in the Mishna:

> Whatsoever is more holy than another precedes that other. [36]
> A man takes precedence over a woman in life saving (*lehaḥayot*).[37]
> (Mishna *Horayot* 3:6–7)[38]

The commentators explain that since a man is obligated by more commandments than a woman is, he is considered more holy, and thus precedes her.[39]

Similarly, read the next *mishna*:

> A priest takes precedence over a Levite, a Levite over an Israelite, an Israelite over a *mamzer* (bastard). (Mishna *Horayot* 3:8)

The Israelite is inferior[40] to the Levite, and the latter to the Cohen[41] as he is not permitted to sacrifice in the Temple.[42] Likewise, handicapped persons are lesser humans than healthy people are, as their commitment to the commandments is weaker.[43] Thus, we expect a caste structure, based on biological elements. The physical is the basis for the religious status.[44] The greater potential for observance of commandments entails superiority. Accordingly, the high priest bears the loftiest rank, as he is in the position to observe the maximum number of commandments.[45]

However, this is not the true hierarchy in Talmudic culture. The absolute echelon assigned to an individual is a result of activity (*talmid ḥakham*—the scholar, sage), or passivity (*am ha'aretz*—the ignoramus)[46] in the field of observance. Between these two extremes there is a middle rank, i.e., the one who behaves in accordance with the laws that obligate him (*haver*).[47] The latter is superior to the boor, who is obligated, but does not perform the laws, and inferior to the scholar who not only performs the commandments but is also distinguished by his knowledge of them (Torah study).[48]

This different ranking can be discerned in Tosefta:[49]

> R. Judah says: Man must recite three benedictions every day:
> Praised [be Thou, O Lord . . .] who did not make me a gentile.
> Praised [be Thou, O Lord . . .] who did not make me a *boor* (ignoramus).
> Praised [be Thou, O Lord . . .] who did not make me a woman.
> A gentile—as Scripture states, All the nations are nothing before him, they are accounted by him as less than nothing and emptiness. (Is 40:17)
> A *boor*—for a *boor* does not fear sin. (Mishna *Avot* 2:5)
> A woman—for women are not obligated [to perform all] the commandments. (Tosefta *Berakhot* 6:18, 40)[50]

The principle of the progression is clearly that of *mitzvot* (commandments). Nevertheless, it is not the potential to perform them which is important, but their realization. Obviously, the gentile, as exempt and non-observing is inferior.[51] However, the order of ignoramus and woman is inverted.[52] Even though what is required of the female is less, her position is superior, since the ignoramus, as a result of his poor knowledge of the Torah, is not wary of sin. The difference between the socio-biological inferiority of the gentile or woman and the purely sociological imperfection of the *boor*, was the reason for the tendency in post-Talmudic sources to replace the latter by "slave," which reduces the imbalance of the text.[53] Our text, at least,[54] assumes that the position of the *boor* was almost biological, as transition to another position is extremely improbable.[55] However, we learn from the order in Tosefta: woman-ignoramus, that the omission of action gives sufficient grounds for denial of the natural status of the Jewish man.

This may also be compared with the end of the Mishna quoted above:

> Whatsoever is more holy than another precedes that other ... A priest takes precedence over a Levite, a Levite over an Israelite, an Israelite over a *mamzer* (bastard) ... This order of precedence applies only when they are all equal, but if a *mamzer* is a scholar (*talmid hakham*) and a High Priest is ignorant (*am ha'arez*) the scholarly *mamzer* precedes the ignorant High Priest. (Mishna *Horayot* 3:8)

Obviously, following this tannaitic logic it is not far-fetched to claim that a pious woman elevates herself above an *am ha'aretz*.[56] The ultimate capability for annulment of natural socio-biological priority is not situated within the realm of observance, but within the realm of Torah study. Thus, a *mamzer* may precede only through the Torah. Sociobiology pales when countered by scholarly achievement. This is not true only for the *mamzer* in particular, but also in general. As Maimonides articulated: "the one greater in wisdom precedes the other,"[57] including the lowest castes such as gentiles.

Thus we find in the Talmud:

> R. Joseph said: He stood and measured the earth; he beheld and drove asunder the nations (Habakkuk 3:6). What did He behold? He beheld the seven commandments which had been accepted by all the descendants of Noah, and since [there were clans that] rejected them He rose up and granted them exemption. Does this mean that they benefited [by breaking the law]? And if so, will it not be a case of a sinner profiting [by the transgression he committed]? Mar the son of Rabana thereupon said: It only means that even were they to keep the seven commandments [which had first been accepted but subsequently rejected by them] they would receive no reward. Would they not? But it has been taught: Whence can we learn that even where a gentile occupies himself with the study of the Torah he equals [in status] the High Priest? We find it stated: "which if Man do he shall live by them" (Lev 18:5), it does not say "priests, Levites and Israelites", but "Man" which shows that even if a gentile occupies himself with the study of the Torah he equals the High Priest. I mean [in saying that they would receive no reward] that they will receive reward not like those who perform commandments having been commanded, but like those who perform commandments without having been commanded. For R. Hanina has stated: "Greater is the one who, having been commanded, performs commandments, than one who, not having been commanded, performs commandments." (BT *Bava Qama* 38a)[58]

Here we see the gentile in relation to both dimensions: commandments and Torah study. The unsuccessful attempt of the Talmudic discussion to tie the two to each other actually stresses the imminent separation between them. This means that the area of commandments concerns the relationship between commander and commanded. Thus, the difference between the ranks of obligation creates the status viz.: "Greater is the one who having been commanded performs commandments, than one who, not having been commanded performs commandments." The Talmudic discussion interprets the application of the status differences as applied to reward. However, in the area of Torah the rank of obligation is not the issue, but: "if Man (*adam*) does/pursue[59] [the laws—Torah] he shall live by them," i.e., any individual—*adam*, who will pursue them. The socio-biological starting point, which creates the status in the area of commandments, does not make sense in the area of Torah. Thus, "it does not say Priests, Levites and Israelites, but Man, which shows that even if a gentile occupies himself with the study of Torah he equals the High Priest." When entering the circle of Torah study, there is no preconditioned status, rather all are (potentially) equal: Priests, Levites, Israelites, *mamzerim*, gentiles, and so on. However, as we learnt from Mishna *Horayot*, the status is determined according to the inner principles of Torah by the activity of the individual inside that area, and his achievement in regard to Torah itself creates the status. Thus, even a *mamzer* who has achieved high standards of Torah study will precede the priest who is not equal to him in the area of Torah study, and this creates the status with implications as to his human value.

This reading seems to be articulated by Maimonides, although neither he nor his commentators refer to our Talmudic sources. In his conclusion, when discussing the rules concerning the election of the Levites, Maimonides writes that this depends on their special obligation to serve God and teach his Torah:

> Not only the Tribe of Levi, but also each and every individual of those who are living in the world (*mikol baei olam*), whose spirit has caused him to dedicate himself, and his knowledge has made him understand that he should set himself apart in order to stand before the Lord, to serve Him, to worship Him, and to know Him . . . such an individual is consecrated to a higher degree of sanctity. . . . The Lord will grant him . . . the same as he granted to the Priests and to the Levites.[60]

Maimonides' articulation that "Each and every individual of those who are living in the world" could opt for the status of the Tribe of Levi,[61] seems to be an adequate reading of the *baraita* in BT *Baba Qama*: "it does not say Priests, Levites, and Israelites, but Man/*Adam*," which does not leave anybody out of it.

Thus, excellence in Torah study creates a non-societal path, in which the power of devotion and intellectual creativity form a composite product: Torah and scholar (*talmid ḥakham*). At this level, any barriers between Torah/God's words as an object of study and the sage as the learner have fallen, and they become a mutual presence for each other. With these barriers fallen, the wise man loses his socio-biological identity and becomes one with Torah, wisdom itself, an eternally present spiritual entity, which is not subject to circumstances of place and time.

This understanding of the Talmudic approach to Torah as separated from the commandments' system, and to this special relationship between Torah and its learner, was developed in the response of an 18th c. Aleppo scholar.[62]

The Talmud says:

The scholars propounded: Must one rise before a Scroll of the Torah? R. Hilkiah, R. Simon and R. Elazar say: It follows a fortiori (*kal vahomer*): if we rise before those who study it, how much more before that itself (BT *Kidushin* 33b)

Accordingly, he determines in his Responsa that the scholar is equated with the Torah scroll, and that the respect that he deserves derives from that of the Torah itself, and not as part of human respect, or of being commanded.[63] As a result he rules:

I should comment that I chanced on a manuscript from the *Pri Ḥadash*[64] ... one must rise in honor of a *ḥaver*'s wife ... and on the question of a wise woman, in respect of her wisdom, requires further study ... But I, the humble slave, see clearly that one must rise before her wisdom, and in honor of the Torah, just as in the case of a scholar, so in her case ... If she does not know Torah we honor her husband's Torah, even more if she is a wise woman ... to honor her in respect of herself and her Torah ... and one may not say that as she is not commanded and thus she is observing without being commanded, and is not at the same level. Even if she does not receive the same reward as a man, who is commanded and performs, it does not mean that others are not required to honor her. As to us: What does it matter whether man or woman, we are confronted by respect of the Torah.[65]

So, as we understand the Talmudic approach, within the domain of Torah-study it is not natural attributes such as gender, race, physiological defects, nation and so on, that determine status. In this domain, the individual acts without parental ties, without his socio-biological personality, without the external reality. True, his/her social-biological personality might be the subject of his/her halakhic study. The blind might study the blind's laws,[66] the woman hers.[67] However, as the social dimension is irrelevant to the sage's personality qua sage, he is able to discourse objectively on his own social existence, much as he expounds on Purity and Impurity laws.[68] At his degree of devotion, the sage is no longer human, but part of his Torah. His personality is only that of a sage, devoid of genealogy.[69]

Why is Torah distinguished from other active commandments, in which there is a clear distinction between those commanded and those exempt, as well as a distinction between the various degrees of those commanded?[70] We suggest that Torah study is indeed an unlimited commandment. The socio-biological aspect is satisfied even for those obligated (adult, sane males) by very little.[71] At this minimal level of study there is truly a dissimilarity stemming from caste difference. There is however, no upper limit to study and this becomes a goal in itself. It cannot be demanded of Man, because it is not mandatory, but, rather, wholly individual. Though Torah study, unlike most other commandments, does not carry a sanction or penalty for its transgressors, it bears profound halakhic authority, superior to standard commandments. Thus, according to the logic of precedence presented in the Mishna,[72] in the case of a wise High Priest, and a wiser *mamzer*, the life of the latter precedes.[73] In spite of the fact that both have fulfilled the requirement of Torah study, and though the priest has the edge in genealogy and commandments, supremacy in Torah is crucially important.

Here we are exposed to a revolutionary element, which is reflected in the Talmudic sources. Man is linked to his creator through Torah—that is to say *hora'ah*—instruction of *mitzvot*.[74] The commandment is the core of human status. Consequently, we find the essential discrimination between those obligated and those exempt, and the precedence of the former. Nonetheless, the elitism of those persons who are engaged in maximal Torah-study is not focused on duty, and is thus devoid of stratum. Our explanation of the source of this paradoxical approach is theological. Torah study is the study of God's method. The inter-relation between God and Man is not God-based, but constitutes Man's search for God. Essentially, this is not compulsory but voluntary, not universally imposed but individually chosen, not biological but spiritual. Therefore, we find blurred boundaries between Priest and *mamzer*, Jew and gentile, male and female. Thus not the source, but the theological product is of interest.

This concept of Torah and its learner-scholar can be expressed also in the dimension of the absurd, for Torah bears its independent spiritual value even in the absurd case of the sinning scholar. When the Torah scholar becomes an apostate (as in the case of the second century scholar Elisha ben Abuya),[75] his own personality ceases being that of the Torah, and becomes a new subversive entity. Nevertheless, this new form cannot destroy the former entity. Torah creativity is an act of cessation of the self, which gives the spiritual qualities an intrinsic significance. Although Torah-learning needs an external kindling of the process, the result becomes independent of the initiator. If the sage leaves the spiritual circle, he only quits his creativity and becomes, instead of a vibrant organism, its casing. He cannot cancel the entity of Torah within him. Thus R. Meir, Elisha's disciple, holds that "They may save the casing of the scroll together with the scroll [and] the casing of the phylacteries together with the phylacteries. Elisha—Aḥer (the other)[76] will be saved through the merit of his [study of the] Torah."[77] Or, as the Talmud says about R. Meir himself in his relating to his apostate Rabbi: "He ate [the fruit] within it, and the peel he threw away."[78]

The transcendental aspect of Torah obviates the criteria distinguishing the student, class, beliefs, etc. This can be either through a total devotion of the scholar, through which he is identified with Torah, or through apostasy, in which he loses his personal relevance to his former creation as a scholar.

Notes

33. Most and not all, see BT *Kid.* 34a, and Rashi and Tosafot *ad loc.*; Maimonides, *Commentary on Mishna, Ḥag.* 1:1 (Jerusalem: Mosad Harav Kook, 1963), *id. Mishne Torah (MT), Laws Concerning Idolatry and the Institutions of Heathen Nations,* 12:3 (traditional edition, Warsaw 1781), and R. Abraham ben David (RaBaD) *ad loc.* Regarding this exemption see R. S. Goren, "Women are Included in Temporal Commandments," Mahanaim 98 (1965): 10–6. There he argues that this rule of exemption is R. Shimon's opinion (2nd c. *tanna,* a disciple of R. Akiva), and was not accepted by all the Sages.

34. Such as Torah-study and Procreation, BT *Kid.* 34a.

35. See Mishna *Hor.* (immediately following), and the Benedictions in Tosefta above p. 10. In the later ruling, this Talmudic principle was applied with severity. Based on BT *MQ* (25a) it was ruled that one does not rend clothes in mourning if present at the death of a sinner, nor should his relatives mourn (cf. *Beit Yosef* and *Shulḥan Arukh, Yoreh De'ah* 340).

36. Although, the Mishna, simply, applies this rule to holy objects (in this case the offering), the Talmud (BT *Hor.* 12b) applies it also to persons like the Cohen.

37. The term: *lehaḥayot* is not clear whether it means saving life, or providing food. BT (*Hor.* 13b) seems to support the first meaning, while JT (*Hor.* 3:4, 48:1) the second. Because the second meaning contradicts the conclusion of the Talmud in another place (*Ket.* 67a), most commentators on the Mishna (Maimonides, Bartenura, Tiferet Yisrael, Albeck) understand the *mishna*

as referring to saving from drowning. This reading was adopted by the Aharonim (*Beit Yosef* on *Tur, Yore De'ah* 251, *Sifte Cohen* on *Shulḥan Aruch* 251:11, *TaZ* on *Shulḥan Aruch*, 252:6). Compare Meiri (BT *Hor. ad loc.*) who supports the second meaning. Maimonides *(MT, Laws Concerning Gifts to the Poor,* 8:17) does not rule specifically on this issue, though it seems that he follows the mainstream view. However, in some circumstances, especially at the time of the Mishna, both meanings were the same.

38. The translations of the Talmudic text are eclectic, based on the Soncino Press and Schottenstein (ArtScroll) editions of the Talmud and on my own translation, unless otherwise indicated.

39. See Maimonides in his *Commentary* on that *mishna*, Meiri, BT *Hor. ad loc.*

40. This inferiority applies in regards to everything when there is not enough for all: the redemption of captives, clothing. *Lehaḥayot* means feeding/saving life, honoring (see JT *Sab.* 12:3; 13:3). See also, Maimonides, *MT, Laws Concerning Gifts to the Poor,* 8:17.

41. Even among the Cohanim there is a clear hierarchy (Tosefta *Hor.* 2:10, BT *Hor.* 13a, JT *Hor.* 3:2, 47:3, Maimonides, *MT, Laws Concerning Vessels of the Sanctuary and those who Minister Therein,* 4; 19).

42. BT Hor. 13a, Maimonides, *MT, Laws Concerning the Sabbatical Year and the Year of the Jubilee,* 13:12.

43. For the case of blind men, see BT *BQ* 87a. Compare Tosafot *ad loc.*, and in BT *Eru.* 96b, with RITBA (R. Yom Tov Ashvili, Spain 13th–14th c.) BT *Kid.* 31a. The Tosafot teach that the involvement of the blind with the laws derives from rabbinical obligation and is not scriptural. This fact has implications for his status vis-a-vis the woman e.g., his ability to exempt her from scriptural commandments by which she is obligated, such as *kiddush* on Friday night.

44. See Z. Guthold, "Legal Status of women," *Mahanaim* 98 (1965): 20. He too reviews the status of women in the early sources out of concern for with a general definition that the one most obligated by the commandments is the most highly ranked. Even though Guthold's introduction of the Talmudic data and their primary reading is similar to mine, there is a vast difference in their further analysis. Guthold places the breaking of the biological circle within the individual, while the breaching itself remains within the sociological circle. In my reading, the individual's action connects with the theological nature of the Torah circle, as opposed to the socio-biological circle with which the commandments are connected.

45. See above p. 10, the end of Mishna *Hor*.

46. Urbach, *Sages,* 585, 632ff. argued that originally, the term *am ha'aretz* referred to those who were not careful with the commandments of Purity and Tithes. Later it extended to lack of Torah study and knowledge, and to disrespect for other commandments or the Sages. According to Urbach, the beginning of the change in the term *am ha'aretz* had already left an impact at the time of the temple. See also, S. Safrai, "The Pious (*Ḥasidim*) and the Men of

Deed," *Zion* 50 (1985): 152–4. Cf. A. Oppenheimer, *The Am Ha'aretz, A Study in the Social History of the Jewish People in the Hellenistic-Roman Period* (Leiden: Brill, 1977), 103ff. who argued that the change in the term began only after the destruction, at the time of Yabne and especially at the time of Usha.

47. See Urbach, *Sages*, 583–4, 632ff. about the concept of *haver* as referring to those groups of people who took upon themselves to observe what the *am ha'aretz* does not respect. The concept of *haver* developed, similarly to that of *am ha'aretz*, from Purity and Tithes to general observance, and Torah knowledge. For a further discussion of the terms *haver* and *am ha'aretz* see D. Rokeah, "Am Ha'aretz, The Pious (*Hasidim*), Jesus and Christians," *Mehkerei Talmud, Talmudic Studies dedicated to the Memory of Professor Ephraim Urbach* (Jerusalem: The Magnes Press, 2005), 876–903.

48. See Urbach, *Sages*, 587–8, Oppenheimer, *Am Ha'aretz*, 170ff. about the relationship between the concepts: "sage" and *haver*, which at some stage became synonymous. The concept of *haver*, in terms of one who observes commandments, but does not know much Torah, and is thus inferior to the sage, was linked by research to the terms: Pious men (*Hasidim*) and *Perushim* (See Safrai, "Pious," Rokeah, "Am ha'aretz"). Since we doubt their comprehension of the concept *hasid* and its contrast with the sage (see "Fire," 278–316), our claim regarding the meaning of *haver* as a middle rank requires further elaboration.

49. About this tannaitic composition (3rd c.) and the dispute regarding its date, see H. Albeck, *Introduction to the Talmud Bavli and Yerushalmi* (Tel Aviv: Dvir, 1987), 51ff.

50. *The Tosefta, Zeraim, Berakhot*, 6:18, ed. J. Neusner (Hoboken: Ktav, 1986), 40.

51. Cf. Rashi, s.v. *kuli hai*, BT *Men.* 43b. Perhaps, this principle is the basis for R. Shimon's famous *midrash* (BT *BM* 114b) on *Ezekiel* (34:31): "'And ye my flock, the flock of my pastures are Man I am your God' only ye are named Man (due to "I am your God") and not the gentiles who are not named Man/*adam*" (since they are excluded from that relation).

52. Cf. S. Lieberman, *Tosefta Ki-fshuta, Zeraim, Berakhot* (New York: Jewish Theological Seminary of America, 1955), 119, 121.

53. Cf. Rashi BT Men. 43b, Maimonides, *MT, Laws Concerning Prayer and the Priestly Blessing*, 7:6, *Kesef Mishne*, ad loc. *Tur* and *Shulhan Arukh, Orah Haim* 46.

54. Though we will not dismiss here the historical question regarding the class status of *am ha'aretz* at the time of R. Judah, see Oppenheimer, *Am Ha'aretz*, 184ff. about the numerous statements regarding the ignoramus at the time of Usha, which reflected an abyss between the classes.

55. Compare *Beit Yosef, Tur, Orah Haim* 46, that a proselyte may not make the benediction "who did not make me a gentile," because benedictions refer to the original creation and not to the new personality he had chosen afterwards.

56. In BT *Shv.* 30b: "the wife of *haver* (here meaning a sage) is like a *haver* himself," therefore she precedes an *am ha'aretz* for honoring. Most of the

Rishonim read that honoring a *ḥaver's* wife derives from her relation to her husband (Tosafot, Nahmanides, BT *ad loc.*). However, a very late ruling from the eighteenth century concludes that a *ḥaver's* wife is like a *ḥaver*, independently and on her own account, and thus precedes an *am ha'aretz*. For honoring and other issues see R. Yehuda ben Yosef Ashkenazi, *Maḥane Yehuda*, "*Hilkhot Dayanim*" (Salonica: M. Naḥman, and D. Israelija, 1793), 17, 4b. See also above p. 13.

57. Maimonides, *MT, Laws Concerning Gifts to the Poor*, 8:18, based on I. Klein translation, *The Code of Maimonides, book 7: The Book of Agriculture* (New Haven: Yale University Press, 1978), 84.

58. See also BT *AZ* 2b.

59. See the translation of this verse: "by the pursuit of which man shall live," in J. Neusner, *Sifra: An Analytical Translation* (Atlanta: Scholars Press, 1998), 3:80.

60. Maimonides, *Code, Laws Concerning The Sabbatical Year and The Year of The Jubilee*, 13:13, trans. Klein, 403.

61. Obviously, he does not refer to the commandments, which those who do not belong to the tribe of Levi are not allowed to perform, but Maimonides refers here to Torah, which was one of the Levites' main missions to study and to teach.

62. Y. Atiyah, *Zera Yitzḥak*, "*Palpelet Kol Shehu*" (Livorno: J. Nunis and R. Mildola, 1793–4), 6:88d. We have not cited this late source in order to prove any general approach to the feminist question by the so-called Sephardic rabbis or any other traditional rabbis (for that approach see: Z. Zohar, "The Attitude of Rabbi Yosef Masas Towards Women's Torah Study," *Pe'amim* 82 [1999]: 150–62). Rather, we have cited this interpretation because of its understanding of the concept of honoring the sage as deriving not from the social standing of the sage, but as part of the ontology of the Torah. Within this logical limit, the question of honoring a female sage is discussed outside the political-feminist question, but within the epistemological borders of the Talmudic literature as we understand it.

63. Thus, he concludes also that one must stand in honor of a blind sage, who is oblivious of the action.

64. *Pri Ḥadash*, R. Hizqiahu de Silva, Livorno (17th c.)

65. Atiyah, *Zera Yitzḥak*, in free translation. The original is of course in Rabbinic Hebrew. This source was discussed by R. Eliyahu Medini, *Sede Ḥemed*, "*Peat HaSadeh*" (New York: Friedman, 1966), 1:183, 59, in which he cited a few more Aḥaronim, who rule that there is no difference between learned men and learned women.

66. Rav Joseph (a blind Babylonian scholar from the 4th c. CE), BT *Kid.* 31a, is interested in the final result of the halakhic discussion, and will celebrate a favorable conclusion. See also BT *Pes.* 116b, where R. Joseph and R. Sheshet (Babylon 3rd–4th c., who was also blind), accept the halakhic ruling, and act accordingly.

67. See below p. 54, our reading of the text about Beruria and R. Jose the Galilean (BT *Eru.* 53b, 8*). We could add to this list: the proselyte (see the attitude of Shma'aia and Abtalion to themselves, BT *Yoma* 71b), and paradoxically *am ha'aretz*, see BT *Pes.* 49b, R. Akiba relating to his past as being an *am ha'aretz*.

68. This topic is considered as the field of Halakha par excellence. See BT Ḥag. 14a, Rashi *ad loc.*, and BT *San.* 67b.

69. As can be found in BT Ḥag. 15b, in the *midrash* on Ps. 45:11; see also Hoshen, "Fire," 89.

70. Compare limited commandments, such as Sabbath, *nidah*, *lulav*, which can be fulfilled without changing one's status. By being strict concerning the commandment of Sabbath one may receive a greater divine reward, but not a change in class.. A woman may fulfill a commandment, which she has not been commanded. However, she does not receive an equal reward, and cannot make the benediction for men. See also Tosafot, *Eru.* 96b.

71. E.g., reciting the *shema* according to R. Shimon, BT *Men.* 99b. See also *Shulḥan Arukh*, *Yoreh De'ah*, 240:1, and *Sifte Cohen ad loc.*

72. Mishna *Hor.* 3:7–8.

73. Either by precedence in "distribution of charity funds, or the redemption of captives when there is not enough for all" (ArtScroll, BT *Hor.* 13b, n. 62), see JT *Hor.* 3:4, 48:4, and Maimonides, *MT, Laws Concerning Gifts to the Poor*, 8:18, Meiri.

74. The etymological connection between the words: "Torah" and *hora'ah* does not link it only to the sense of commandment-instruction, but also to that of teaching-doctrine. This sheds light on the relationship of God and human as deriving from the entity of the Torah.

75. This scholar has been the subject of considerable research. For recent example see A. Goshen-Gottstein, *The Sinner and the Amnesiac: The Rabbinic Invention of Elisha ben Abuya and Eleazar ben Arach* (Stanford: Stanford University Press, 2000), D Hoshen, "Elisha ben Abuya, Avoidance and Realization of the Absurd in R. Akiva's Theology," (unpublished).

76. See BT Ḥag. (15b), for the Talmud's explanation for this name.

77. JT Ḥag. 2:1, 77b, *Talmud of the Land of Israel*, trans. J. Neusner (Chicago: University of Chicago Press, 1996), 50.

78. BT Ḥag. *op. cit.*

Chapter Two

Beruria and the Theological Theory of Torah

The conclusion of the theory presented in the previous chapter was that the religious status and value of any socio-biological group in the Talmudic sources is based on a two-dimensional system. According to this theory, the system consists of both the obligatory actions based on socio-biological criteria, and the voluntary system of actions based on individual theological criteria. The second dimension is more important, and can supersede the other in discerning the spiritual status of an individual. In such a case, the individual's background is relevant merely as it determines the divine reward for his deeds.

We would now like to take the challenge of applying this theory to the well-known Talmudic figure, Beruria the *tannait*[79]—daughter of the *tanna* R. Ḥananya ben Teradion and wife of the *tanna* R. Meir (BT *Pesaḥim* 62b).[80] It is risky because this figure has become easy prey for a political (feminist) agenda in various disciplines (Talmud, history, folklore, and so on).[81] Therefore, the sources from Talmudic literature mentioned here are frequently quoted and interpreted in that light. In spite of our desire to transfer the analysis of these sources from the political realm to the epistemological framework mentioned above, we may still be misinterpreted as working within the feminist epistemological framework. Therefore, in this study we shall follow a dialectic style, namely, contrasting the present reading to the other by thesis, anti-thesis, and synthesis.

According to our reading, the figure reflected from the Talmudic sources (tannaitic and amoraic) is a Mishnaic sage, a *tanna*, who like the other Tannaim, devoted herself to Torah, and whose devotion and great creativity have supreme halakhic importance.

"Tanna" does not mean here a label demonstrating scholarship, social status or an empty space, used as a historical datum for denying or asserting her reality. Rather, "Tanna" is interpreted in its full meaning of presenting a specific conception or method, and capabilities, which is integrated into the studies of the Talmudic universe.[82] Our study of the Beruria texts has shown their strong affinity to the *tanna* R. Eliezer ben Hyrcanus (halakhically, in their conception of the Torah, as well as in the handling of various subjects). This is contrary to the relations between these two figures as they have been understood both in post-Talmudic literature and in modern research.[83]

The case of Beruria the *tannait* illuminates the rule of all such exceptional individuals. If we ask, hypothetically, the historical question: "How many women like Beruria were there in the tannaitic period?" one could answer as Tal Ilan: "Obviously all this is beyond historical fact and deep in the realm of speculation."[84] The answer, according to the analysis offered in the previous chapter, would be virtually the same for blind men,[85] boors,[86] or gentiles who became sages. The spiritual arena of individuals does not comprises statistics and quantity, but rather singularity and quality.

Indeed, the historical question of realism in Talmudic literature is a general question, pertinent to all its named personalities.[87] However, we do not aim to describe a historical figure in this study, beyond the figure emerging from the texts. We relate to the historical issue only when its implications have a crucial impact on the direction of research, as in the following case.

It was David Goodblatt[88] who was the first to challenge the Babylonian Talmud's identification of Beruria as the second century daughter of R. Ḥananya ben Teradion, the wife of R. Meir (BT *Pesaḥim* 62b).[89] He proposes that this genealogy was actually the Talmud's elaboration.[90] Consequently, he related to the texts as not reflecting a single figure. His claim was based on a comparison of parallel sources from the 2nd–5th c. CE, checking whether Beruria is mentioned or not and, if so, how. Later research adopted his conclusion almost unanimously.[91] Goodblatt's conclusion does not provide an understanding of the historical Beruria, since his reconstruction of the Talmudic texts is refutable,[92] but does provide a basis for explaining the Talmudic motivation. The essential question emerging from Goodblatt's conclusions was bluntly phrased by Judith R. Wegner: "So we may be forgiven for wondering whether she is a figment of the Talmudic imagination and, more importantly, what literary purpose she serves?"[93] This question invited political answers, which analyzed the attributed Beruria texts through a prism of feminism. Thus even an innocent text, which Wegner presents in order to answer her question, does not escape this area. The text from BT *Pesaḥim* (4*) talks about Beruria's learning three hundred *halakhot* from three hundred rabbis. Wegner asks whether it should be read as "tokenism (Women are allowed to study Torah!"), or functions as a cultural countertype, proving the very rule sages wish to enforce ('women should not study Torah, Mishna *Sota* 3:4' ").[94] The central issue of this text, which deal with the exclusive status of Aggada and its relationship to halakhic knowledge, and with Beruria as embodying this combination (three hundred *halakhot*, why not *aggadot*?)[95] has disappeared in the light of the feminist focus. Goodblatt's attempt to undermine the historicity of Beruria, which posited the Talmudic invention of the daughter and wife, has led to superficial textual research, which reduces complex tannaitic disputes (1*, 2*) about *taharot* (Purity) to feminine kitchen issues.[96] Similarly, another text in which Beruria quotes Mishna *Avot* (8*), is read not as a scholarly assertion, but as a reflection of a wife's awareness of her husband's colleagues' misogyny.[97] By Goodblatt's reading of Beruria's texts, we are guided to view the woman behind each text, not its substance. Even in her scholarly texts, Beruria seemingly merely mimics rabbinical methodology. It is not necessary to seek insight into it, nor examine its unique interpretation or conception, as we would have done if the text had not borne Beruria's name.

Goodblatt's followers followed this approach. Meir Bar-Ilan says of Beruria's exegetical dispute (Is 54:1) with the *min* (6*): "the story demonstrates how an observant Jew outsmarts a heretic, and how a woman outsmarts a man through verbal virtuosity."[98] The same attitude we find towards her exegetical dispute in BT *Berakhot* (5*) regarding the verse in Psalms (104:35). Ilan reinforces Goodblatt's de-historicizing of Beruria's figure in this text, by comparing it with a similar Talmudic text where Beruria's name is missing. There, the woman is the wife of Aba Hilkia (1st c. CE), and the exegetical process is also missing from the text. In spite of Ilan's admission of the difference that "Beruriah is a scholar, and Aba Hilqia's wife is a pious woman," she concludes: "However, it is obvious that we are dealing here with the same literary composition, which therefore, has no historical significance."[99] Beyond her feminist conclusion about the pious woman, as opposed to a scholarly one, there is no need to examine the exegetical process of the Beruria text. However, the historical hypothesis of these texts' composition makes a more profound examination obligatory, in order to come to a conclusion as to whether they actually reflect the same conception.[100]

Even when followers of Goodblatt's a-historical approach were aware of the necessity of literary analysis of Beruria's texts, their research lacked penetration. The literary foci were not applied in a free analysis of Talmudic texts, but were shackled by a political feminist reading. Yifat Moonikandem articulated it:

> As there is no clear evidence of the marriage of the daughter of R. Ḥananya ben Teradion to R. Meir, the focus of reading moves to the discussion of her literary figure. Our question in the discussion may be articulated: Why did the Talmud fictitiously marry Beruria the daughter of R. Ḥananya ben Teradion to R. Meir? And why did it attribute to R. Meir's real wife the symbolic name: Beruria?[101]

The Beruria texts, according to this approach, are pre-motivated. They are nothing but a token of something else,[102] an example, an object utilized by the Talmud. Here we return to Wegner's question: for what purpose? Moonikandem's answer would be that the Talmud chose Beruria to be R. Meir's wife, to contrast her with R. Meir himself. Even the detailed literary analysis provided by Moonikandem is deaf to the text. In BT *Berakhot* (5*), Beruria is "reacting unlike a woman of her period—quoting a verse and making a *midrash* of it."[103] The sort of exegesis and, possibly, philosophy that Beruria does present in this text is not worth mentioning, as she is but "using" the verse in order to criticize R. Meir morally, for not "using" Torah (properly) in order to solve his life problems.[104] The main interest in this text, according to Moonikandem, is the reversal of the platonic functions between man and woman, and consequently the power that Beruria gains over her husband. Similarly in her analysis of the subsequent dispute of Beruria with the *min* (6*), it is not the exegetical process which is the main focus,[105] but its result, that is Beruria gaining power over the opponent. In this case, the adversary is a Christian Jew, and the arena is that of ideology and nationality. Moonikandem reminds us, however, that in addition, the overall meaning of the text also gives Beruria a feminist advantage over her husband who, unlike her, did not succeed in defeating a *min* who was none other than Aḥer—his Rabbi—Elisha ben Abuya.[106]

So, according to the feminist reading, when relating to Beruria's texts we enter the arena of power and of power struggles.[107] The Talmud employs Beruria for a specific purpose, and she herself exploits the Sages' technique of "using" verses to demonstrate her feminist abilities.[108] Her precise analytic-synthetic exegesis, which is founded on other Talmudic, or biblical texts, and her understanding of the topic itself, are considered uninteresting or irrelevant to the analysis of the texts in which she appears. This approach maintains that the Talmudic text, in general, is a male composition. Any notice taken of women in it is nothing but the male's attitude towards the female, as Wegner concludes:

> A literature produced by men offers very little testimony to the actual experience of real, historical women. The Talmud rarely speaks of individual women, treating them for the most part in a generic and stereotypical way. What we get, in the end, is the rabbinic understanding of women's nature and place in the social fabric, along with a set of rules delineating the (perhaps theoretical, perhaps actual) legal status of women in a patriarchal culture.[109]

In this masculine culture of Talmud the composition of Beruria's texts derives, so Adler teaches, from the male consciousness, which is basically the psychoanalytical fear of anomaly ("the other").[110] This fear influences two kinds of Talmudic texts: the "good" and the "evil", which is more common—those texts which encourage submitting to the fear, and thus accept women, and those texts which encourage grappling with the fear, and thus reject them.[111]

This doctrine was applied perfectly in Ilan's research on Beruria:

> The Beruria of the Mishnah and the Beruria of the Babylonia Talmud simply reflect two different reactions to the one piece of historical information about Beruria . . . in the Tosefta. However, while the Mishnaic rabbis preferred to eliminate all memory of her, the Babylonians chose conversely to blow up her scholarship out of all proportion, making Beruria into a grotesque fantasy. This too would ensure that Beruria the scholar would remain an anomaly.[112]

This is not the place to argue in detail with the political methodology in general and the feminist in particular, as it relates to Talmudic literature.[113] However, we would like to stress that the reduction of this literature to the "masculine" challenges not only its historical, but also its literary, philosophical, and religious value.[114] This conclusion does not accord with the results of our reading of that literature.[115] For us, the Talmudic literature reflects a high quality and unique product of culture and the human spirit (in various dimensions), even though it is still obscure to occidental eyes and thought.[116] In this perspective, we return the Beruria Talmudic texts to their independent literary analysis, where they are released from political shackles. This, I believe, may lead eventually also to an understanding about the historical question of Beruria's genealogy.[117]

As stated, the broader context of this study, the question of woman's status in the Talmudic sources, will be treated here by applying our general theory about human status, comprising dual dimensions (commandments/ Torah study), to texts attributed to Beruria and to the figure which emerges from them. Since we see Beruria as a true *tannait*, we believe that her nature was determined by the centrality of Torah and, therefore, like the other Tanaim, she viewed the socio-biological dimension of any object, including herself. In addition, she is revealed through her texts as a *tannait*, who integrates Halakha and Aggada, whose conception of Torah is that Torah encompasses all strata of life and that the Midrash, in the sense of the exegetical process, is the substrate upon which this ideal entity of Torah is revealed. These characteristics of Beruria (as well as of her father R. Hananya ben Teradion) in relation to the Torah demonstrate, as mentioned above, a great affinity with the *tanna* R. Eliezer ben Hyrcanus, whose "fire conception" reflected this very nature of Torah.[118]

According to our theory, the question of status (of any kind) is irrelevant when tracing the Talmudic figures within their Torah qualification. This is also the case with Beruria, who is reflected in the Talmudic literature as a bona fide scholar.[119] The question of the relevance of status would arise in the mentality of post-Talmudic culture, in which the secularization process of certain branches of Torah began, and with it the incursion of foreign influences. This process is not always manifested fully and consistently in the post-Talmudic sources, owing to their traditional adherence to the Talmudic sources.

Notes

79. In BT *Pes.* 62b, the Talmud uses the form: *tannait* as a female form of the verb: *tanna* (to study) as regards Beruria's study. Similarly, I used the female form *tannait* in parallel to the masculine *tanna*.

80. Concerning this genealogy of Beruria see also BT *AZ* 18a. Later on, we will deal with the historical appeal of this genealogy, which has become very popular in research.

81. For a broad bibliography about Beruria see T. Ilan, "The Quest for The Historical Beruriah, Rachel and Imma Shalom," *AJS Review* 22, no. 1 (1997): 1–17, nn. 1–4. For further bibliography, see *id. Integrating women into the Second Temple History* (Tübingen: Mohr Siebeck, 1999), 175–94, J. Gerwin, "Lucid is God, Beruriah and the Subversion of the Patriarchal Discourse," *Mosaic* 14 (1993): 8–24, Y. Moonikandem, "Beruria and Rabbi Meir—Parallels and Contrasts," *Pathways through Aggada* 2 (1999): 36–63. For the feminist view as expressed also in the field of theatre, see D. Urian. "'Our Teachers break our heart:' Beruria, Theatre Company of Jerusalem," in *Theatre and Holy Script*, ed.

S. Levy (Brighton: Sussex Academic Press, 1999), 222–37. In part of this list we can see a shift from a generally political perspective to a specifically gender-based one. See D. Boyarin, "The Diachronic As Against the Synchronic in the Tale of Beruria," *Studies in Jewish Folklore* 12–3 (1990): 15, and its adaptation in Boyarin, *Carnal Israel*, 181ff.

82. See Ilan, *Integrating women*, 181–9, who concludes that Beruria is a sage in the Babylonian Talmud, but gives this conclusion a cynical evaluation. Rather than examining the texts in terms of their midrashic or halakhic function, she evaluates them solely on the basis of her impression that they demonstrate a considerable amount of learning on Beruria's part. Then she moves to reasoning from an outside political footing, namely, the reaction of the Talmudic rabbis to information about a female *tanna*.

83. We will relate to this issue in detail below.

84. Ilan, *Integrating women*, 179.

85. Among the Tannaim there were no known blind sages, while among the Amoraim there were two: R. Joseph and R. Sheshet (see above n. 66).

86. See R. Lacks, *Women and Judaism Myth, History and Struggle* (Garden City, NY: Doubleday, 1980), 25, that as opposed to women "unlearned men often became great scholars." However, if Lacks is right, the benediction of the boor is really inexplicable; see also, Oppenheimer, *Am Ha'aretz*, on this subject.

87. On this question see, Hoshen, "Fire," 27; *id.* "Suffering and Divinity in R. Akiva's philosophy," *Da'at* 27 (1991): 6–7.

88. D. Goodblatt, "The Beruriah Traditions," *JJS* 26 (1975): 68–85.

89. This genealogy was accepted by Talmudic scholars; see Goodblatt, ibid., n. 4, A. Goldfeld, "Women as Sources of Torah in the Rabbinic Tradition," in *The Jewish Woman, New Perspectives*, ed. E. Koltun (New York: Schocken books,1976), 276.

90. His final hypothesis (Goodblatt, "Beruriah Traditions," 81–4) is that there was an unlearned woman called Beruria in the second century, and there was a learned unnamed woman in the 5th c. The connection between the two is the elaboration of the Babylonian Talmud, which derives from folklore.

91. See Ilan. *Integrating women*, 179; L. J. Archer, "Her Price Is Beyond Rubies," *JSOT* supp., 60 (1990): 97–9, Moonikandem, "Beruria and Rabbi Meir," E. Ahdut, "The Status of The Jewish Woman in Babylonia in the Talmud Era," (PhD diss., The Hebrew University, 1999), 118ff.

92. In spite of his general agreement with Goodblatt's claim, Boyarin raised some concerns, *Carnal Israel*,183, n. 3. See also, S. Tov, *Characters from the Talmud* (Jerusalem, S. Tov, 1988), 73.

93. J. Wegner, "The Image and Status of Women in Classical Rabbinic Judaism," in *Jewish Women Historical Perspective*, ed. J.R. Baskin (Detroit: Wayne State University Press, 1991), 76.

94. Ibid. See also Adler, "Virgin in the Brothel," 30: "R. Yohanan uses the example of Beruriah . . . to discourage . . . to insult . . . Rabbi Simlai whom (he) does not wish to teach."

95. More about this text, see below p. 39.

96. Goodblatt, "Beruriah Traditions," 83. It is interesting to note that scholars adhere to Goodblatt's hypothesis of the Talmudic invention of Beruria, even when they have been convinced that his "kitchen-lore" theory is incorrect, and therefore conclude that the *tosefta* does reflect historical information about Beruria the sage (*Integrating women*, 178–9). The Talmudic invention then becomes a reaction (derived from anti-woman complexes) to that *tosefta* (Ilan, 189). This is unlike Goodblatt's conclusion that the text reflects a historical situation of a learned woman in the time of the Talmud.

97. Goodblatt, "Beruriah Traditions," 82.

98. M. Bar-Ilan, *Some Jewish Women in Antiquity* (Atlanta: Scholars Press, 1998), 47. See also, M. Benovitz, *BT Berakhot Chapter 1, in Talmud Ha-Igud*, ed. S. Friedman (Jerusalem: The Society for the Interpretation of the Talmud, 2006), 443.

99. Ilan, "Historical Beruriah," 4; *id. Integrating women*, 182–3.

100. See H. Malter, *The Treatise Ta'anit* (New York: American Academy for Jewish Research, 1930), 101, about this suspect text from BT *Ta'anit* (23a). He sees it as a supplement, which had been transferred from the Beruria story in BT *Berakhot* 10b, and was inserted into the mouth of Aba Hilkia's wife in BT *Ta'anit*. Therefore, Malter places the entire text in brackets. However, even without Malter's philological view, it is obvious that Beruria's text in BT *Ber.* introduces a wide and rich view, as opposed to that of *BT Ta'anit* which adopted its external layer. In order to understand the differences, one should go through the exegetical process. See Goldfeld, "Women as Sources of Torah," 268ff. who reads the supplement by BT *Ta'anit's* redactors as an insight into the character of the two women. Cf. Benovitz, *Berakhot*, 441, who argues that BT *Ber.* is a reworking (*inter alia*) of BT *San.* 37a. However, the stories express different theological conceptions as reflected by the different verses appearing in the texts. In BT *Ber.* it is the relation between "sin" and "sinners," while in BT *San.* it is the relation between the "public" and the "congregation" as regards the sin.

101. Moonikandem, "Beruria and Rabbi Meir," 41 (my translation). For the same style of questions from the historical perspective, see Ahdut, "Status of The Jewish Woman," 122.

102. Or, in Boyarin's psychoanalytic phrasing: "a symptomatic reading of the Talmud" (*Carnal Israel*, 169).

103. Moonikandem, "Beruria and Rabbi Meir," 43 (my translation).

104. Ibid., but on p. 42 we find a slightly different claim. In any case, in both claims she missed the text which assumes that R. Meir's behavior derived from his exegesis of the verse.

105. Due to this fact, it seems that Moonikandem wrongly attributed to the Midrash methodology the motif of bareness, while, actually, it is the symbol of the verse in Isaiah. Consequently the whole exegetical process was missed. The originality which Moonikandem attributes to Beruria's *midrash* on this basis is also unexplained except as a polemical achievement.

106. Moonikandem, "Beruria and Rabbi Meir," 44.

107. The political analysis of Talmudic texts is teeming with violent terminology. See for instance, Boyarin, *Carnal Israel*, 179, the repetition of the word "power" beside: "control," "monopoly," and "authorities" in one little passage. See also other terms taken from psychoanalysis, which build the political discourse: suppress, dissent, threat with their inflections and synonyms (ibid., 169, 170, 174, 189, 195).

108. This relation is blatantly applied in Moonikandem, work, but seems to be raised almost by definition in all feminist works we have seen.

109. Wegner, "The Image and Status," 88.

110. The post-structuralist use of the term: "the other" is developed by Adler in her paper "Toward a Jewish Feminist Theology of Self and Other," *Tikkun* 6, no. 3 (1991).

111. Adler, "Virgin in the Brothel," 29, 31, regarding the male's imagination (fantasies).

112. Ilan, *Integrating women*, 189. Note in Ilan here, and elsewhere (for instance p. 193), the common area that the historical discipline shares with the political discipline, especially when it comes to reasoning and text analysis.

113. For an example of such an approach to the Talmudic literature, see Boyarin, *Carnal Israel*, *id. Unheroic Conduct, The Rise of Heterosexuality and the Invention of the Jewish Man* (Berkeley: University of California Press, 1997), *id. Dying for God* (Stanford: Stanford University Press, 1999).

114. See Adler, "Virgin in the Brothel," 29, who said that rabbinic legends as male creations "are necessarily andocentric."

115. See Hoshen, "Fire," which studies the Talmudic philosophy through the literary form of its texts, and *id.* "Agnon's Writing," which studies the Talmudic texts through their philosophical principles.

116. See Hoshen, *Agnon*, 58-69, for the comparative study of the Talmudic textuality in relation to modern and post-modern philosophy, literature and linguistics.

117. See Hoshen, "Fire," 272–6, and below chap. 5, about the conceptual linkage between R. Ḥananya ben. Teradion and R. Eliezer ben Hyrcanus.

118. See Hoshen, "Fire," chap. 1.

119. We say "bona-fide" and not "ideal" scholar (see Ilan, *Integrating women*, 181), as we do not think that the Talmudic literature has room for such an image. The characters of the Tannaim are described conceptually very differently from each other. As to their behavior, which derived from their scholarly nature, no one is described as more ideal than the other. If such were the purpose, the details in the texts would quickly destroy the ideal image. Indeed, this was a failure of nineteenth-century Talmudic research, which clung to such details in order to examine the tannaitic figures according to external moral and intellectual criteria (see Weiss, *Zur Geschichte der Judischen Tradition*, 2:74ff. in regard to R. Eliezer), just as contemporary research is now doing with Beruria. However, for us "bona fide" scholar means one of the other Tannaim—neither token nor subversive.

Chapter Three

The Teachings of Beruria the *Tannait*

"Beruria the scholar" is neither a mere name, nor a diploma of evaluation, but designates the proponent of a specific school of thought. When delving into the details of Beruria's attributed texts we are exposed to a whole doctrine. If we follow its applications in the various branches of tannaitic teachings of Midrash, Halakha, and Aggada, Beruria's doctrine is portrayed before us by the fire measure we know from the method of the *tanna* R. Eliezer ben Hyrcanus. Furthermore, the scholarly character of Beruria as she appears in Talmudic texts is imprinted with the "fire traces" of R. Eliezer's theological conception. To this, she adds her own original and specific flavor.

Halakha

We shall commence our discussion with two debates from the Mishnaic volume, which deals with the laws of Purity—*Seder Taharot*:

1*
 (A stove)[120] when does it receive uncleanness?
 When it will have been heated sufficiently to bake sponge cakes in it.
 And R. Simeon declares [it] unclean forthwith.
 Rabban Simeon ben Gamliel says in the name of R. Shila, When its manufacture will be completed.
 [If] one plastered it in a state of insusceptibility to uncleanness and it became unclean, from what time is its purification?
 R. Halafta of Kefar Hananya said, I asked Simeon ben Hananya, who asked the son of R. Hananya ben Teradion, and he said, When one will have moved it from its place.

And his daughter says, When he will have removed its garment (*haluko*).
And when these things were reported before R. Judah ben Baba, he said, Better (*yafe*)[121] did his daughter say (rule) than did his son. (Tosefta *Kelim Baba Qama* 4:17, 15)[122]

2*

Clostra (a door bolt), R. Tarfon declares unclean, and Sages declare clean, and Beruria says: One removes it from this door and hangs it on another on the Sabbath. When [these] things were reported before R. Judah (Joshua), he said Beautifully (*yafe*) did Beruria say (rule). (Tosefta, *Kelim Baba Metzia* 1:6, 30)

There are feminist readings of these Beruria texts, viewing them as nothing but superficial halakhic knowledge by the woman-daughter.[123] This approach does not take into account the formal structure of the sources. These texts, like other tannaitic texts, are not structured logically according to their ruling element. Their very structure reflects halakhic positions, which potentially bear seeds for broad Talmudic discussion. They are unlike both the post-Talmudic codification style and the modern "question to the rabbi." Hence, we cannot deduce, as Goodblatt does, any historical hypothesis from the absence of Beruria's name in one of the tannaitic debates, and her being addressed as the daughter of R. Ḥananya in the other.[124] Due to the great similarity between the structures of the two texts, we cannot accept the conclusion that the figure in both is not the same. Such a claim ignores the literary structure of the text, which talks not only of the daughter but also of the son, and ends: "Better did the daughter rule than did his son."[125] Above all, in regard to the tool's nature, we see a consistency in the two debates between the daughter's and Beruria's conception (as opposed to that of the other disputants), pointing to these being one and the same person.

We read the first *tosefta* (1*) as a continuation of its preceding *tosefta*.[126] That one speaks of a broken barrel (*pitas*),[127] which was made into a stove, and then mended with plaster. In spite of having the required measure of impurity on its sides (fractures),[128] this stove (*pitas*) is considered pure.[129] Following this case, the above *tosefta* (1*) queries: "when does it receive uncleanness?" i.e., from what stage does such a stove becomes a tool, and consequently is susceptible to impurity? The first opinion says that only after the regular process of heating, which is estimated as sufficient for baking sponge cakes, i.e., quick baked bread.[130] The second (R. Shimon) says: immediately, since it had already been a barrel and been heated.[131] After plastering, its manufacture is completed, and the *pitas* is susceptible to impurity. The next question of the *tosefta* is: "[If] one plastered it in a state of insusceptibility to uncleanness and it then became unclean, from what time does its purification apply?"[132] i.e., from what stage is it no longer to be considered a tool? At this point the members of R. Ḥananya ben Teradion's family were asked to give their halakhic opinions. The son requires the physical moving of the stove from its place, while the daughter (Beruria), in contrast, holds that removing the plaster is sufficient.

Beyond the fact that attracted the readers' attention, that it was the daughter's opinion which was praised and accepted, as opposed to the son's, we have to consider also the conceptual differences.

The daughter holds that the tool's definition is determined by its essence. The plaster unites the stoves' parts.[133] Hence, when removed, there is nothing to combine them and the stove is considered broken. Accordingly, the removal of the plaster makes the stove pure in accordance with the verse in Leviticus (11:35): "An oven or stove shall be smashed."[134] Differing from the daughter, the son focuses on human action, during the process of the breakage, which may define the stove as a tool or not and consequently determine its purity.

Comparing this *tosefta* to Mishna *Kelim* (5:7) which talks about purification of an ordinary stove, we find the following: The first *tanna* says: the stove should be divided and the plaster combining the fractures should be removed. R. Meir thinks that we could ignore the plaster only by reducing the stove to less than four handbreadths from within the stove. R. Shimon says: the stove should be moved from its place.[135]

If we read the *tosefta* as discussing a broken barrel which was plastered, the opinion of Beruria, that the plaster should be removed from the fractures,[136] corresponds with that of the first *tanna*, who said that the stove should be divided (which means a manner of smashing it), and the plastering scraped off. This opinion of the first *tanna* (Beruria) is opposed to that of the other disputants. R. Shimon, like Beruria's brother, requires the shifting of the stove. Like her husband, R. Meir, who requires neither the plaster removal, nor the division, nor the cutting or breakage of the stove down to the ground, unlike the first *tanna*, R. Shimon only requires its reduction to four handbreadths from the ground.

The acceptance of Beruria's opinion as the first opinion in the *mishna* (*tanna kama*), which is usually considered to be the majority opinion, should not be interpreted only as a socio-political "victory" over her brother/husband, but should throw light on her conception. This might help explain the philological and historical difficulties that this figure and her attributed texts attracted.

As in the *tosefta*, the conceptual difference between *tanna kama*—Beruria versus R. Meir and R. Shimon is that which bases the definition of the tool on itself, rather than on Man's relation to it. R. Meir and R. Shimon embody in contrasting ways the same principle. R. Shimon says: no matter what is done to the stove, the biblical requirement of smashing (*yutatz,* Lev. 11:35) is fulfilled only when extreme action was taken towards it, i.e., when it was severed from the ground. R. Meir is satisfied with an almost symbolic action of cutting, even though the parts are still united, either due to the incomplete cutting or to the plaster. Against these two opinions, says the first *tanna kama*—Beruria—Sages, the definition of the broken tool depends only on the oven's nature. Neither symbolic, nor extreme human action is needed. When the plaster is removed from the broken barrel, or from the completely broken oven, this establishes its breakage by definition, since nothing unites it. If, in fact, the oven stands, it is like an object standing in the air. Hence, there is no need to separate the parts or, needless to say, to remove it from the ground.

Beruria's opinion, which was accepted by the Sages, reminds one of R. Eliezer's opinion which was rejected by the Sages in the famous dispute known as the oven of Akhnai,[137] found in both Talmuds and also in Mishna *Kelim* (5:10). In that dispute, the cuts between the sections of the oven are filled with sand. R. Eliezer says it is unsusceptible to impurity, as it is not considered a tool, but considered a broken one. Since the sand separates the sections, the plaster does not assist in combining them.[138] At any rate, even if it actually stands due to that plaster, the oven is considered broken due to its structure and its very nature.[139] The Sages say: the plaster does help make this oven a tool, hence it is susceptible to impurity.

Although this *mishna* was discussed in both Talmuds, the Talmudic discussion does not go into details as it usually does, but begins with the very last sentence, viz. "this is the oven of Akhnai," afterwards relating a horrible and beautiful *aggada* (especially in the Babylonian Talmud version).

In a detailed analysis of this *aggada* elsewhere,[140] we concluded that it presents two different approaches to the Torah. On the one hand, R. Eliezer maintains the Torah's divine nature that had continued to function in life, overwhelming all reality, since Sinai. Therefore, Man should try to look for the Torah's original meaning, adhering to its ideal nature, and taking it as part of his existence. On the other hand, the Sages and R. Gamliel in particular, maintain that since Sinai, the Torah's meaning was to be determined by Man's limited reason.

These approaches, which could be described in terms of existentialism[141] versus rationalism, or in terms of idealism versus pragmatism, are applicable to the halakhic dispute between R. Eliezer and the Sages in the *mishna* of Akhnai, as well as to the dispute between Beruria and the other *tannaim*.

According to R. Eliezer, the definition of the tool is independent of the user[142] and depends on its ideal nature i.e., the original rules that God, the Creator, imprinted on it. Thus, the halakhic status of the tool is determined by God's original intentions, as all the laws of the Torah are said to be determined by the original intentions of God, and not limited to the human perception. The other approach is not idealistic like that of R. Eliezer, but pragmatic. This approach holds that Man determines the tool's status, as Man determines all the other laws of the Torah.[143] Even though the tool in itself is broken, the important thing is the plaster that Man put around it in order to combine it. The artificial human act determines its very nature.

As we know from the end of the Akhnai text, R. Eliezer's idealistic conception of Torah, founded on the Sinai revelation, which we called "the fire conception," was rejected after a great struggle that ended by his being excommunicated. However, it seems that in our *mishna* R. Eliezer's "fire principle" was accepted, since it was applied by *Tanna Kama*—Beruria—and Sages.[144]

The conceptual proximity of Beruria to R. Eliezer's halakhic way is reinforced in her next dispute quoted above. (2*)

Clostra[145] is a peg, which has a knob at its top. R. Tarfon thinks that, because of that knob, the peg is a tool, as it may be used for pounding and, as a result, it is susceptible to impurity. The Sages do not consider it a tool and, therefore, consider it not susceptible to impurity. Here, Beruria's opinion transfers from another subject—the Sabbath laws—instead of learning directly from the laws of Purity. She says, somewhat obscurely "One removes it (pulls down and drags along) from this door and hangs it on another on the Sabbath."

Once again, many modern readers focus on the fact that Beruria's opinion was praised and made law by R. Judah/Joshua,[146] but the question is really, what was so special about Beruria's opinion? After all, aside from applying her opinion in the laws of the Sabbath to the laws of Purity, was it not the same opinion as that of the Sages in the dispute with R. Tarfon?[147]

Reading Beruria's opinion carefully, we learn a general halakhic principle. As the commentators say, regarding the same opinion brought in the name of R. Joshua in the parallel *mishna* (*Kelim* 11:4): "Just as he considers it a tool for Sabbath issues, it is the same regarding purity issues."[148] This halakhic method of similar principles applying to different issues (*hashva'at hamidot*—standardization of the rules/principles) was specifically identified by a few *tannaim* with R. Eliezer's methodology, as opposed to that of R. Joshua.[149] Indeed, the early commentator R. Simshon of Sens (RS) raised a crucial question regarding this ruling attributed to R. Joshua, although it is not articulated as a methodological refutation.[150] According to the Talmud (BT *Shabbat* 124a), we must make one of two assertions. We may say that this rule refers to the time before carrying tools on the Sabbath was permitted and that, even though R. Joshua considers *clostra* as impure, implying that he considers it a tool, he will prohibit its carriage. Or else, one might say that this ruling applies to moving tools in a courtyard with an *eruv* around it, where permitted according to R. Joshua. This is in spite of the fact that in the Tosefta R. Joshua does not consider it a tool as regards purity. Accordingly, R. Joshua does not standardize rules between Sabbath and Purity. RS leaves this conclusion for further contemplation. Undoubtedly, the version: "R. Joshua" rather than "R. Judah" in the Tosefta contributed to the difficulty raised above. However, the *mishna* itself, even if explained as dealing with Sabbath rules rather than with Purity, is stylistically linked to the Tosefta ruling by Beruria who, like R. Eliezer, standardized the rules. Consequently, the assignment of the *mishna* to R. Joshua is problematic.[151]

Against this background, returning to the Tosefta, it seems that Beruria's opinion does not necessarily tally with that of the Sages.[152] The Sages might agree with the 3rd–4th c. *amora* Abaye's statement in his dispute with his comrade Rava: "Are you casting (implying) from Purity to Sabbath?"[153] Namely, these are two different matters. In order to be subject to the laws of Purity, an object needs to have the definition of a tool, while in order to be an object the removal of which is permitted on Sabbath, it needs only a function, some usage. Accordingly, the Sages might not consider a *clostra* as a tool by Purity Law standards. As the Jerusalem Talmud (JT) says, the knob is dispensable for the peg and is not essential for its definition. However, since it has some utility (pounding with) it could be considered as a tool permitted to be moved on Sabbath.[154] Unlike the Sages, Beruria does standardize the principles in both issues. Just as the *clostra* is not a tool for the law of Purity, so it is not for the law concerning its being removed on Sabbath.

Yitzhak D. Gilat analyses the foundation of R Eliezer's method of standardization of the rules:

> This basic method first analyses the specific laws according to their own logic and considers them in the light of their own principles and

then takes their common features as the decisive factors in determining a unified *halakhah*. It is this method that fostered his habit of applying uniform standards (*hashvaat hamidot*) and served him as an intellectual basis guiding him in his acceptance of various law, and in adopting and in formulating them as practical *halakhah*.[155]

Gilat links this method of R. Eliezer to his inclination towards the early Halakha, which was more uniform and did not have the development of differentiation that later Halakha purportedly acquired.[156] Unlike Gilat, we explain this method of R Eliezer as deriving from a philosophical inductive approach, which follows from his "Fire-Sinai conception" in its idealistic feature. Torah itself, namely the specific features of the detailed law, will determine its common definition, or its own nature, rather than that the latter be determined by rules external to the specific law—logical or attitudinal.

Following R. Eliezer's method as applied in Beruria's second ruling, we find the same idealistic conception as against the pragmatic. This means that the definition of a tool, and consequently its status implications in various fields of law, derive intrinsically from its own nature, rather than being established by the human-related function. Hence, *clostra*'s status as a tool for both Sabbath and Purity will be determined by its very definition, rather than by external human usage.

Halakha and Aggada

In our research on R. Eliezer[157] we analyzed this idealistic (fire) conception of Torah, as applied not just to Halakha and Aggada separately, but also to their mutual relations, which led to a new understanding of the nature of both. Unlike the Geonim who viewed these two fields as ontologically separate, and even unlike those who recognized a linkage between the two,[158] we read the Talmudic Aggada as an extreme Halakha.

Tracing R. Eliezer's halakhic character, we observed how the text's nature changed to aggadic when halakhic process was exhausted. The BT version of the dispute of Akhnai begins "he (R. Eliezer) had given them (his opponents) all answers in the world,"[159] which means all possible halakhic answers. At this ultimate stage of the Halakha, it continues to exist beyond limitations of reality and then it moves to Aggada.[160]
Hence, all the proofs that R. Eliezer gives, refer to the symbols of Torah:

If the Halakha agrees with me, let this carob-tree prove it!

> If the Halakha agrees with me, let the stream of water prove it!
> If the Halakha agrees with me, let the walls of the schoolhouse prove it!
> If the Halakha agrees with me, let it be proved from Heaven! (BT *Baba Mezia* 59b)

The tree, the water, the academy's walls, and the voice from heaven reflect the same logical principles revealed in the halakhic dispute in the *mishna*, viz. the Torah itself will determine its legal nature. However, these proofs were considered aggadic (or popularly called miracles), since their symbols express the idealistic nature of Torah as given at Sinai. They are thus closer to the Divine area than to the human.[161] From that extreme stage, for the halakhic scholar who is in union with this idealistic conception of Torah, the overwhelming and infinite nature of Torah becomes part of his existential being, at which very moment the halakhic scholar becomes an aggadic scholar.[162]

This perspective of Halakha and Aggada, as nourished from the same ontological principles, is strongly connected with the feature of multiplicity that the Sinai conception of Torah creates. R. Eliezer's tendency towards multiple, rich Torah is well known in regard to the quantity,[163] but is less known in regard to the quality of Torah.[164] Richness of Torah in terms of quantity is expressed especially in R. Eliezer's wide knowledge of transmitted Halakha from the recent generations back to Sinai.[165] This does not merely help to reconstruct the original Sinai Torah, but the quantity also helps to apply the Torah's principles in various patterns and dimensions of life and text, such as in the standardization of the principles, and the relationship between the fields of Halakha and Aggada. Richness of Torah in terms of quality is expressed in R. Eliezer's review of the multiple interpretations that should be applied to the multiple *shemuot (halakhot)*,[166] viz. the area of Midrash, and his concept of the "fertilized scholar" who is obligated to intensive hermeneutic creativity. Once again, this approach of R. Eliezer does not merely help to connect the scholar to the Sinai Torah, and thus to the idealistic nature of Torah, but also reveals R. Eliezer's vision of the text itself as potentially fertile.

Beruria the Halakhist-Aggadist

This introduction brings us to the next source, in which Beruria is introduced as an aggadist from the perspective of her strong relation as a halakhist. Note that the text presents Aggada not merely as Midrash, i.e., as a technical exegetical methodology which could be taught to everyone, but rather as a field which requires a multitude of Torah-learning in both Aggada and Halakha, and thus becomes the realm of elite scholars.

The feminist reading assumes that the Babylonian Talmud could have chosen "any number of male sages who frequented the academies during her time, earlier or later" instead of the "woman Beruria."[167] We maintain however that the text refers specifically to the field of Aggada, from that very perspective of Halakha, which was a very hard standpoint to adopt even in the tannaitic time.[168] Nonetheless, the Beruria figure which arises from this and other texts seems to meet these specific requirements of the field, which apparently leads once again to the idealism inherent in the "fire conception" of R. Eliezer.

3*

R. Simlai came before R. Johanan[169] [and] requested him, Let the Master teach me the Book of Genealogies. Said he to him, Whence are you? He replied, From Lod. And where is your dwelling? In Nehardea. Said he to him, we do not discuss it either with the Lodians or with the Nehardeans, and how much more so with you, who are from Lod and live in Nehardea! But he urged him, and he consented.

Let us learn it in three months, he proposed. [Thereupon] he took a clod and threw it at him, saying, if Beruria, wife of R. Meir [and] daughter of R. Hananya ben Teradion, who studied three hundred *shma'atteta* (Halakha) from three hundred Rabbis in [one] day, could nevertheless not do her duty in three years, yet you propose [to do it] in three months!

As he was going he said to him: Rabbi, What is the difference between [a Passover offering which is sacrificed both] for its own purpose and for a different purpose? He said to him: since you are a scholar, come and I will tell you (BT *Pesahim* 62b)

4*

R. Simlai came before R. Jonathan [and] said to him: Teach me Aggada. He said to him: I have a tradition from my ancestors not to teach Aggada to Babylonians or to Southerners, for they are *gasei ru'ah* (haughty) and *mi'utei Torah* (short in Torah) and you are Nehardean [by origin] and live in the South. He said to him tell me one thing: what is the difference between [a Passover offering which was sacrificed both] for its own purpose and for a different purpose? (JT *Pesahim* 5:3, 32:1)

Goodblatt is inclined to view the BT version as a reworking of the JT.[170] The most important difference for him is that JT does not mention

Beruria, and so the tradition about her is, as his followers put it: "a Babylonian choice rather than an authentic ancient tradition."[171] Since the issue of authenticity of the Babylonian tradition about Beruria is unresolved here,[172] the most important point for us is that in BT Beruria's figure is reflected through her unique conception of Aggada, expressed also in JT. In addition, in both versions the domain of the Aggada is depicted as a field exclusive to scholars.[173]

As stated, the question which strikes everyone in Talmudic studies is why R. Simlai, who was known mainly as a scholar of Aggada,[174] when asked to be taught Aggada, was rejected, since he was suspected of lack of knowledge in Halakha? From the reaction of the R. Simlai in both versions, we may understand that Halakha was a prerequisite for entrance into the field of Aggada. Thus, we may ask, what is the relevance of the Halakha to Aggada?

In the Babylonian version, this point is emphasized by the example of Beruria, who is not characterized directly as an aggadist, but rather as a halakhist scholar. More specifically, Beruria "who studied three hundred *shma'atteta* from three hundred Rabbis," was presented as skilled especially in the transmitted Halakha, as learned from the term: *shma'atteta—shemu'a*—the traditional law (Halakha)[175] which she had been taught and heard from the Rabbis. The last characterization of Beruria as adhering to the transmitted Halakha makes for an immediate analogy to R. Eliezer. However, what reveals their affinity to each other is the description in this version (BT) of the extreme halakhist who is rich in Torah, and the unique conception presented in both versions (BT and JT), which situates the field of Aggada at the very limit of Halakha.

The BT version teaches us, albeit indirectly by the example of Beruria, about the prerequisite for the study of Aggada. This is the prerequisite of multiple Torah from its quantity perspective, as expressed in the transmitted Halakha from Sinai ("three hundred *shma'atteta*"). Against BT, JT explicitly mentions the prerequisite of multiple Torah for the study of Aggada. However, JT also attaches to it a second prerequisite, which sheds light on the concept of "multiple Torah" from its quality perspective. Accordingly, R. Jonathan did not want to teach R. Simlai Aggada, because he assumed that R. Simlai was one of those who are "short in Torah" (*mi'utei Torah*), which apparently means that he was not rich in Torah. R. Simlai's reaction in demonstrating his knowledge of Halakha, stresses the importance of quantity (short/rich) in Torah-learning expertise. Similarly, we find in the BT version (3*), after R. Simlai demonstrates his halakhic knowledge, that R. Johanan "said to him: since that you are a scholar," meaning that he was "full of Torah." However, as stated previously, in JT the phrase: "short in Torah" is brought alongside the phrase: "being haughty (*gas ru'ah*)." This makes for the possibility that the contrary concept of multitude or richness of Torah refers also to methodology and not only to quantity. Thus, the phrase "short in Torah" means limiting Torah study to certain ways of studying, and not being open to various interpretations or multiple readings that Midrash methodology suggests for scriptures. Accordingly, the richness of Torah, or the avoidance of shortage of Torah, depends on the quantity of Torah knowledge, as well as on the scholar's interpretational creativity, which extends and multiplies the Torah itself. For its part, a large quantity of Torah knowledge enables the scholar to be "multiple" in his extensive application of creative interpretation, thus enriching the text of the Torah.

This vision of the "multiple Torah" in its double meaning, reminds us of R. Eliezer:

> Concerning the garment, I know only about the one in which there is room for spreading. A garment in which there is not room for spreading, how do I know [that it is susceptible]? Scripture says: "And the garment" (Lev. 13:47) the words of R. Eliezer. Said to him R. Ishmael: Lo, you say to the Scripture, be silent by the time (*ad she*)[176] that I am making interpretations (*doresh*). Said to him R. Eliezer: Ishmael, you are a mountain-palm. (*Sifra Negaim* 13)[177]

R. Ishmael's claim is that Scripture cannot bear R. Eliezer's multiple interpretations,[178] and he is like one who is silencing the text from uttering what it wishes to say, while loading it with interpretations (*midrashim*) that are detached from the text itself.[179] The answer of R. Eliezer is "Ishmael! You are a mountain-palm." As we know from Mishna *Bikurim*,[180] the mountain palm is considered unproductive, since its fruits are inferior. The application of this metaphor in our textual environment means, as RaBaD explains: "As it (the mountain palm) does not keep its fruits, and its fruits are meagre, so you Ishmael cannot bear many interpretations/ *derashot* of the text."[181] Accordingly, the meaning of the peculiar metaphor used by R. Eliezer: "a mountain palm" is none other than the term: "short in Torah," which appears in the parallel of the Beruria text, in JT (4*). "Mountain palm" reflects infertility, either in regard to the scholar's creative interpretational ability, or in regard to his vision of the texts' richness and multiplicity. Hence, those who applied numerous interpretations/*midrashim* are a target for haughtiness: "Lo, you say to the Scripture, be silent at the time that I am making interpretations." Here we could also hear something of a literary rudeness towards the methodology of Midrash, which is derived ideologically from the vision of the text and, therefore of Midrash and interpreter as limited.[182]

This limited view of text as an interpreter was considered by R. Eliezer as barrenness (in all dimensions: philosophical, literary, hermeneutic), or in the JT terminology as "shortage in Torah," in both dimensions: quality (methodology), and quantity. Since R. Eliezer was known to have multiple knowledge of *Shemu'a*, his vision of the text and his hermeneutic keenness were motivated by that extensive halakhic knowledge.[183] A lack in quantity of Torah, in his view, would cause textual insensitivity and thus haughtiness towards the field and the scholar of Aggada.

We now return to Beruria's texts. Although BT (3*) does not generalize this conception of the Aggada as does JT (4*), it seems that it is imprinted on the BT structure. By wishing to study Aggada in a short time (three months), R. Simlai demonstrated his attitude towards Aggada as a field which does not require prior or profound knowledge and richness of Torah. Therefore, he was suspected of being haughty (*gas ru'ah*) towards this domain in general.

Against this background, the appearance of the Beruria figure in BT (3*) should not be taken as external to the text, and simply as another example of a great scholar whose name was added to the BT version for this or that reason. Rather, Beruria presents that very special conception of the Aggada and the aggadist scholar, which emerges from both versions.

Beruria appears to us as a sage whose multiple knowledge of Halakha has an implication for her interpretative ability. Furthermore, the quantity dimension of her multiple Torah, creates the vision of a multitudinous text. True, the phrase: "three hundred *Shma'atteta* (*halakhot*) from three hundred rabbis" seems to be a figurative formula of "three"—which is not free of polemics, following the rudeness of R. Simlai, who asked to learn Aggada in "three" (months). However, this should not stop us from seeing it as referring to the issue itself.

Interestingly, R. Eliezer uses the same phrase in regard to his multiple Torah:

> He then put his two arms over his heart, and bewailed them, saying, Woe to you, two arms of mine, that have been like two Scrolls of the Torah that are wrapped up. Multiple Torah have I studied, and much have I taught. Multiple Torah have I learnt, yet have I but skimmed from the knowledge of my teachers ... Multiple Torah have I taught ... Moreover, I have studied three hundred *halakhot* on the subject of a deep bright spot, yet no man has ever asked me about them. Moreover,

I have studied three hundred (or, as others state, three thousand) *halakhot* about the planting of marrows. (BT *Sanhedrin* 68a)[184]

We can clearly see in this passage the concept of richness in Torah, in regard to the Torah itself and to the scholar's knowledge of it.[185] The expression "three hundreds/thousands *halakhot*" does not specify an amount or quantity of knowledge of Torah, which is contained in the potential of the text, or which is achieved by the scholar, but rather emphasizes its inexhaustibility. The same is true regarding Beruria's Torah. The phrase: "three hundred *shma'atteta*, (*halakhot*) from three hundred rabbis" does not express the full extent of knowledge or efforts required for Aggada study, but rather claims that no quantity of knowledge is sufficient. Accordingly, even Beruria who, like R. Eliezer, maintained the extreme approach of "multiple Torah," did not exhaust the Aggada studies "in three years," i.e., in any amount of time. Thus, both texts (BT 3* and JT 4*) demonstrate a great affinity to the Sinai conception of R. Eliezer as applied to the area of Aggada. The fact that in BT it is Beruria who is presenting this special Torah conception does not seem strange, considering the great affinity we have already found in her relation to R. Eliezer's principles and opinions in the area of Halakha.

In the following few texts, too, we will observe how the tendency to multiple Torah of R. Eliezer (as well as other features of the Sinai conception) was applied by Beruria in Midrash and in other dimensions of Torah and the scholar.

Sins and Repentance

5*
>
> There were once some highwaymen in the neighborhood of R. Meir who caused him a great deal of sorrow. R. Meir was asking for mercy (prayed) on them so they should die. His wife Beruria said to him: what do you think? [on what have you based yourself in that prayer] Since it is written: Let *hataim* cease? (Ps. 104:35) Is it written *hot'im* (sinners)? It is written *hataim* (sins). Further, lower yourself[186] down to the end of the verse (*shfel leseifei dikra*) "and let the wicked men be no more." Because the sins will cease, there will be no more wicked men! Rather ask for mercy (pray) for them so they should repent, and there will have been no more wicked. He did ask for mercy (prayed) for them, and they repented. (BT *Berakhot* 10a)[187]

We must read this text as reflecting the concept of the scholar's personality, as previously discussed.[188] Both Beruria and R. Meir, as true scholars, act only according to the all-engulfing entity of Torah-study. Beruria assumes that R. Meir's prayer is derived from a certain exegesis, i.e. *midrash*, and in that area she disagrees. Some readers who have cited this text as an example of Beruria's superiority, (emotional or intellectual) to R. Meir, seem to have missed the exegetical and conceptual differences between them.[189] R. Meir's exegesis seems to be based on the Bible. In all of Scripture we find that the word: *hataim* means "sinners", except for a single occurrence as a plural of the noun: *het*, in which case the word: *hataim* means "sins."[190] The form: *hot'im* as "sinners" does not appear at all in Scripture. Consequently, Beruria's query: "is it written *hot'im*,"[191] which is the opening for her midrash, seems totally inexplicable. Without doubt, she knows that Scripture never uses this form of *hot'im* as "sinners"? If we leave this puzzle for a moment, and concentrate on her interpretation, it seems that she is applying a midrashic methodology of expounding superfluity in Scripture, in order to extract from it a multiple meaning: "Let *hataim* cease / and let the wicked men be no more" (Ps. 104:35). If we are not relating to both parts of the verse as synonymous parallelism, the second part of the verse is superfluous.[192] Thus, the first part must bear a less obvious meaning. However, against the background of the problematic scriptural meaning of *hataim* as "sins," applying the midrashic methodology by Beruria in this case seems to derive from her strong tendency to multiple Torah, which affects not only her methodology, but also her vision of the text, and most important, her exegetical results.

In addition, Beruria's use of the phrase: "lower yourself to the end of the verse" (*shpel leseifei dikra*) does not seem to be figurative, as in the case of the only other two *tannaim* to whom this formula was attributed.[193] Rather, she coins the phrase: "lower yourself to the end of the verse," in order to express her extreme approach of "multitude" [194] viz., when making a *midrash*/interpretation, one should adopt a wide vision of the text. This does not refer only to the known midrashic methodology, according to which the reader should enrich the text's content through its extended context. That is to say that the reader should take into consideration not only the word itself, but also the entire verse, and maybe the entire chapter.[195] Rather, it means that the reader should enrich the text by reading multi-directionally. Thus, one should look at the later parts of the text in order to interpret the earlier, applying a backwards reading. This view extends the content of the text to other dimensions, and so deepens its general meaning.

Looking at Beruria's interpretation, we find that instead of understanding the verse as repeating the idea of the death of the wicked (sinners), by her multiplying the meaning of the verse and thus reading *ḥataim* as sins, she transforms the text from being declarative to being "relational." Therefore, the verse does not tell us only about the end of the sins/sinners, but also teaches about the relationship between them. Thus, the textual vision is enriched from its quality perspective by reflecting complexity. In addition, Beruria's methodology and vision give us a new understanding of the concepts "sins" and "sinners" themselves. We conceive the entity of the sin as separate from its bearer—the sinner.[196] Hence, destruction of the sinners is not a prerequisite for elimination of sins. The latter are a non-essential and non-permanent dimension of human personality. This understanding logically explains the possibility of the concept of repentance.[197] Thus, Beruria derives that the appropriate behavior is: "Rather ask for mercy (pray) for them so they should repent, and there will be no more wicked men." This sensitive reading of the verse by Beruria is not due only to her fruitful character as a scholar of Aggada who is not haughty (*gas ru'aḥ*). Rather, her sensitive reading becomes possible due to the extreme multiple methodology she applied i.e., "lowering herself" not only to the end of the verse, but also to the entire relevant chapter in Psalms 104. Reading the verse as a whole enables her to read it backwards and forwards, and thus to feel the conditional relationship between the parts. Reading the whole chapter, which describes the complete harmony between God's overwhelming presence and all of Creation (including human beings), leads to her philosophical interpretation of this verse, which ends the chapter. In her interpretation, the poet of Psalms is hoping for the end of the sins and not that of the sinners. Since the human being is, basically, in harmony with God's presence, the only obstacle that could interrupt this harmony will be a person's sins that in themselves are a separate entity from him.

Once again, Beruria's conception as presented in the text, takes the Beruria figure very close to that of R. Eliezer, who says in *Sifre*:

> For whosoever doeth these things he (it) is an abomination to the Lord (Deut. 18:12) . . . When R. Eliezer would come to this verse he would say: Alas, for us! Since he who clings to the uncleanness the spirit of uncleanness rests upon him, all the more, he who cling to the *Shekhinah* the holy spirit should rest upon him. What causes this (not to happen?) but your sins have separated between you and your God (Is 59:2). (*Sifre Deuteronomy* 173)[198]

In this *midrash* of R. Eliezer it seems that we find not only the same philosophy of the basic harmony between God and Human, which is interrupted by sin, but also the same midrashic methodology. Here too we see how superfluity of the verse and "lowering oneself" not only to the end of the verse, but also to the next verse, creates an interpretation which does not view the first part as declarative, but relational. Again, this approach causes a backward and forward reading. The verse says: "For whosoever doeth these things it is an abomination to the Lord. And because of these abominations the Lord thy God is driving them out from before thee" (Deut. 18:12). If the only meaning of the first part was to declare God's abomination of the deeds of the people, it would be superfluous, since it is obvious from the second part. The same applies to the beginning of the second part that repeats: "because of these abominations." So, why all this superfluity? A careful reading shows blurriness in regard to the abomination mentioned in the first part, where it is not clear whether it refers to the deeds or to the people themselves.

Against this background, we understand R. Eliezer's interpretation that the first part: "For whosoever doeth these things it (he) is an abomination to the Lord." does not declare anything, but presents the relationship between the people and their abominable deeds, a relation of clinging to the uncleanness until they themselves became an abomination. However, not only superfluity and sensitivity towards the text compelled R. Eliezer's *midrash*, but also the "lowering of oneself" to the second part of the verse, reading it backwards: "And because of these abominations the Lord thy God is driving them out from before thee." If one asks: why did God drive the people out? Apparently, it was because of their deeds, "these abominations." But should it not be something in the people themselves that would justify this total separation from God?

Just as Beruria, who finds the reason for the second part of the verse in the first part, so it seems, does R. Eliezer's *midrash*. He reads a double meaning in "Because of these abominations" as referring to the normal situation wherein the evil deeds are apart from the people who commit them and, simultaneously, to the actual situation wherein the people were clinging to their abominable deeds, and became one with the spirit of uncleanness, i.e., the abominations themselves. Therefore, the Lord drove them out and decreed total separation.

The separation from God is only one part of R. Eliezer's *midrash*, which is intrinsically tied to the other part dealing with unification with God, although the verse itself refers only to the former—the separation. Thus, in R. Eliezer's *midrash*, the relations between the parts actually complete the whole philosophical idea which we found in Beruria's *midrash*: the idea of a basic harmony between Man and God,[199] and of sins as foreign incursions. One might say that the harmony with God is the other implicit aspect of the verse, which talks about the separation of God. Methodologically, as R. Eliezer multiplies the text by interpreting superfluity, finding its meaning in the deep layers of relationship systems, in the same way he extends his interpretation to this complementary aspect of the verse, although the latter is not asserted explicitly. Nonetheless, it seems that the main factor which affected this interpretation was, once again, the multiplicity of the text [from its quantitative respect], or, in Beruria's terms, the lowering of oneself, this time, to the next verse. "Thou shalt be whole-hearted/complete (*tamim*) with the Lord your God" (Deut. 18:13). The requirement of the Torah in this verse simply contradicts the requirement in Deuteronomy (18:12) as interpreted by R. Eliezer: Cling to God, to the Holy Presence, to the *Shekhina*, as opposed to the clinging to uncleanness and abominations. This structural similarity generates the expectation of the same result, as if to say "Because of this holiness, the Lord your God will bring you close to him." This conclusion is however missing from the biblical text. Indeed, from this missing part in the next verse, arises R. Eliezer's interpretation of the previous one: "Since he who clings to the uncleanness, the spirit of uncleanness rests upon him, all the more, he who clings to the *Shekhina*, the holy presence should rest upon him." The question is why "all the more"? Why should clinging to God promise a true union, rather than clinging to the spirit of uncleanness? The answer comes out of the next verse. It is because the natural state of the human being is that of complete union with God: "Thou shalt be whole-hearted/complete (*tamim*) with the Lord your God." Therefore, normally his relation to evil deeds should be as between two entities, and not one, as in the case of those people who themselves became abominations. However, in spite of the differentiation between Man and sins as entities, the latter have the power to separate him from his basic state of a complete harmony with God. Indeed, one could pray cheerfully as the Psalmist in Beruria's *midrash*: "let sins cease" and believe in the power of repentance to cancel the gaps between Man and God. However, it is the actual situation compared with the ideal one which, in this *midrash*, brings about R. Eliezer's elegiac tone: "Alas to us"—to all human beings whose sins prevent them from a total adherence to God. Nevertheless, since it is the harmonious relations between Man and God and the perpetual striving for a complete union between them which characterizes R. Eliezer's Sinai-fire conception of Torah and divinity,[200] in other sources we do hear another voice of R. Eliezer, more optimistic and closer to that of Beruria's interpretation of Psalms.

In Mishna R. Eliezer says:

> A person may bring a voluntary "suspensive" guilt-offering any day and any time he wishes and it is called the guilt offering of the pious. (Mishna *Keritot* 6:3)[201]

And in the Talmud he said:

> Repent one day before your death.[202] His disciples asked him, does then one know on what day he will die? Then all the more reason that he repent today, he replied, lest he die tomorrow, and thus his whole life is spent in repentance (BT *Shabbat* 163a)

These two texts[203] demonstrate how R. Eliezer extends the application of repentance, so that one will partake of that process throughout one's life. According to our reading, this reflects R. Eliezer's true belief in the possibility of elimination of the gaps created by sin, bringing about harmony and the full clinging to the Holy Spirit.[204]

The Aggadist: The Fertile Scholar

In the following text Beruria is revealed once again as master of Aggada in the style of R. Eliezer, i.e., she shows an extreme tendency to multiple Torah, while applying fruitful methodology, with brilliant results.

6*

> A certain *min* [205] said to Beruria: It is written: Sing, O barren, thou that did not bear (Is.54:1). Because she did not bear is she to sing? She replied to him: You fool! Lower yourself down to the end of the verse, where it is written: For the child of the desolate shall be more than the children of the married wife, saith the Lord. But what then, is the meaning of "a barren that did not bear?" Sing, O congregation of Israel, who resembles a barren woman, for not having borne children like you[206] for Gehenna. (BT *Berakhot* 10a)

It seems that the political-feminist analysis has shifted the focus of this text from its center.[207] The question of the *min* should not be read as referring simply to the verse by itself: "why should she rejoice . . . because she is barren?"[208] Indeed, it seems as if the *min*, too, knew how to read a verse within its biblical context, and the end of the verse simply explains the barren's rejoicing. The question of the *min* should be understood in the context of the dispute of the heretics (Christians or others) about the Midrash methodology of interpreting superfluity instead of accepting synonyms in Scripture.[209] Although the *min* is challenging the Sages in general, and so his question is not free of a polemical element, Beruria, who was an extreme applier of the multiple approach in Midrash, seems to transmit the dispute from the polemical sphere to the conceptual one. In other words, a mild version of the *min's* question could be raised within the Sages' circles,[210] as implied by R. Ishmael's comment to R. Eliezer's multiple interpretations, and echoing the warning against teaching Aggada to those who are short in Torah and haughty. Therefore, rather than defending the Sages' methodology, Beruria is presenting here a specific stream within it, and thus unveiling the theoretical principles of the method.

The *min's* criticism is reflected in his artificial question, which is extrapolated by him *ad absurdum*. Hence, it is exposed in its mimicry of the midrashic exegesis.[211] Since, according to the midrashic method, "barren woman" and "thou that did not bear" are almost synonymous, an additional meaning must be derived. The *min* concludes that the latter reflects a more severe state than the former, i.e., being permanently, rather than temporarily, barren. Consequently, he raises the question whether the joy of the barren woman is a result of not bearing. Or, in the text's words: "Because she did not bear is she to sing?" The rhythm of the *min's midrash* resembles somewhat the rhythm of Beruria's previous *midrash* on Psalms: "Since the sins will cease, there will be no wicked," except for the question mark, which the *min* applies to his *midrash*, but which is also drawn on Beruria's previous *midrash*.[212] However, the absurdity betrays the mockery and triviality he felt towards his midrashic results, reflecting his contempt for the Sages' midrashic world in general, and Beruria's in particular.

Beruria counterattacks on all fronts:

First, the *min* has failed to imitate the midrashic methodology of interpreting redundancy and superfluity, not, as he thought, because he applied the Sages' "false" view of the text as rich, but because he did not apply this view with sufficient rigor. Therefore, he is a "fool!"

The extreme vision of the multiple text requires in Beruria's phrase: "lowering oneself to the end of the verse," or to larger textual units. We have already seen how applying this approach affected a text's meaning in various dimensions. However, Beruria here is extending its application to the choice the interpreter should make of the exegetical process. Namely, this multiplicity will determine which novel meaning may be found in that redundancy. In this case, the text from Isaiah, the end of the verse prevents one from following the exegetical direction of severity. The second part, "thou that did not bear," could not be explained as a more severe state than the first part, "barren," and as an absolute barrenness,[213] because it explains the reason for elation: "for more are the children of the desolate from those of the married wife." Thus, the *min's* pseudo-*midrash* is logically false, as the exegesis must lead to the opposite direction, not towards severity but, rather, towards leniency. Namely, the second part comes to limit the barrenness and not to extend it. This methodology will lead the interpreter to explore the novel meaning in other layers of the text. Instead of positing the meaning on the textual surface whose subject is merely the quantity of children and a physical barrenness, she burrows into the quality dimension, which refers to the kind of children and spiritual barrenness. Beruria therefore teaches that the favorable infertility is that which prevents unworthy and hence undesirable children. As Scripture would have said in midrashic logic: "Did not bear" those sorts of children, but rather "Did bear" these sorts. The fresh meaning infused by Beruria's *midrash* is no longer illogical as it was reflected through the *min's* eye. It once again enriches the text, transferring the motivation for rejoicing from mere non-existence of childbirth to its qualitative significance.

Actually, the richness of the textual resolution achieved by Beruria in this case was not caused solely by applying the methodology of superfluity interpretation, but once again by applying her principle of "lowering oneself," not only to the end of the verse, but to the end of the whole chapter. There we find: "And all your children are God's students" (skilled in God's studies—Torah) (Is 54:13). Reading the chapter backwards, it becomes clear that the multitude of children, which are described at length in the first part of the chapter, does not reflect merely quantity but also quality. Hence, the barrenness parable in our verse has a dual meaning, physical and spiritual. Since the eventual fertilization was concerned with children skilled in Torah, the initial barrenness (which was physical) was also concerned with this. Thus, the relations between these two dimensions of barrenness (the physical and spiritual) created, according to Beruria, the "Joyous" of the barren, as saying: "O! Sing physical barren! Who has not borne spiritual barrens, i.e., children who are not skilled in Torah."

At this point, the polemics of Beruria's *midrash* become overt, as she interprets the (spiritual) barrenness in the verse as referring to the infertile study of the *min,* who attacked the Midrash and its methodology of multiplicity. By this, she extends the meaning of the barrenness to apply to the congregation of Israel and to those outside. She explains: Sing, O congregation of Israel! Thou that did not bear children who are not skilled in God's studies, like that *min* and such who do not know how to study Torah, which is Midrash, and attribute their own barrenness in studying to those who are actually fruitful in it, due to their creative vision of the multiplicity of Torah (in all respects). However, the style of her response: "Sing . . . for not having borne children like you for Gehenna" does not leave the *min*'s error merely in the intellectual field, but associates it with the moral one. This she does by referring to the haughtiness and rudeness reflected from the *midrash* of the *min*, who mocked the Rabbis as representatives of the whole congregation of Israel. Mocking the Rabbis deserves the fire of Gehenna[214] and thus leaves the sinner no hope, and incapable of repentance. The question is Why?

Once again, what seems like Beruria spitting fire, rather than deriving from a harsh character, actually reflects, as in the case of R. Eliezer, her conception of the Torah in its oral respect as transmitted by the Rabbis, namely the Sinai conception. Thus, disrespect for the Rabbis is denial of the Sinai conception from its national aspect,[215] while the contempt for the Sages' exegetical methodology of multitude denies the divine character of its revelation aspect. Thus, children of Gehenna are at the other extreme from children of Sinai, the congregation of Israel. Unlike the fire of Sinai, which cancels gaps and brings harmony between Man and God, the fire of Gehenna consumes everything: sin and Man, detaching the latter from God and preventing repentance.[216]

The Engulfing Presence of Torah and the Scholar's Union

In the next text, we will identify Beruria's "fire conception" of the Torah, her exegetical method and the scholar's behavior that derives from it, which is compatible with R. Eliezer's approach.

7*
> Beruria once encountered a student who was studying in an undertone (whisper/*lehishah*): she kicked him. She said to him: Is it not written, *arukhah* (ordered/set) in all things (*bakol*), and *shemurah* (kept/secure)? (Samuel II 23:5). If it is ordered in your two hundred and forty-eight limbs it will be secure, otherwise it will not be secure. (BT *Eruvin* 53b, 54a)

The subject of Beruria's *midrash* is the covenant of the House of David with God: "Does not my house stand so with God?[217] For he has made with me an everlasting (*olam*—literally: universal) covenant, Ordered *(arukhah)* in all things, and secure *(shemurah)*" (Sam II 23:5). The origin of the meaning of the term: *berit olam* (literally: the covenant of the universe) as "everlasting" is probably connected, as the *Targum* understood it, with the everlasting quality of the universe's natural ordinances.[218] However, the Tannaim understand that the covenant with the ordinances of the universe depends on something external to them.

Basing himself on the verse in Jeremiah,[219] R. Eliezer says:

> Great is the Torah, since if not for Torah, heaven and earth could not endure, as it is written: If not for my covenant by day and night I would not have appointed the ordinances of heaven and earth (Jer. 33:35) (BT *Nedarim* 32a)[220]

R. Eliezer's disputants[221] understand *berit olam* in Samuel as referring to circumcision.[222] Beruria, on the other hand, follows R. Eliezer's well-known opinion[223] that the covenant, on which earth and heaven are dependent, is the Torah. Thus, *berit olam* refers to the Torah in its fire perception, i.e., Torah as the essence of the universe, which encompasses its whole strata,[224] and requires a total union with its multiple presence.

We can explain Beruria's *midrash* and behavior in our text accordingly, as they derive from this "fire conception." By studying Torah in whispers, the student was ignoring its spiritual presence, and thus was creating gaps in the required union. "Is not it written?" She is rebuking the student as if to say: have you not noticed the Torah's encompassing presence? This is the same conception underlying the style we saw her apply in regard to R. Meir (5*): "what do you think? Since it is written,"[225] assuming R. Meir's behavior towards his evil neighbors derived from his *midrash* of Scriptures. However, unlike R. Meir who interpreted the Torah differently, this student ignored or forgot the Torah presence, i.e., the *midrash*, and consequently acted against the law—the *halakha* that one should study aloud.[226] Thus, the situation naturally requires the burning feature of the Torah,[227] and Beruria, like R. Eliezer in similar cases, spits fire:[228] "She kicked him. She said to him: is it not written?"[229]

How does this law illustrate a total union of the scholar with the Torah? For this, we need to delve inside Beruria's *midrash*, which places the Torah text in the flames of her conception in all its strata: its basic vision, its exegetical methodology, and its content.

Although the words of the verse in Samuel: *arukhah* and *shemurah* are frequently understood in two different meanings: "ordered" and "secured," respectively,[230] and are thus very close to Beruria's basic interpretation,[231] it seems that Beruria's *midrash* reacts to a possible textual superfluity. This reads *arukhah* and *shemurah* as synonyms,[232] which means (the covenant was) "set in all,"²³³ i.e., maintained by all and kept (observed)²³⁴ by them.²³⁵ Thus, one of these descriptions is superfluous, or the second one merely strengthens the first one, namely: the Torah was not merely "set" and maintained by the House of David, but also kept/maintained very well.

At this stage, we encounter the same methodology and exegetical results we met in Beruria's other *midrashim*. The vision of text multiplicity does not merely deny superfluity by extending the meanings of the Torah applying them to further textual parts, but also by enriching all the textual strata. Instead of relating to the verbs as descriptive only, she reads them as relational. This becomes possible due to her method of multiplicity, i.e., "lowering oneself" to the end of the verse, reading the later part before the first. According to her reading, the second verb is not an intensification expressed by the conjunctive sixth Hebrew letter (*waw*—and), but on the contrary, the second is weakened and conditioned by the first. Thus, the reader is guided to interpret the first part of the verse, not in its limited meaning, but in a more extensive one.

Following her midrashic style and logic, we would say also here: "it is secure" because "it is ordered (or set) in all (things)." The word: "all" (*bakol*) describes specifically the way the Torah was set, and in its most extreme situation. "Set in all (*bakol*)" is interpreted by Beruria as "Set in two hundred and forty-eight limbs," which will be aware of the Torah study through the voice. Possibly, the phonetic similarity of the words *kol* (all things) and *kol* (voice) plays some part in the raw material of this reading, which is not limited to the mere vocal resemblance. But the resemblance is then extended to the meaning: Studying with all—*b'khol* (the organs) is vocal, i.e., spoken *b'kol* (with voice). ²³⁶ The human voice will pass the Torah's words, either physically or consciously, throughout the human body. Consequently, in this extreme situation when the Torah "set in all," it will be secure, i.e., will not be forgotten or ignored thus attaining the total union of the scholar with the Torah presence.

It is significant that the following two stories brought in the Talmud immediately after this one of Beruria illustrate R. Eliezer's maximalistic conception of the Torah, which maintains: Study in all or deserve burning fire!²³⁷

> *Tanna* (one taught): R. Eliezer²³⁸ had a disciple who learned in an undertone (whisper—*laḥash*). After three years,²³⁹ he forgot his study. (BT *Eruvin* 54a)

> *Tanna* (one taught): R. Eliezer had a student who deserved heavenly burning,[240] they said:[241] Leave him alone; he attended on a great man.[242] (ibid.)

This extreme reaction illustrates R. Eliezer's typical conception. The price of learning in a whisper, and thus failing the utmost requirement of studying in all (body and soul), is a total withdrawal, a gap, amnesia, the loss of connection at any level with the Torah.[243] From that chasm the appropriate punishment bursts out; the student was liable to a heavenly burning. The burning, (the death, or Beruria's kicking 7*) reflects the diversion of the student from total union with the Torah and his being out of its encompassing presence.[244]

Sexuality, Existentialism, Torah

We now approach a text[245] which is an extreme example of the "fire conception" and shows Beruria to be one of its indubitable adherents. Long before the feminist movement in research, this text was considered from a feminist aspect. Consequently, the debatable theme reflected within it was missed and not scrutinized.

8*
> R. Jose the Galilean was once on a journey when he met Beruria. By what road, he asked her, do we go to Lydda? Foolish (*shote*) Galilean, she replied, did not the Sages say this: Engage not in much talk with women?[246] You should have asked: By which to Lydda? (BT *Erubin* 53b)

In 1940 Robert Gordis wrote about Beruria's "rejoinder to Jose the Galilean which is most probably to be taken sarcastically."[247] Observing this text in the light of sarcasm, irony, and mockery, implies that one should not take Beruria's conversations seriously as Torah talk, as a teaching about the matter at hand. Rather, her quotation of the Sages' assertion should be taken as a means of displaying contempt towards the Sages, quite similar to the *min's* method in the previous text. Accordingly, Beruria's figure is relocated from the arena of Torah, the state of the *tannait*, the scholar to the socio-biological one: the female, the woman, and this is set in the wide arena of politics: females struggling against males.[248]

According to our investigation, this approach does not suit the figure we have found in the texts. Analyzing the text, not as a token for something else, but as a source for a novel understanding of the subject matter introduced there, we find the same conceptual principles with their great affinity to R. Eliezer. As with R. Eliezer, who envisioned Torah presence as infiltrating and overwhelming all layers of life—a vision which shapes the scholar's behavior and sometime appears harsh and extreme[249]—so it is with Beruria, who embodies the extremes of the scholar's personality, going beyond the direct intellectual activity towards the existential behavior.

Indeed, the framework of this text is unique, as it illustrates the encounter between the sage as sage, and the sage as a member of a sociobiological grouping. From this observation, we see Beruria, who does not burst out of her scholarly entity, but views herself merely as the object of study, through her halakhic eyes.[250] Apparently, R. Jose was asking an innocent question in a purely social context.[251] This is the very point of the argument. Beruria, like R. Eliezer, maintains that there is no part of life which the Torah does not penetrate. This refers to Torah in its broad sense, Written and Oral, and in its various patterns, Halakha, Aggada, Midrash, or, as in this case, even rabbinical guidance.

As we find in R. Eliezer's warning in Mishna:

> And warm thyself by the fire of the Sages, but beware of their glowing coal, least thou be burnt, for their bite is the bite of a fox, and their sting is the sting of a scorpion, and their hiss is a hiss of a serpent, and all their utterances are like coals of fire. (Mishna *Avot* 2:10)[252]

The Torah, which is fire, fills reality. The scholar, who unites with this entity of Torah, himself reacts like fire. Therefore, one who ignores, or is not aware of the Torah presence, is burnt by it, or by the scholar.[253] From this conception, Beruria's reaction bursts out: "Foolish (*Shote*) Galilean." The same assumption we find in the text describing Beruria's dispute with R. Meir, her husband (5*). There, she interprets his behavior concerning his evil neighbors, as deriving from his *midrash*: "how do you make out . . . because it is written?" However, in this case it does not end with spitting of fire, since no one has transgressed the Torah presence—rather the Torah was interpreted differently.[254] This is not the case with R. Jose, who was not wary of the Sages' hiss: "Did not the Sages say?" Did not R. Eliezer say that: "all their utterances are like coals of fire?" Hence, R. Jose was burnt by Beruria's fire. But here Beruria expands R. Eliezer's conceptualization. On reading Beruria's interpretation of the Sages' utterance: "Engage not in much talk with women" we observe how brilliantly and creatively she applies the whole method.

Initially, when reading the dialogue, it seems that the question of R. Jose: "By what road do we go to Lydda?" is not much different from Beruria's correction: "By which to Lydda" in which she drops the words; "road" and "we go." This reading has led to the conclusion that we are dealing here with irony on Beruria's part. Actually, in a second reading the difference not only makes sense, but also reveals Beruria's novel application of the Sages' saying. The Hebrew verb: *nelech* (we will go), when said to a woman, may be understood as referring to her with a great intimacy (walk together), while the whole sentence means: "one road for both of us," which increases the intimacy. Hence, we comprehend Beruria's interpretation of the Sages' advice as avoiding potential sexual light-headedness, not only through direct chatting with women in superfluous talk,[255] but by extending it also to unconscious layers of speech. Not only the content of speech (the "What") should be safe from light-headedness, but also the form (the "How") should be clean of sexual connotations. A scholar must, by Beruria's extension, be wary in all possible levels of conduct, including the misuse of innocent language in delicate contexts.[256]

Here, too, upon donning her scholarly garb, Beruria is contemplating her biological aspect like any other halakhic object. These reflections of Beruria fit R. Eliezer's in every respect: First, in her extreme rejection of licentiousness and harlotry, whether in their non-practical manifestations, or in permitted relationships. According to R. Eliezer, foreign thoughts[257] or a contemptuous attitude[258] can turn relations between man and wife into harlotry.[259] Indeed, the essence of harlotry signifies to R. Eliezer lack of intimacy in a situation based on intimacy, while for Beruria, immodesty means intimacy, where there should be none. This difference in emphasis arises from the different situations they are considering (between man and wife, or between two strangers), and does not obscure the fact that both of them find the possibility of licentiousness in the very deep and unconscious layers of relationship. Second, the strict reaction towards licentiousness which they have in common, derives, methodologically, from their shared "fire conception," that all strata of life are overwhelmed by the presence of the Torah.[260] In our investigation of R. Eliezer,[261] we presented this point in various dimensions: from magic, through dreams, social relations, miracles etc., all reality's elements, including transcendental, subconscious, terrestrial and extra-terrestrial, are observed through his halakhic mind. Beruria joins the force brilliantly and creatively, by extending the Torah presence to the unconscious as expressed through the language dimension. As language is a permanent phenomenon in life, especially for a scholar, the unconscious is ever active in the shadow of the divine presence. On one hand, this ultimate application of "the fire conception" makes it almost futile for one to avoid burning others or being burned by his own or others lack of awareness of the Torah presence.[262] Accordingly, like R. Eliezer she spits out fire in her reactions when she faces this lack of awareness. On the other hand, this application of the awareness of Torah to the deep layers of consciousness makes Beruria one of the standard-bearers of the "fire school."[263]

Notes

120. We dropped the word: *tanur* (oven), at the beginning of the *tosefta*, following the gloss of R. Eliyahu of Vilna (GRA, Vilna 18th c.)

121. Literally, the word: *yafe* here means "beautiful." In rabbinic language, it has various meanings: "appropriate," "good," "right," etc., see M. Jastrow, *Dictionary of the Talmud* (New York: Pardes, 1950), 585.

122. The Tosefta, *Tohorot*, trans. J. Neusner (New York: Ktav, 1977).

123. Cf. Goodblatt, "Beruriah Traditions," for instance, and his "Kitchen-lore" theory. In addition, we do not maintain Ilan's feminization that: "the only anomaly in this tradition is the gender of the transmitter" (Ilan, *Integrating women*, 176).

124. Goodblatt, "Beruriah Traditions," 77, 75, Moonikandem, "Beruria and Rabbi Meir," 39–40, Ilan, *Integrating women*, 176–7. There is no basis either for the hypothesis identifying the daughter in this text with the other daughter of R. Hananya just because she quoted verses (see *Sifre on* Deuteronomy, 307:4, ed. L. Finkelstein [New York: The Jewish Theological Seminary of America, 1969], 346, and BT *AZ* 18a), since the wife also recites a verse before her death (see below p. 127, for our reading of these quotations). See also, Ilan, *Integrating women*, 191, who identifies the daughter of the two last sources with Beruria. For our response to this suggestion, see below n. 273.

125. Cf. the version in R. Judah ben Kalonimus, *Yehuse Tannaim ve'Amoraim*, ed. J. L. Maimon (*YTA*) (Jerusalem: Mosad Harav Kook, 1963), 31: "better . . . than he" (the father—R. Hananya). I would like to thank D. Boyarin for showing me this source many years ago. See also GRA's gloss, Tosefta, *ad loc*. However, the version which deals with the son rather than the father seems preferable, as we will see that Beruria tends, like her father, towards R. Eliezer's method. Regarding the epilogue of these two texts of the Tosefta, see Ilan, *Integrating women*, 177–8, who concludes: "In this last respect, the two traditions resemble one another, but do not resemble most other *halakhic* traditions, perhaps suggesting that the gender of the transmitters made it necessary to specify that a higher authority sanctioned them." Indeed, this epilogue exists in other tannaitic texts, e.g. Mishna *Ket*. 13:1,2, Mishna *Nazir* 7:4, Tosefta *Kil*. 1:3, Mishna *Neg*. 3:4, and so on. Hence, it seems more

plausible to investigate the function of this phrase within the circles of the tannaitic decision, rather than speculate within feminist concerns.

126. See S. Lieberman, *Tosefeth Rishonim* (Jerusalem: Bamberger and Wahrmann, 1939), 3:17, and Neusner, *Tosefta*, 15.

127. See Lieberman's gloss, *Tosefeth*, 17: a *pitas* (a large jar, barrel) *shekiro*, as *shekirzelo*. According to R. David Pardo, *Ḥasde David* (HD, Italy 18th c.) Tosefta, *ad loc. shekirzelo* means "broke its margins" and became capable of being a stove. GRA's gloss, Tosefta *ad loc.*: *shepara oto* (tear/destroy) is explained in his commentary: (*pitas*) which he broke and made a stove and plastered it as the stoves are done. But see Lieberman, *Tosefeth*, 17: "prepared and smoothed it."

128. See GRA, Tosefta *ad loc.*

129. See HD, Tosefta *ad loc.*, it is not yet a barrel but neither is it a stove, and since the impurity has gone from it for a moment, it has gone forever.

130. *Gaonic Commentary on Mishna Tohorot, attributed to R. Hay Gaon*, ed. J.N. Epstein (Jerusalem, Tel Aviv: The Magnes Press, 1982), 15, *Aruch Completum*, s.v. *safgun*, Maimonides, *Commentary*, *Kel*. 5:8.

131. See commentators, Tosefta *ad loc.*

132. It seems more likely that this question refers to the broken barrel (see also, Neusner, *Tosefta*, 15). However, most of the commentators understood it as the beginning of a new case, which refers to an ordinary barrel (maybe because of the *mishna*'s parallel). See GRA and others on the Tosefta *ad loc.*, in the Vilna edition, and in Lieberman.

133. *Ḥaluko*, might mean as translated: "its garment," i.e., the plaster is like a garment, an external covering of the stove (see YTA, HD, GRA, Lieberman). However, the version in MSS appearing in Tosefta Zuckermandel is *ḥalukan*, which means "fractures." In that case, Beruria is saying, it is pure from the time of the removal of the plaster from its fractures.

134. See *YTA*, the "smash" in Scripture does not refer only to the stove itself, but also includes its plaster's shell.

135. See Maimonides, *Commentary*, *Kel*. 5:7. However, compare R. Asher (ROSH), R. Shimshon the son of Abraham of Sens (RS, France 13th c.) on this *mishna* (his commentary appears at the end of BT *Nida*), and R. Ovadia of Bartinoro (Italy, 15th c. popularly called Bartenura), who reads: "to separate the fractures."

136. See HD who explained Beruria's opinion as referring to an ordinary stove, requiring only plaster removal with no pre-division. *YTA* oddly identifies Beruria's opinion with that of R. Shimon, who was interpreted as requiring, like Beruria, plaster removal and in addition shifting. However, see Maimonides, *Commentary*, on R. Shimon's opinion in the *mishna*, and *YTA* on R. Ḥananya ben Teradion in *tosefta* (whose opinion is attributed, in our version of Tosefta, to his son).

137. See BT *BM* 59ab.

138. See Tosafot, BT *BM* 59a, that in a case of no sand between the sections, R. Eliezer agrees that the oven is susceptible to impurity, since the plaster is around it.

139. See Maimonides, *Commentary*, *Kel.* 5:10, and Bartenura *ad loc.* Compare Rashi, *BM* 59a, that according to R. Eliezer it is not considered a tool made of earthenware, but rather a construct, like a tool made of dung, and soil.

140. See Hoshen, "Fire," 90ff.

141. I use here the term: "Existentialism" to describe how an object, in this case Torah, becomes part of one's existence (physical and spiritual), in this case the scholar. For the development of this usage regarding the "fire conception," see Hoshen, "Fire," 89–99. For a comparative study of our usage of "Existentialism" in the Sages' thought with that in Philosophy, see *id.* "Agnon's Writing," 36–45, *id. Agnon*, 37–47. For more about "Existentialism" in connection with R. Eliezer and Beruria, see below nn. 185, 254, and pp. 37, 54.

142. See above p. 37, how this halakhic logic was reflected in the proofs, or what was called miracles, which R. Eliezer provided in the dispute of the Akhnai oven.

143. See Hoshen, "Fire," 95, for other examples of this approach.

144. See "Fire," where I claim that Rabban Gamliel was the main character in this debate, even though, from the text, it seems that he is but a representative of the majority, or what is considered to be the Sages' opinion.

145. From the Latin: *claustrum* and in Greek: χλεστρον. In other sources: *glostra*, see e.g. Mishna, *Eru.* 10:10. See also, *Aruch Completum*, s.v. *Glust*, Jastrow, s.vv. *Glostr*, *Clostra*.

146. In Tosefta, ed. Zuckermandel, 579, the version is "Judah." Lieberman, *Tosefeth*, 3:35, upholds the version: "Joshua" according to R. Ḥananel's version (BT *Sab.* 124a) and others, but see J.N. Epstein, *Prolegomena ad Litteras Tannaiticas* (Jerusalem, Tel Aviv: The Magnes Press and Dvir, 1957), 1:135, n. 64, who rejects it on chronological grounds, and maintains the version of "Judah." See Ilan, *Integrating women*, 177–80, who uses this philologically debatable basis to support Goodblatt's argument concerning the chronological separation of the two figures (daughter and Beruria) in the two texts of the Tosefta. Ilan also uses this attribution of the Tosefta to support her feminist reading of the parallel Mishna, which assigns Beruria's ruling to R. Joshua. However, we support Epstein's decision, as the *mishna* assigned to R. Joshua is problematic methodologically, see further below p. 90.

147. The definition of not being a tool means that, under Sabbath laws, moving it is forbidden but, under Purification laws, the object is not susceptible to impurity. See RS (Mishna), HD (Tosefta), Epstein, *Prolegomena*, regarding the similarity between Beruria, the Sages and R. Joshua of the *mishna*.

148. See commentary on Mishna *Kel.* 11:4 (RS, Bartenura et al.)

149. See Tosefta *Yeb.* 13:3,4. About this principle see Y. Gilat, *R. Eliezer Ben Hyrcanus: A Scholar Outcast* (Ramat Gan: Bar-Ilan University Press, 1984), 128.

150. See RS on Mishna *Kel.* 11:4.

151. I tend to say that the *mishna* and our *tosefta* had two separate traditions of this law (see Albeck, *Introduction*, 77). The Mishna's tradition was earlier (R. Eliezer?) than the Tosefta's (Beruria, R. Ḥananya ben Teradion?) which had been confirmed by R. Judah ben Baba (see one of the possibilities raised by Sarah, "A Suitable Case," 17). This is preferable to the feminist speculations about the deliberate omission of the Tosefta tradition by the Mishna (see Sarah, "Beruria: A Suitable Case," 18, Ilan, *Integrating women*, 180). If one is speculating, it should be about why the Tosefta's editor preferred the later tradition. One possible answer is that, when there is a tradition which is Halakha (the Law), it is preferable, and here we do have the acknowledgment that this is the *halakha*. The second possible answer is, if we are right as regards the affinity of this *mishna* to R. Eliezer's method, the ruling according to him is problematic as he was considered banned (see Tosefta *Nida* 1:5 and BT *Nida* 7b).

152. See also R. I. Lifshitz, *Tiferet Israel*, below n. 154.

153. BT *Sab.* 123a, the dispute refers to a broken needle which has no hole.

154. JT *Eru.*10:10, 26:3. R. I. Lifshitz, *Tiferet Israel* on Mishna *Kel.* 11:4. Basing oneself on GRA's version raises the possibility of difference in the opinions of the Sages as well as of Beruria, but from another direction.

155. Gilat, *R. Eliezer Ben Hyrcanus*, 137.

156. Ibid., 132.

157. See Hoshen, "Fire," chaps. 3, 4.

158. Ibid., 14ff; *id.* "Agnon's Writing," 126–7, and notes, see about this approach.

159. BT *BM* 59b.

160. See Hoshen, "Fire," 93–4.

161. See in Hoshen, "Agnon's Writing," 130ff.; *id.* "Midrash and Genres," in *Encyclopedia of Midrash, Biblical interpretation in Formative Judaism*, ed. J. Neusner, A. J. Avery-Peck (Leiden: Brill 2005), 121–48, where we etymologically based this understanding of both terms. Halakha, reflects the walker (*holekh*), human being, who performs the Law/Torah. Haggadah, reflects the teller (*magid*), God, who is the teller of the Law. Thus, we find the same issue discussed from two different angles: the human, and the divine.

162. For more about this principle and the transmissions between Halakha and Aggada, and vice versa, see Hoshen, "Fire," *id.* "Midrash and Genres."

163. See BT *Suk.* 28a, for R. Eliezer's assertion about himself. Also, see Gilat, *R. Eliezer Ben Hyrcanus*, chap. 1, and in the second part of his book.

164. For how these two perspectives function in "the fire conception" of R. Eliezer, see Hoshen, "Fire," 162ff., part of these sources will be presented later.

165. See for instance Mishna *Yad.* 4:3, BT *Pes.* 38b.

166. See Mishna *Neg.* 9:7.

167. Ilan, *Integrating women*, 181; For Ilan it is an unsolved problem, and, in this text, Beruria is "an ultimate example of serious scholarship," not specifically in the field of Aggada, as in this context.

168. See BT *San.* 38b and above n. 173.

169. See R. Rabbinovicz, *Variae Lectiones Mischnamet in Talmud Babylonicum* [*Dikdukei Sofrim*], BT *Pes. ad loc.*, the version in MS Munich is "Natan." (For the same version see, MS JTS 1623, MS Colombia X893–T141). Following Rabbinovicz, see S. Lieberman, *Hayerushalmi Kiphshuto* (New-York and Jerusalem: Jewish Theological Seminar of America, 1995), 558, that "Johanan" is a printing mistake and it should read "Natan." However, compare the version "Johanan" in MS Vatican Bibliotheca Apostolica 125, 134, and in the first edition, Venice 1520–23. In MS Vatican 109 the version is "Jonathan" as in JT (*Talmud Text Databank*, CD-ROM [Saul Lieberman Institute for Talmudic Research, Bar-Ilan University]) and as in *YTA*, 32. More about it see below n. 170.

170. Goodblatt, "Beruriah Traditions," 70–1, basing himself on the changes between the names "Johanan" in BT and "Jonathan" in JT. However, see above n. 169, MS Vatican 109, which reads "Jonathan," and other name changes in the other MSS.

171. Ilan, *Integrating women*, 181, although Ilan (ibid., n. 12) admits the plausibility of other readings, she interprets all of them as falling within the political-feminist speculations about the editorial erasing of the name of the woman Beruria. However, the authenticity and accuracy of the JT version is questionable (see Goodblatt, "Beruriah Traditions," n. 7) also in regard to the place of the male hero, R. Simlai, which, we think, seems to favor the BT version. More about this see previous and following notes.

172. In addition to the above doubts (nn. 170, 171) we raised in regard to Goodblatt's conclusion, if we consider the specific text which poses this special conception towards Aggada, we see that it gives preference to the BT version "Johanan" over that of JT "Jonathan." R. Jonathan studied very little Halakha, while R. Johanan gave both the same significance. Nonetheless, this needs further investigation.

173. See also BT *Ḥag.* 14a, BT *MQ* 28b.

174. See Albeck, *Introduction*, 190, and others.

175. See Jastrow, *Dictionary*, s.v. *shma'atteta*, 1600, see also *Aruch Completum*, s.v. *shama*, 108.

176. One meaning of "*ad she*" in rabbinic language is "until" (as in the biblical usage. See the commentary of R. Hillel on the *Sifra ad loc.*, also see, Neusner's translation). But it could be understood also as "while," "during," or "by the time" (see Jastrow, and M. Sokoloff, *A Dictionary of Jewish Babylonian Aramaic* [Ramat Gan: Bar-Ilan University Press, 2002]).

177. Based on *Sifra*, trans. Neusner, 312.

178. According to RaBaD *ad loc.*, the previous interpretations are also R. Eliezer's. GRA *ad loc.* maintains that the whole *baraita* is R. Eliezer's, see also Gilat, *R. Eliezer Ben Hyrcanus*, 87.

179. For another reading possibility, see R. Hillel's commentary on the *Sifra*, GRA *ad loc.*, Neusner's translation.

180. In Mishna *Bik.* (1:3) the term is "mountain dates," but see the version of the Mishna in BT *Pes.* 53a: "mountain palms."

181. See RaBaD, *ad loc*. In other versions, R. Eliezer calls R. Ishmael: "Uprooter (*doker/oker*) of mountains," which has the positive meaning of a sharp-minded scholar. Accordingly, R. Eliezer was inviting R. Ishmael to create a *midrash* in order to base the Torah law.

182. This literary rudeness covers a wide range, beginning from within the field of Midrash, including sages who believe in the limited Midrash, and ending with the sectarians who did not believe in Midrash at all. About the latter, see above p. 48; regarding R. Ishmael's methodology, see Weiss, *Zur Geschichte der Judischen Tradition*, 2:93, Gilat; *R. Eliezer Ben Hyrcanus*, 88.

183. See also Mishna *Neg.* 9:7, Hoshen, "Fire,"165.

184. See the various analyses of this text in Hoshen, "Fire," 89, 109.

185. Ibid., for analysis of this text from the perspective of existentialism and Torah.

186. The textual usage of the metaphor means: go down in the text from the top, the first part, to the continuation in the second part. In other words, read the following.

187. BT *Ber.* 10a.

188. See above p. 13. Cf. Benovitz, *Berakhot*, 435-443, who reads this Beruria text (5* and 6*) as the editors' fabrication. This methodology leaves too many nuances unresolved regarding the editorial motivation and the comprehension of the midrash's exegetical and philosophical principles.

189. See Goldfeld, "Women as Sources of Torah," 265, 268, Aschkenasy, 180–1, Moonikandem, "Beruria and Rabbi Meir," 42–3, Benovitz, *Berakhot*, 439. 441.

190. Ecclesiastes 10:4. There, the vowel is *ḥataf-pataḥ* for a noun, as opposed to *pataḥ* for an adjective. See also, Rashi, BT *Ber.* ad loc.

191. See also M. H. Goshen-Gottstein, *Fragments of Lost Targumim* (Ramat Gan: Bar-Ilan University Press, 1989), 2:84. There, the verse was translated in both ways: *ḥataim—rashiaya* (sinners), another version: *ḥataim—ḥobaya* (sins).

192. The fact that the vowel in Psalms is not *ḥataf-pataḥ*, as is proper for an adjective, is obviously irrelevant, since the Masoratic vocalization came centuries later and reflects a contradictory reading. Cf. Benovitz, *Berakhot*, 440-441, who views this text as an invention of the Babylonian editor. Benovitz speculates that the Masoratic rules ceased to be followed at that time. He argues that this midrash was originally similar to the 10th c. Midrash on Psalms (104:27) on the word *yitamu* (sinners/sins will cease), which was interpreted as *temimim* (sinners will become devoid of sin), but the Talmudic redactor changed the exegetical emphasis to *ḥataim* and attributed it to Beruria. However, it seems, quite the contrary, that the late midrash changed the Talmudic exegetical emphasis, due to the total adoption at that time of the Masoratic rules.

193. This phrase appears five times in BT, two of them are attributed to Beruria, the two others: one to R. Joshua (BT *Eru.* 101a) the other to Rabbi (BT *Ḥulin* 87a). In both cases, the use of the formula does not depart from the polemical context, i.e. as an answer to the heretics, while exegetically it is not

convincing at all. In the case of R. Joshua, the second part actually strengthens the heretic's view and in the case of Rabbi, he himself is not satisfied with his answer to the heretic, and only the miraculous death of the heretic saves him from being refuted.

194. We tend to attribute the originality of this phrase to Beruria since, unlike the two other tannaitic examples (see above n. 193), Beruria's usage of the formula has very deep hermeneutic consequences in both cases: the polemical one, and the academic one (see analysis 6*, above p. 48). Hence, one can say that this phrase was coined by her, and was transferred technically to the other *tannaim* due to the polemical context. In amoraic sages this phrase appears once (BT *Suk.* 52b), not in a polemical context. There, the usage of the phrase reflects a very high standard of the scholar as an aggadist. Methodologically it seems to follow Beruria's method of reverse reading. See also R. Gordis, *The Universal Jewish Encyclopedia* (below n. 247): "Her canon in Biblical interpretation, 'Look to the end of the verse' (*Ber.* 10a) became axiomatic with later authorities." However, Gordis attributes this principle to Beruria, without giving it any support, or explaining the unique meaning of this principle. Furthermore, we truly tend to attribute to Beruria this particular phrase however as regards the principle, we are not sure of her originality, since we saw that this principle was already in use in R. Eliezer's *midrash* (see above p. 46) and also in R. Ḥananya ben Teradion's *midrash* (see below p. 124).

195. About this analysis principle as regard to R. Eliezer and in general, see Hoshen, "Agnon's Writing," 2:437, n. 901.

196. About this idea, see BT *BQ* 60ab, Hoshen, "Agnon's Writing," 127ff.; *id.* "On the Quality of the Rabbinic text."

197. See Hoshen, "Fire," chaps. 3, 4, about this concept in regards to the "fire conception," as applied in the biblical characters of Jonah and Elijah.

198. Based on *Sifre a Tannaitic commentary on the book of Deuteronomy*, trans. R. Hammer (New Haven: Yale University Press, 1986), 201. See BT *San.* 65b, for a parallel *midrash* in another style, in the name of R. Akiba (for an analysis of this Midrash, see Hoshen, "Fire," 119, n. 335).

199. Later on, we will mention this basic principle as part of the "fire conception" of R. Eliezer, and his followers: Beruria and her father, R. Ḥananya ben Teradion.

200. For more about the features that characterize the "fire conception" of R. Eliezer, see Hoshen, "Fire," chap. 1; *id.* "Semiotics"; *id.* "Fire in Revelation."

201. About the early piety concerning the "fire-conception" of R. Eliezer, see Hoshen, "Fire," Section 1, chap. 6, Section 2 chap. 6.

202. See Mishna, *Avot*, 2:10.

203. For a detailed analysis of these two texts, see Hoshen, "Fire," 119ff.

204. See JT *Sota*, 9:16, 24:4, that R. Eliezer was deserving that the Holy Spirit would rest upon him; see also, Hoshen, "Fire."

205. See Jastrow s.v. *min*: "a Jewish infidel mostly applied to Jew-Christians. In editions controlled by censors, often substituted by Sadducee *and kuti* (Samaritan)," as in that text in the printed editions. Also, see *Aruch*

Completum, for the spectrum of references of this term. Historically it is hard to identify to which sect this *min* belongs (see the text following). The exegetical emphasis of the dispute renders it reminiscent of the Sadducees, but historically this would be impossible. According to the content of the verse, this text could be read as referring to the congregation of Israel in relation to redemption and Messianic elements (see the text which follows). Hence, it could be identified with a Jew-Christian *min*.

206. In two versions the word *kevataykho* ("like you") is missing (cf. Benovitz, *Berakhot*, 444, n.28). Hence, Friedman argues that this omission reduces the polemical tone (ibid. 443, n.28). It is, however, clear that Beruria refers here personally to the *min* himself, with or without "like you."

207. Green, "Lucid is God," 15, Adler, "Virgin in the Brothel," 30.

208. See for instance, E. Sarah, "Beruria: A Suitable Case," 18.

209. We learn from the *aggada* brought immediately after in BT Ber. 10a that the heretics (*minim*) did not interpret closeness of verses (*smuchin*) and so undermined the order of the Torah text., See the commentary of R. Shmuel Eliezer ben Judah haLevi Adels (MaHaRSha) on BT *Ber.* (ibid.)

210. See the short version of this text in Midrash *Song of Songs Rabba* 1:37, ed. S. Donski, (Jerusalem, Tel Aviv: Dvir, 1980), 30. There, the *min*'s question and Beruria's answer became one midrashic union.

211. See R. A. Steinsaltz in his edition to BT *Ber.* 10a, who deciphered the mocking factor of this *aggada*. However, compare with commentators on *Ein Ya'akov* on that BT who read otherwise.

212. It seems that in seeing Beruria's first *aggada* as a question, a few commentators were influenced by the structure of the *min's* reading in Beruria's second *aggada*. However, if we are right and such an ironic question about Beruria's *midrash* did exist, the ironic question of the *min* could not be reconstructed within the logic of Beruria's answer, but only from the logic of the *min*.

213. Actually the verse: "And Sarai was barren, she had no child" (Gen. 11:30) was interpreted severely by BT *Yeb.* 64b, in that the second part came to say that Sarai was not simply barren but, more seriously, lacked a vessel for an embryo (uterus).

214. See the fire punishment in R. Eliezer's saying in Mishna *Avot* (above p. 55) to those who are not aware of the Rabbis.

215. See Hoshen, "Fire," Section.1, chap. 6, about the national aspect as part of the fire-Sinai conception.

216. Cf. Friedman (Benovitz, *Berakhot*, p. 443, n.28), who suggests that there is a difference between *minim* (heretics) and ruffians (who are Jewish).

217. There is another reading, which drops the question mark from this sentence, and refers it to the previous verse.

218. See *Targum Jonathan*, Samuel *ad loc.* that God will secure his kingdom as the natural rules of creation (*sidrei bereshit*). About the Aramaic root of *sdr* as opposed to the Hebrew: *arch* in connection with creation see, E. Van Staalduine-Sulman, *The Targum of Samuel* (Leiden: Brill, c2002), 677.

219. The tannaitic reading considerably changes the meaning of the verse.

220. In a few MSS of BT *Ned.* 32a (see Lieberman, Virtual, MSS: Vatican 110, Munich 95, Moscow Ginzberg 1134) all this passage of R. Eliezer is missing. However, it appears in Geniza fragments, Venice edition, and others (see *The Babylonian Talmud with Variant Readings, Tractate Nedarim*, [Jerusalem: Institute For The Complete Israeli Talmud, 1985]). In BT *Pes.* 68b, it is brought under the name of "Elazar" (and accordingly it was changed in the notes of BT Ned.) It is "Elazar" also in various Mss. However, "Eliezer" appears in MS Columbia 141; MS Sopron 1554, and the Venice edition.

221. See the other opinion of Rabbi, Mishna *Ned.* 3:11, BT *Ned.* 32a, BT *Sab.* 137b.

222. Or possibly as idolatry, see *Mechilta d'Rabi Ishmael, Masekhta de'Bahodesh* 2, ed. H.S. Horovitz (Jerusalem: Shalem, 1998), 208, for the meaning of *berith* although not *berith olam*. However, in Samuel, this sense, as avoidance of idolatry, could fit easily as the central principle that the House of David observed before God.

223. See BT *Ned.* 32a, which confronts Rabbi's opinion with that of R. Eliezer.

224. See Hoshen, "Fire," 110.

225. BT *Ber.* 10a.

226. See BT *Eru.* 54a, for a direct legal application of Beruria's reaction; and for the same in the Rishonim, see Maimonides, *MT, Laws Concerning the Study of the Torah*, 3:12. For the application in the name of Beruria, see R. Simhah of Vitry, below p. 72.

227. For the definition and application of the burning feature of the Torah to biblical and Talmudic figures, see Hoshen, "Fire," throughout.

228. Ibid., 75ff. cf. also BT *Beza* 15b.

229. See above p. 54, for her similar reaction toward R. Jose the Galilean.

230. All the translations to the verse read: *arukhah* as "ordered"/ "arranged," and *shemurah* as "secure"/"sure." See also, the biblical dictionaries: *Gesenius' Hebrew and Chaldee Lexicon to the Old Testament Scriptures*, trans. S. P. Tregelles (Michigan: Wm. B. Erdmans, 1950), L. Koehler, *Lexicon in Veteris Testamenti Libros* (Leiden: Brill, 1953).

231. Modern commentators apply these meanings to the legal subject: *arukhah* as ordered in details legally (the covenant as any contract), and *shemurah* as secured of injury (see J. Kill, *Da'at Mikra*, [Jerusalem: Mosad Harav Kook, 1981], M. Z. Segal, *Torah Neveim ketubim* [Tel Aviv, Dvir, 1948], S.R. Driver, *Notes on the Hebrew text and the Topography of the books of Samuel* [Oxford: Clarendon Press, 1913]).

232. See Z. Hardi & H. Rabin, *The New Bible Dictionary* (Jerusalem: Keter and Yavneh, 1989), s.v. *arukh* who refer to the meaning of "secure" or "promised," and thus, we have a common meaning between *arukhah* and *sehmurah* in terms of "observed."

233. See Exodus 21:1: "These are the judgments which you shall set (*tasim*—put) before them," and R. Akiba (*Mechilta, Masekhta de'Nezikin*, 1, 246) who explains the verb: *sim* (put) as "sit" (order).

234. "Observed" is, of course, the meaning of the verb: *shmr*, see *Gesenius' Hebrew and Chaldee Lexicon*.

235. See the commentaries of R. David Kimḥi (RaDaK), and R. Levi ben Gershon (RaIBaG) on Samuel *ad loc.* who expounded these two words as synonyms in terms of "maintain," although not as referring to Torah, but to the covenant of David's kingdom.

236. See MahaRsha, *Ein Ya'akov*, BT *Eru. ad loc.*, that the voice, in passing, brings feeling and motion to all limbs.

237. See BT *Beza* 15b and its analysis in Hoshen, "Fire," 75, for this view of R. Eliezer.

238. Although in MSS Vatican 109, Oxford 366, Munich 95 read: "Eliezer ben Jacob." In the old editions (Pizaro, Amsterdam) and MS 466 in Adler's collection (18th c.) the version is "Eliezer." Also, the next text (BT *Eru.*), which the above MSS also read "Eliezer ben Jacob," is read by R. Ḥananel (10th c. Morocco) *ad loc.* "Eliezer," and its style testifies to his being R. Eliezer. (The first story about the forgetful disciple is missing in R. Ḥananel, *loc cit.*)

239. See above p. 39, "three years" for Torah study, in regard to Beruria.

240. Soncino and ArtScroll translate it as saying that this student "deserved burning [for an offence] against the Omnipresent," probably because burning is one of the punishments carried out by human court, in contrast to death through heavenly decree (like *kareth*, etc.) However, we understand this phrase as similar to death through heavenly decree (*mitah lashamyim*). See the attribution of this phrase to R. Eliezer, in *ADRN* 1, 25. Also, we find burning as a punishment by the heavenly court in the case of Aaron's sons' death (see the commentary *Iyun Ya'akov, Ein Ya'akov,* BT *Eru. ad loc.*, who connects this death by burning with R. Eliezer's opinion on the death of Aaron's sons (BT *Eru.* 63a) and the story about his disciple who incurred the death penalty.

241. Soncino ed., interprets: "they say—the Sages," while ArtScroll: "they say—in the heavenly court." The impersonal style: *amru* in the stories about R. Eliezer, brought under the name of *tanna* (one taught, see BT *BM* 59a), needs further investigation.

242. Compare BT *BM* 59b, the story entitled *tanna*, which relates the great respect paid to R. Eliezer in the heavenly court, which said: "what business do you have with R. Eliezer whom the law follows in every place."

243. See also BT *AZ*, below chap. 5, regarding R. Eliezer, and R. Ḥananya ben Teradion, Beruria's father.

244. See Hoshen, "Semiotics"; *id.* "Fire in revelation," about the burning feature, which is directed toward those who are standing outside the harmonic circle of Torah.

245. Note that BT *Eru.* 53b juxtaposes this text (8*) before the previous text we quoted from BT *Eru.* 54a (7*).

246. Based on Mishna, *Avot*, 1:5.

247. R. Gordis, *The Universal Jewish Encyclopedia*, s.v. "Beruriah (Valeria)" (New York: *The Universal Jewish Encyclopedia*,1940), 243. Gordis uses this story along with Rashi's story (*AZ* 18b) as "some evidence that Beruriah resented the restrictions placed upon her sex and the low opinion of women's power held in certain quarters."

248. See Ilan, *Integrating women*, who extended the ironic reading of Beruria in this text to the context, i.e. to the subversive voice of the Talmudic editors, which is "contrary to the hegemonic rabbinic discourse." These editors actually think "that it is in fact very fruitful to converse with a wise woman . . . wisdom is an inborn rather than an acquired trait. Women, children, slaves . . . may posses it from birth. Dicta claiming the opposite are ridiculous" (ibid., 186). Beruria as the ultimate sage was chosen to raise this ironic counter-voice. Naturally, according to Ilan, the editors tucked away this voice safely between "heaps of other traditions, which shield it from the undiscerning reader" (ibid., 187).

249. See Hoshen, "Fire," where we exemplified this throughout the thesis.

250. A similar encounter can be found in the story of R. Joseph the blind in BT *Kid.* 31a.

251. We do not accept the feminist reading, which views this question as mocking Beruria the woman, see Adler, "Virgin in the Brothel," 31.

252. The translation is based on *Mishnayoth, Order Nezikin*, trans. P. Blackman (New York: The Judaica Press, 1963), 502. About this *mishna* see, Hoshen, "Fire," chap. 1.

253. About the burning feature of the "fire conception," see Hoshen, "Fire," throughout.

254. Ibid., chaps 3:4, for illustrations of the rationalist halakhic situation, which remained inside the disputable dimension, versus the existentialist one, when fire is spit out from within the halakhic personality of the scholar, and the transitions between them.

255. This is the most common understanding of the phrase, whether it refers to one's wife (see the second part of the *mishna*), pure or impure, the strange woman, or the poor woman (see the commentaries on the Mishna). See also, BT *Ned.* 20a, on this phrase: "that you come in the end into fornication." Indeed, there is another explanation that connects this phrase with the first part of the saying. This saying deals with kindness to guests and women's miserliness in regards to guests (BT BM 87a).

256. One should not confuse Beruria's extension of the saying in Mishna *Avot*, as we read it from the Talmudic source, with extensions of this saying that are found in Geonic and later sources. For the latter, see *Masekhet Derekh Eretz*,13, which includes within this advice any talk with woman, whatsoever: "that all woman's talk is nothing but words of fornication"; Maimonides, *Commentary, Avot* 3:5; R. Zemah, Duran on his commentary on Mishna *Avot* (*Sefer Magen Avot*, [Jerusalem: Makhon Haktav, 2003]): "Not only length of talk is prohibited but also an extra word (bar)." Echoes of such extension and the resistance to it are found in 20th c. Responsa. E.g., R. Ben Zion M. Uziel, *Piske*

Uziel, Besheélot Hazman, 44 (Jerusalem: Mosad Harav Kook, 1977); R. Obadia.Yosef, *Yabia Omer, Orah Ḥaim*, 6, 13 (Jerusalem: Porat Yosef, 1974). However, Beruria herself did not mince her words when rebuking R. Jose—on the contrary. In addition, we do not notice that she is unusually brief in her conversations with the Sages. Hence, we must say that Beruria is talking about the modesty of the sage's language that should take into account delicate circumstances, e.g., the nature of the person to whom the speech is directed could influence the range of dubious meanings which burst out unintentionally from the deep layers of language.

257. Cf. BT *Ned.* 20ab.

258. Cf. BT *San.* 66a.

259. About these and other sources, see Hoshen, "Fire," Section 1, chap. 6; *id.* "Sexual Relations," and below chap. 5.

260. About the connection between the theology of R. Eliezer and sexual relations, see Hoshen, "Fire."

261. Ibid., chaps. 4–6.

262. For this case we have an example of Beruria's father R. Ḥananya ben Teradion in a text in which Beruria plays a minor part, see below chap. 5, for analysis of BT *AZ* (17b–18a).

263. See BT *AZ* (16b), and below p. 115, for a similar demand in the story of R. Eliezer and the Christian Jew.

Chapter Four

The Post-Talmudic Beruria and Talmudic Culture:

"The Beruria Incident"

At this stage, we must traverse a side path, cross the cultural border, far from these flames of the Talmudic Beruria, and be cooled off by a medieval commentary/story about her. We are moving the focus away from the Talmudic sources because of the influence this late story has had on later generations of readers of Talmud, both traditional and scholarly.[264] These readers saw the Talmudic Beruria through post-Talmudic eyes and consequently viewed the different types of cultures reflected from these two figures as one continuous pattern.

In order to understand what relevance this late commentary has to the Talmudic Beruria or to Talmudic culture, we must cross the border to the post-Talmudic side, and view these two from that perspective. However, the conceptual criterion for our "texto-cultural" criticism will be the portrait of Beruria and Talmudic culture which we have drawn in the previous chapters from the Talmudic texts.

> Once, she (Beruria) mocked the saying of the Sages: women, *da'atan kalot hen alehon* (their mind is light upon them), and he (R. Meir) said to her, by your life, in the end you will admit to their sayings. He sent one of his students to seduce her and forced her into a (sexual) transgression. And he beseeched her for many days until she obliged, and when she found out (this conspiracy) she strangled herself, and R. Meir fled because of the shame.[265] (R. Shelomo ben Isaac of Troyes—Rashi, commentary on BT *Avoda Zara* 18b)

If this story were not situated in the commentary on the Talmudic page, and were not attributed to the great commentator Rashi,[266] its fate, obviously, would have been like that of many other bizarre stories scattered in late Midrash collections. Rather than Midrash, they are actually folk legends[267] attributed to Tannaim and Amoraim,[268] which were eventually revealed as medieval products situated outside the Talmudic literature.[269] This late story about Beruria does not fit the Talmud from any aspect, either as a commentary to the Talmudic text in tractate *Avoda Zara*, or as an independent Talmudic piece, as we shall now show.

"The Beruria Incident" as a Commentary to the Talmudic Text

10*
>Beruria, the wife of R. Meir, was a daughter of R. Hananya ben Teradion. Said she (to R. Meir), It is debasing for him (*zilah beih milta*)[270] that my sister is sitting in a brothel. So he took a *tarkab*-full of denarii and set out. If, thought he, she has not been subjected to anything wrong, a miracle will be wrought for her, but if she has committed anything wrong, no miracle will happen to her. Disguised as a knight, he came to her and said, Prepare thyself for me. She replied, The manner of women is upon me. I am prepared to wait, he said. But, said she, there are here many, many prettier than I am. He said to himself, that proves that she has not committed any wrong; she no doubt says thus to every corner. He then went to her warder and said, Hand her over to me. . . . At the end the matter became known to the government . . . and [the warder] on being brought [for judgment] . . . and he told them the incident that had happened. They then engraved R. Meir's likeness on the gates of Rome and proclaimed that anyone seeing a person resembling it should bring him there. One day [some Romans] saw him and ran after him, so he ran away from them and entered a harlot's house. Others say he happened just then to see food cooked by heathens and he dipped in one finger and then sucked the other. Others again say that Elijah appeared to them as a harlot who embraced him. God forbid, said they, were this R. Meir, he would not have acted thus! He then arose and fled and came to Babylon. *Ika de'amrei* ("some say") it was because of that incident (that he fled to Babylon), *ika de'amrei* (some say) because of *ma'ase deBeruria* (the Beruria incident). (BT *Avoda Zara* 18ab)

Two reasons are stated for R. Meir's flight, both of which are headed *Ika de'amrei* ("some say").[271] The first is "because of that incident." The other is because of "the Beruria incident"—*ma'ase d'Beruria*. In Rashi's commentary, we find his explication of the second reason, *ma'ase d'Beruria*.[272] But is any explanation needed?[273] And is it necessary to interpret the two opinions titled *Ika de'amrei* as referring to two different issues,²⁷⁴ in which the first *Ika de'amrei*—"because of that incident"—refers to the whole text about Beruria's sister and the Romans pursuing R. Meir, and the second *Ika de'amrei*—"because of the Beruria incident"—refers to another incident concerning Beruria, external to that Talmudic text in tractate *Avoda Zara*? Rather, one could read the two opinions of the *Ika de'amrei* as referring to the same text, and to two different incidents described in it. Thus "because of that incident" means the last incident described in the text, i.e., the saving of R. Meir in the brothel, either by being seen apparently eating Gentile cooking, or by apparently being embraced by a prostitute (who, according to this text, was Elijah who came miraculously to save him).²⁷⁵ In both instances, the Roman hunters said "God forbid . . . were this R. Meir, he would not have acted thus!" Hence, the first opinion of the *Ika de'amrei* interprets R. Meir's escape to Babylon as deriving from the shame before the Romans (some sort of blasphemy),²⁷⁶ because his salvation came by being taken for a transgressor (either by eating forbidden food or associating with a prostitute). Therefore, the flight from "that incident" will be understood not as flight because of "the Beruria incident" (whatever that means), but rather as flight because of his own incident at the brothel. Accordingly, the second *Ika de'amrei* refers, simply, to the "fear" of the Romans, which was caused by the entire "Beruria incident," which consists of her sending R. Meir to release her sister and its results, including its main—and sub-stories. Hence, there was no need for any commentary on "the Beruria incident," since the Talmud had fully described it previously.

Indeed, it seems that the generation before Rashi also read the Talmudic text without knowing this commentary/story about Beruria: R. Nisim of Kirouan's rewriting of this story (Morocco 10th–11th c.)²⁷⁷ in *Hibur Yafe MehaYeshua*—a moralistic book based on adapted aggadic and halakhic texts—mentions no word about this end. On the contrary, he ends the story with "He (R. Meir) went, took his wife and all he had, and moved to Iraq."²⁷⁸ This epilogue, following the story of R. Meir and the prostitute,²⁷⁹ matches our reading that the flight was due to shame before the Romans, even though there is fear of them, too. At any rate, according to R. Nisim, the wife went with him, and in no way was the cause for his going. Also, in R. Nisim's moral deduction from the story about Beruria's sister (BT *Avoda Zara* 18a), the above story about Beruria is missing:

> Pay attention to this righteous woman, how, because she was wary of her soul, the Lord heard her and saved her. This is what the Wise man said "Grace is false and beauty vain. A woman who fears the Lord, she

should be praised" (Prov. 31:31). Thus grace and beauty are seduction, and the God-fearing woman is to be praised and commended.

And the righteous women should be like those women and learn from them, and similar women, and not be of the kind of whom it is said: And a woman I did not find in all these (Ecc. 7:28). (*Hibur Yafe MehaYeshua*, 29–30)

This moral is part of a general moral deduced from a series of tales found in the *Hibur* about good or evil women (mainly from the sexual aspect) and the test of their chastity, a folkloric motif,[280] which appears in the Geonic midrashim, probably imported from Arabic literature. In one of these Midrashim,[281] the protagonist is R. Meir, who himself sinned with a seductive married woman.[282] It might seem from these Geonic midrashim that this R. Meir probably was not the *tanna*, or Beruria's husband, but rather a later Geonic rabbi.[283] However, this is not obvious from the *Hibur*,[284] which seems to connect the perfidious woman's story to the *tanna* R. Meir.[285] This is different from the case of Beruria for whom R. Nisim did not have such a story. It is unlikely that R. Nisim would have let such a story slip away! He would surely have grabbed this textual prey for his folkloric moral composition, as he did with other Talmudic texts. Moreover, R. Nisim lived at the twilight of the Geonic era, and had strong scholarly connections with the latter Babylonian Geonim.[286] If such a commentary on the Talmud was common among them (or among previous generations), he would not have ignored it, as he himself had a commentary on Talmudic tractates.[287]

In addition, we do not find any reference to this story in the 11th–13th centuries[288] among Rashi's students and followers. R. Simhah ben Samuel of Vitry, who was Rashi's student, refers to Beruria's *midrash* (7*) in his commentary to Mishna *Avot*.[289] R. Judah ben Kalonymos (end of 12th c.) who based himself on Rashi's commentary to the Talmud,[290] when writing his genealogy of Tannaim and Amoraim, does not include this story in his chapter about Beruria (whom he considers as one of the Tannaim).[291] In thirteenth-century Spain, R. Yonah ben Abraham Girondi,[292] who was influenced by the France-Provence school of the Talmud and was himself one of its commentators, and his follower R. Zemah ben Duran (14th c.),[293] who based himself on Rashi's commentary, both refer to Beruria in their commentary on Mishna *Avot*. They learn from her meeting with R. Jose (8*) about the specific sexual modesty required in the Sages' saying: "Engage not in much talk with women" (Mishna *Avot* 1:5). If they had known this story about Beruria, they would by no means have referred to her as a model of sexual modesty. The absence of references before Rashi, during the period of the Babylonian Geonim, and immediately after him, raises severe doubts as to whether Rashi himself knew this story,[294] which hardly warrants a commentary. Hence, the plausible hypothesis is that this piece infiltrated Rashi's commentary, [295] having been expropriated from a very late medieval source, maybe not originally Babylonian, and which was probably one of the pseudo Midrashim that blossomed at the time. [296]

The possibility that we are dealing here with a very late source explains why the medieval story is incompatible with the Talmudic source, even as a self-sufficient text, as we shall now demonstrate.

"The Beruria Incident" as an Independent Talmudic Piece

Some traditional and modern[297] scholars have related to the late story as a lost Talmudic text. However, the epistemology of this text is not of a Torah nature, unlike the typical Talmudic text. Thus, ontologically its characters, unlike Talmudic characters, are acting within another arena and are motivated by different considerations than Torah. In the Talmudic text, for instance that of Beruria and the *min* (6*), the mocking motif is absorbed within the hermeneutic complexity of Midrash. This complexity is the underlying basis of all the Talmudic texts concerning her name.[298] Thus, even if we assumed "mocking the Sages" to be an acceptable Talmudic subject, neither the behavior of Beruria, nor of R. Meir of the late story hints at a midrashic basis. In contrast to a Talmudic text, their dialogue is shifted from the theological sphere (Man's relationship with God, as was found in BT *Berakhot* 6*) to the socio-political and folk sphere (Rabbi against ignoramus/ woman). R. Meir too, in the late story, is not a specific rabbi, but an instance of the whole camp of the academy, as illustrated by the function of the student in the background. In addition, in the late story, Beruria does not seem to be a specific woman, obviously not a scholar, but a representative of the other camps: ignoramuses (women) who could be handled by one of the students. Hence, since the representatives of rabbis in the late story are not scholars, although they are standing up for the rabbis, they make their way much like the ignoramus, i.e., not in the intellectual arena, but rather in the experiential one. This essential deviation of the late story from the Talmudic one, giving rise as it does to folkloristic motifs (the seduction, the test by ordeal for good and evil women, and the suicide),[299] and thus undermining the entire world of the Sages, exposes the un-Talmudic nature of this late story. Indeed, in order to defend the Rabbis, the story has gone so far as to attribute to their models blatant transgressions of the Torah itself.[300]

It is true that other Geonic-medieval stories also apply this deviation from Talmudic ontology, but they draw scant attention, as they are scattered in separate midrashic collections, and most of the time remain within traditional bounds.[301] However, the crossing of the lines by the late story of "the Beruria incident," and its place as a commentary to a Talmudic text, are an inducement to investigate its content as well.

Once again, the alienation of the medieval from the Talmudic Beruria is very clear. Mocking the Sages cannot be associated with the Talmudic Beruria, for whom we know from the Talmudic texts that the Sages are part of her Sinai conception, as transmitters of the Torah and its true learners.[302] For her, the Sages' sayings are reflections of the overwhelming presence of the Torah, which extends to all strata of life. More specifically, in her meeting with R. Jose in BT *Eruvin* (8*), Beruria was the one who interpreted the Sages' saying: "engage not in much talk with women" as referring to the prevention of sexual transgression, a strictly halakhic interpretation, without encumbering it with feminist notions of female inferiority.[303] Attributing feminist baggage to the Talmudic Beruria, with regards to another sages' saying, arouses suspicion of a medieval insertion.

The medieval nature of the post-Talmudic Beruria is disclosed not only in its general content, which does not fit the Talmudic figure, but also by its specific details, which do not fit the Talmudic methodology.

The late story interprets the Talmudic phrase: "Women, their mind is light upon them" according to the post-Talmudic commentary, which states that women are easily seduced,[304] or generally have a weak nature[305] (lightheaded).[306] However, in the Talmudic context this phrase is ambivalent, and its status as a saying of the Sages is questionable. In one place[307] it means that women cannot bear great torture or pressure, which may refer also to sexual acts like rape. There, it does not seem to have the status of a saying of the Sages.[308] In another place, which refers to the Mishna (*Kiddushin* 4:12) prohibiting a man being alone and secluded with two women, the Talmudic editing[309] seems to allude to the sexuality of women,[310] which has a legal implication, but there is no word of explanation. This ambiguity perhaps gives leeway to the post-Talmudic commentary on the weak character (lightheadedness) of women to take hold of the Talmudic phrase and to allow it to be adopted by the late story,[311] whilst in actual fact the Talmudic phrase seems to refer specifically to the great sexual desire/sensitivity of women.[312] Thus, even if we assume the existence of the saying of the Sages, such as: "Since women's mind is light upon them, one man should not be alone with two women," which Beruria mocked, does the story fit the Talmudic Beruria, as we know her? Do the socio-political chit-chat with the husband and the preceding temptation, sexual chat, with the student correlate with her philosophy or teachings? We saw previously that she was very strict about sexual matters (8*), even in such settings that might potentially lead to sexual connotations. Would she ignore this main principle and come close to a sexual transgression, i.e., allowing a man to be alone with one woman (in this case herself), when in the case of the *mishna* a man cannot be alone even with two women?

And finally, could this same figure who did not discriminate in favor even of R. Jose the Galilean (8*), allow "one of the students" to seduce her into a sexual transgression "for many days," without burning him right away; Would she let him come near at all to the fire circle of Torah, to be burnt by its prohibition of adultery? The seduction in the late story is described too simply and too naively to fit a lapse by the Talmudic Beruria, who kicked the student who she thought was ignoring the Torah presence (7*).

It is obvious that in that medieval invasion of the Talmudic page[313] we are facing (an)other figure(s), another, and also another kind of Judaism. These are very far from the Talmudic mind and figures (tannaitic and amoraic), especially from those who are part of the fire school of the Torah, that of R. Eliezer, Beruria and her father R. Ḥananya ben Teradion (as we will see later).

However, both traditional Rabbis and modern scholars have "dragged" the late story into the areas of Epistemology,[314] Law,[315] Culture,[316] and Biography[317] in Talmudic studies. This "dragging" has obvious implications for the understanding of the quality of the Talmudic versus post-Talmudic culture. This essentially says that the same social powers represented in the Talmuds as contending for hegemony, crossed over to the post-Talmudic culture and were brought to fruition in the late story,[318] i.e., the late story reflects a continuation of the earlier culture. In contrast, our theory (presented in a general manner in the first chapter, and later on specifically in regard to this subject) maintains that socio-political terms are not relevant to the Talmudic text-culture, formed on a theological-hermeneutic base, but are relevant to the post-Talmudic culture which, from its very beginning, was subjected to the secularization process. The great abyss that kept opening between the two cultures is apparent, too, in the difference between the late story and the Talmudic material. However, it is not of much help in facing the theoretical question of the two cultures as a basis for denying the "dragging" of the late story about Beruria into the Talmud text and culture. This theoretical perspective is not effective, because our data are texts, and as such are intrinsically ambiguous and obscure (the Talmudic ones by their very nature,[319] and the post-Talmudic by their claim for continuity with the previous ones), and there is thus much leeway for various readings. Therefore, another implication of this "dragging" seems to discredit itself. This is the implication it has for the understanding of the relationship between the two figures, Beruria and R. Eliezer.

The late story about Beruria was considered in traditional discourse to be Talmudic and to refer to the tannaitic figure. This inspired the discourse to confront the figure of Beruria (in general and the late story specifically) with R. Eliezer. This confrontation is based on his opinion in the Mishna (*Sota* 3:4): "Anyone who teaches his daughter Torah is teaching[320] her *tiflut*" (sex)[321] which, since Geonic times, has become an *obiter dictum* and has been interpreted as reflecting a halakhic opposition to women's studying Torah.[322] Accordingly, it is clear why the existence of a scholarly female figure in the Talmudic texts was considered as contradicting R. Eliezer's opinion, and the story of her end has confirmed this opinion as a law (*halakha*).

Following this confrontation, since "Beruria is, after all, the very paradigm case of a daughter learned in Torah."[323] In his research dedicated to sexuality in the Talmud, Boyarin (1993, 189) attributes this confrontation to the Talmudic (Babylonian) and post-Talmudic (European) culture:

> If R. Eliezer's dictum is true, in the way that the Babylonian Talmud understood it—namely that there is an intrinsic connection between woman's studying Torah and sexual immorality—then Beruria's fall into license is structural necessity. Any other denouement to her biography would constitute a refutation of R. Eliezer.[324]

However, Boyarin has not remained merely speculative, but has taken upon himself "to deepen and extend this reading of the text of Beruria's end as being generated specifically in the intertextual web of the Babylonian Talmudic tradition." This leads Boyarin to focus on the contrast between Beruria's figure and R. Eliezer's saying, this time from within the Talmudic text (BT *Avoda Zara* 18ab): "Beruria had, according to the Talmud, a double, in fact a sister" (190). This Talmudic sister is "an exemplum of the proper behavior of a woman, because she had not studied Torah in accordance with R. Eliezer and thus was not led to lewdness," while, Beruria, her sister, "dies a wanton, because she violated the taboo" (191). In other words, she went against R. Eliezer's position. Thus, according to Boyarin the earlier tale about Beruria "clones itself in mirror image, as it were, to produce the later one" (189, n. 20). This is, apparently, because the latter "is generated by simply reversing the polarity of every element in the sister's story that is told in the text of the Talmud itself" (189). So, although the late story about Beruria was only "tantalizingly hinted at in the Talmud, and told in its margins" it was produced as the "dark double of the story of the sister" (191). Hence, Boyarin concludes that the two sisters' stories form a single paradigm that depicts R. Eliezer's saying, as understood in the cultural setting of the Babylonian Talmud.

According to these conclusions, the validation of the post-Talmudic Beruria as Talmudic (although not historically but culturally) lies in the incongruity between such a feminine figure and the misogynist R. Eliezer. In contrast, according to our conclusions, this very point reveals the alienation of the post-Talmudic Beruria from the Talmudic culture, and the figure of Beruria who appears in its texts. These contradictory conclusions stimulated us to re-examine our reading of the figure of Beruria as an extreme embodiment of R. Eliezer's method in Halakha and Aggada, and his general perception of the Torah.

We will examine the relationship between Beruria and R. Eliezer from two perspectives, which have been raised in both traditional and modern literature. The first concerns the saying of R. Eliezer and the whole tannaitic dispute in Mishna *Sota* (3:4) as read independently or through the Talmudic reading in tractate Sota (20ab–21ab).[325] The second, concerns the text from tractate *Avoda Zara* (18ab), which relates the story about Beruria's sister, and "the Beruria incident" to which the late story about Beruria was attached.

Going deeply into the details of the Talmudic discussions in both tractates (*Sota* and *Avoda Zara*) exposes us, once again, to the cultural infiltration of the medieval commentary. This commentary treats the Talmudic discussion as being of a socio-political nature (regarding the relations between people, e.g., men and women), while actually it is thoroughly theological (regarding the relations between Man and God). Moreover, when the Talmudic sources are interpreted as theological, the conceptual link between R. Eliezer and Beruria is not only strengthened but also extends to R. Ḥananya ben Teradion, who has been genealogically associated with Beruria.[326]

Torah study and the Deviant Wife

As stated above, R. Eliezer's opinion is brought in Mishna *Sota*, which talks about the deviant wife (Number 5:11–31) who drinks the bitter water that is supposed to cause her death in case of infidelity. Accordingly, the Mishna comments:

A*

> If she possessed a merit, it [causes the water] to suspend (*tola*)[327] its effect upon her. Some merit suspends the effect for one year, another for two years, and another for three years.

B*

> Hence declared Ben Azzai: One (*adam*) is obligated to teach his daughter Torah, so that if she has to drink [the bitter water] she may know that the merit suspends (the effect) upon her.

C*

> R. Eliezer says, whoever teaches his daughter Torah is teaching her *tiflut* (sex).[328]

D*

> R. Joshua says: a woman prefers one *kab* sex (*tiflut*) to nine *kabs* sexual withdrawal (*perishut*) He used to say a foolish pious person (*hasid*), a cunning evil person, a celibate woman (*perusha*) and blows (*makot*) of withdrawn persons (*perushin*), those are the destroyers of the world. (Mishna *Sota* 3:4)[329]

On first reading of the *mishna* one wonders: Why was it generalized in later generations to the broad subject of women's studying Torah? The principal disputants are R. Eliezer, the great opponent to women's education in Torah, and Ben Azzai, its great sympathizer. Is not its proclaimed subject the deviant woman? A second reading partially explains the cause for this detachment of the *mishna* from its specific subject. It is the word "Torah," which both *tannaim* use, and which was interpreted by post-Talmudic readers in its broad meaning as the laws of the whole Torah.[330] A careful reading of Ben Azzai's saying (B*) will find that Ben Azzai is limiting himself by reasoning accordingly: Why should one teach his daughter Torah? "Because if she will drink she will know" etc. The reason for teaching Torah is the bitter water. Actually when looking at the biblical context of the deviant woman we do find that the term "Torah" is limited to this very specific law of the bitter water. Numbers (5:29–30), after the ritual of the drinking of the bitter water, reads:

> This is the Torah of *hakenaot* (the law of jealousy), when a wife will deviate from her husband . . . or when the spirit of jealousy cometh upon a man . . . and the priest will execute upon her all this Torah (law).[331]

Following Scripture's style,[332] both *tannaim* in the *mishna* (B* C*) use the word "Torah" in the limited sense,[333] and their dispute circles around this point. Ben Azzai (B*): "One is obligated to teach his daughter Torah"—the law (*torat*) of jealousy, i.e., the law of the bitter water,[334] "so that if she has to drink she may know that the merit suspends (the effect) upon her." This means that she may know that the punishment will nevertheless reach her, if not immediately then after a while. R. Eliezer says (C*): "whoever teaches his daughter Torah," i.e., the law of the bitter water, and especially the law of merit suspending (the effect) upon her, simply teaches her *tiflut*—sex (in this case the prohibited type), namely he is encouraging her to deviate and commit adultery using her immunity from punishment. In short, the dispute between R. Eliezer and Ben Azzai deals with the question: whether this knowledge of the effect of the water will prevent "speaking ill of them," [335] and thus will also prevent the water from losing its threatening effect, whilst maintaining its deterrent effect. Or whether, on the contrary, such teaching on the nature of the water will merely encourage sexual transgression.

How does the Babylonian Talmud deal with this dispute?
In fact, as Boyarin first noted,[336] we have no discussion of Ben Azzai's opinion in the printed editions of the Babylonian Talmud, aside from a quotation of his saying from the *mishna*, which is immediately followed by the quotation of R. Eliezer's saying, together with a brief discussion. This unusual form[337] arouses suspicion that something is missing in the Talmudic text between these two sayings.[338] In contrast to this hypothesis which we will present later, and which is supported by manuscript variants of the Talmud, Boyarin speculates that this missing treatment is a deliberate act of the Babylonian Talmud to marginalize Ben Azzai by ignoring his statement and interpreting only R. Eliezer. This deliberate move of the Talmud follows, according to Boyarin, an initial move wherein

> The Babylonian Talmud refuses to interpret the Mishna's point as being that the merit of having studied will protect[339] a wife in her

> moment of trial—refusing . . . a conclusion that would have been perfectly consistent . . . with generally held opinion on the efficacy of Torah in protecting sinners.
> The upshot is that this Talmud is forced ultimately into displacing the merit of the daughter from her own study of Torah to merit accrued from supporting her husband and male children in their study.[340]

Thus, concludes Boyarin:

> the Babylonians' dual moves of first interpreting the merit . . . as . . . supporting the Torah study of males and then "ignoring" Ben Azzai's statement have had the effect of causing the latter's point to be nearly forgotten. It seems, therefore, that our Babylonian text was at much greater pains to simply eliminate the possibility that women would be considered candidates for the study of Torah.[341]

This rejected possibility, according to Boyarin, is identified by the Talmud with Ben Azzai's opinion. Thus, ignoring Ben Azzai, or objecting to the principle that women have the merit of Torah reflects the same anti-female cultural opinion that is naturally compatible with R. Eliezer's.

However, reading the Talmud on a theological basis, while taking into account other variants of the Babylonian Talmud, shows that the possibility that the woman's merit is of her own Torah study is not rejected outright in the Talmud. Nonetheless, this does not yield a feministic or political result that we might attribute to the Talmud, i.e., favoring the principle of women studying Torah, but theological. That is to say, Torah study belongs more to the divine than to the human, and thus it does not matter who studies, man/woman/gentile/*mamzer*, all have the merit of Torah. At any rate, this theological Talmudic approach (here in tractate *Sota*) to the subject of Torah study (including women) has nothing to do with the opinion of Ben Azzai in the *mishna*, which is not interpreted in the Talmud at all in this context (as manuscript variants of the Talmud show), but within the subject of sexual transgression, where R. Eliezer's opinion is also interpreted.

Thus, according to our reading of this Talmudic discussion in its entirety, there is no conceptual basis for a contradiction between the Talmudic approach and the character of Beruria, who appears in the Talmudic texts as a female taking part in Torah study. We shall now demonstrate this Talmudic approach through a detailed analysis of the Talmudic discussion to this *mishna* in tractate *Sota*, which will include also a philological reconstruction of the Talmudic text. In the first discussion in the Talmud, we will see that the Babylonian reading of the concept of Torah study in general, and regarding women especially, is compatible with the theoretical model that we presented in the first chapters on the relation between status and Torah study in the culture of the Sages (Tannaim/ Amoraim). In the second discussion, we will show that the Talmud reads the dispute in the *mishna* between Ben Azzai (B*) and R. Eliezer (C*) as being about the issue of sexuality. Similarly, within this issue, the Talmud reads R. Joshua, the third opinion in the *mishna* (D*). Finally, we will compare the analysis results of the Talmudic *sugia* with our portrait of Beruria and we will show that, unlike post-Talmudic readings, the *sugia* and the portrait are neither contradictory in their general approach toward Torah study (women included), nor in their specific approach towards sexuality.

Discussion 1: Preference of Torah over Commandments

The Talmud relates to the first part of the *mishna* (A*), which talks about merit suspending the death penalty of the deviant wife, and asks:

> What sort of merit? If I answer merit of [studying] Torah, she is [in the category] of "one who performs a precept without having been commanded to do so"—Rather must it be merit of [performing] a commandment. (BT *Sota* 21a)

Although the subject of the Talmudic discussion is the deviant wife, it seems to be discussed as part of a general theological question, namely, what sort of merit could postpone a person's heavenly death penalty? As we see, the immediate answer of the Talmud is: "Torah's merit." However, since the Talmud seems to interpret the merit's application within the subject of Reward and Punishment, the reading that the Talmud presents first as to the nature of this merit (from now on: "the first reading"), assumes that Torah must be mandatory, not voluntary. Thus, according to our theoretical model of status, (mentioned in Chapter One), the socio-biological parameter is taken into consideration. Since the deviant wife, by studying Torah, is in the category of "one who performs a precept without having been commanded to do so" (BT *Sota* 21a), and because she is doing so voluntarily, it cannot be considered as a sufficient merit for postponing death. For this, according to the first reading, we need the merit to be achieved through another commandment, which, presumably, she is obliged to fulfill.

This conclusion of the first reading, that the merit depends on the obligation to perform the commandment, is immediately confronted by the Talmud (*Sota* 21a) with a *baraita*, which returns the Talmudic discussion of the merit to the theological arena, i.e., it relates to the divine aspect of Torah, without relating to its human (the learner) and thus obligatory aspect. The *baraita* claims that a commandment cannot protect one from death, while Torah study can. Ignoring the aspect of what is mandatory, and relating only to the question of priority, the Talmud settles this problem by attributing to the *baraita* another advantage of Torah study over commandments,[342] while leaving to the latter the feature of defending one from death. This does not mean that the Talmud understood defending against death in the *baraita* as total protection by merit, following Boyarin's translation of the *mishna's* word: "[merit] *tolah*" to mean "[merit] mitigates" [the punishment].[343] But rather, the Talmud understood the merit-induced remit from death to be a temporary one, i.e., postponing the punishment, e.g., for "one to three years" as the *mishna* says (A*). At any rate, the conclusion of the first reading is that the merit, which could postpone the deviant wife's death, is that of a commandment, not Torah-study by which she is not commanded.

After the first reading, the Talmud follows with another reading as to the nature of the merit (from now on: "the second reading"). The second reading seems to follow the *baraita's* preference for Torah Study over commandment, beyond the explanation the first reading lends to this preference, and thus detached from the commandment aspect.

In the second reading, the Talmud says:

> Ravina says: It is certainly (*le'olam*) merit of [the study of] Torah [which causes the water to suspend its effect]. And as to [your objection, that she is in the category of] one who is not commanded and fulfills. Granted (*nehi*) that she is not commanded—For having their sons taught Scripture and Mishna and waiting for their husbands until they return from the Schools, should they not share the merit with them? (BT *Sota* 21a)

The Talmud's statement that "she is not commanded" was understood by most of the Talmudic readers as dependent on what followed in the text. They therefore connected them with words such as "still,"[344] "however,"[345] "but."[346] Accordingly, the total meaning of the second reading is as Rashi explains it:

> It is certainly (*le'olam*) the merit of the Torah—this does not mean that she is herself studying Torah, rather that she sees to it that her son and husband will study. (Rashi BT *Sota* 21a)

Boyarin interprets this tortuous interpretation of the merit psychoanalytically, as a symptom of the Rabbis' refusal to take the "simple path." The "simple path" would be attributing the merit to the woman who is herself studying Torah.[347] According to Boyarin, the reason for the refusal of the Talmud to attribute to the woman herself the merit of Torah study is not necessarily connected to the commandment aspect, as claimed by the Talmud, but actually stems from the fear of the idea that women could be considered candidates for the study of Torah.[348] This fear leads the Talmud to conclude that the woman could achieve this merit only through a male's studying.

However, interpreting the second reading according to Talmudic logic, we find that its solution of "sharing reward" contradicts the criteria of the Talmudic text itself. In these terms, the conclusion means that, although the woman is exempt, she does receive her share of reward, together with those who are commanded, which is enough to postpone the death penalty. Thus, the text first claims that the supremacy of Torah study over commandments is not based on its having the status of a higher commandment, but then somehow associates Torah-study with its commandment factor. Furthermore, this conclusion goes against the dynamics of the Talmudic discussion itself. Since the second reading seems to be stricter about the nature of the merit, it is apparently not satisfied with the first reading's conclusion of a commandment postponing death, despite the fact that the woman is commanded and fulfills the precept herself. By speaking of sharing reward, the second reading goes against this dynamic, by offering, in effect, an easy solution to the question of merit. In spite of the fact that it is Torah study which delays death, and not commandments, Torah study is ultimately considered a non-obligatory commandment, i.e. a commandment which the women herself is not obligated to fulfill.

These immanent problems raise serious questions regarding the Talmudic variant which we have received, and whether we are dealing here with another medieval invasion of the Talmudic page, or at least with Ashkenazi variants of the Talmud.[349]

Maimonides apparently had another variant of this Talmudic text, or at least a different explanation:

> If a deviant wife has the merit of studying Torah, even though she is not commanded to study Torah, her merit causes her punishment to be

suspended, and she does not die immediately, but rather declines gradually, and grave illness comes upon her until she dies a year or two, or three later, depending upon her merit, by way of the swelling of her belly and the falling away of her limbs. (Maimonides, *Mishne Torah, Laws concerning the deviant wife* 3:20)[350]

Accordingly, either Maimonides (12th c.) did not have in his Talmud the last segment we have in our printed edition of the Talmud, which talks about sharing rewards with sons and husbands, or else he did not consider it important.

Meiri (13th c.), who preserved Sephardic variants in his commentary to the Talmud, mentions the last segment, but as a separate possibility:

And they explained in the Talmud that the merit of commandment does not postpone so much . . . rather the merit of Torah whether she occupied herself with Torah, although she is not commanded, or she made the effort for her sons' and husband's studying. (Meiri, *Beit ha-Behirah, Sota,* 45)[351]

Although it is possible that Maimonides influenced Meiri's commentary, it might also be that Meiri integrates another Talmudic variant,[352] which added the last segment to the previous statement with phrases like: "or also" (*i nami*), "another thing" (*davar aher*) etc. At any rate, according to Maimonides or Meiri, when the second reading says:

It is certainly (*leolam*) merit of [the study of] Torah [which causes the water to suspend its effect]. And as to [your objection, that she is in the category of] one who is not commanded and fulfills, granted (*nehi*) that she is not commanded. (BT *Sota* 21a)

the second reading means that it is not a commandment, but Torah-study, which can postpone death. Regarding the commandment aspect, the answer of the second reading would be: "granted that she is not commanded, what of it?" The power to influence death is interpreted in that Talmudic text as deriving from another dimension of Torah study, not that of Reward and Punishment.[353]

Actually, the approach adopted by the second reading seems to have originated in a reading of the *baraita* other than that presented by the first reading. As stated, the *baraita* does not present the concept of Torah study in terms of commandments. Otherwise, the total preference it gives to Torah over commandments is meaningless, since, in the end, the preference is of a specific commandment (Torah study) over commandments in general. Rather, it seems to claim a preference for one religious category (Torah = knowing God) over the other (commandments = obeying God). Furthermore, the *baraita*, when interpreting the biblical sources which concern this preference, reveals the nature of Torah study as independent of the commandment principle. The first source, which actually establishes the preference, is from Proverbs (6:23): "for commandment is a candle, and Torah is light." The *baraita* is asking about this preference of Torah, and follows with a very detailed and functional interpretation, that Torah keeps a person in this world, in the world to come, and from death.[354] This enables the first reading, in contrasting the *baraita*, to ignore the non-commanding aspect of Torah, and to attribute the preference of Torah, introduced in the *baraita*, to a quantitative advantage over commandments.[355] This explanation of the first reading ignores the fact that the *baraita's* style seems to refer to the ontological advantage of Torah over commandment, the engulfing presence of Torah against the limited presence of commandments.[356] This ontological characterization of Torah strongly reminds us of "the fire conception,"[357] and is reinforced in the second source in the *baraita* which emphasizes the ontological preference of Torah in metaphorical terms of fire.

The *baraita* quotes a verse from Song of Songs (8:7): "Many waters cannot extinguish love," which it interprets as meaning that "a transgression[358] extinguishes[359] a commandment, but a transgression cannot extinguish Torah." Accordingly, Torah study is the love mentioned in Song of Songs (8:6), that is "strong as death," and "its flashes are flashes of fire—God's Fire."[360] Therefore, its essence is in the divine sphere, and, as such, it has an existence independent of its bearer's persona. Hence, a transgression derived from human action cannot extinguish the realized entity of Torah, nor its effect on the "grey" area where the person joins this entity. Consequently, the natural result of the transgression (death) is postponed, not as a reward for that specific person, but as a causative product of the divine nature of Torah which inspires all who come in touch with it. However, this is not the case with commandments. The ontology of those is determined entirely by the human individual who is commanded (although by God). Thus, when an individual transgresses, the commandment's presence does not prevent the transgressor's action. On the contrary, the commandment is extinguished by it, since both (commandment and transgression) derive from the same ontological level, which is purely human.

This is the very point of the second reading. The merit that postpones death must be Torah study, since only Torah is strong as death. One might argue that the woman is not commanded. Yes. Indeed! "She is not commanded," but that is irrelevant, as the postponing power does not derive from the person's power, and thus it does not matter whether he or she is commanded, or not. In terms of Mishna *Horayot*, that we have discussed previously,[361] we can also say here: all that exist in the radius of Torah study, whether woman, Gentile or Cohen, their lives receives the divine quality of Torah, and their flash are flashes of fire—God's fire.

The Talmud discussion continues to interpret the *baraita*, while eventually adopting the second reading's approach to Torah study in general, and to the merit that postpones death in particular:

> Another explanation: a transgression extinguishes a commandment but a transgression does not extinguish Torah. R. Joseph[362] said: R. Menahem son of R. Jose expounded that verse as though [it were interpreted] from Sinai, and had Doeg and Ahitophel expounded it [similarly], they would not have pursued David, as it is written, saying: God hath forsaken him, [Pursue and take him, for there is none to deliver him] (Ps. 71:11). What verse did they expound?— [For the Lord your God walks in the midst of your camp to deliver you and to give your enemies over to you; therefore your camp shall be holy,] That He may see no unclean thing in thee, [and turn away from you. (Deut. 23:15)]. They did not know, however, that a transgression extinguishes a commandment but a transgression does not extinguish Torah. (BT *Sota* 21a)

Although in this discussion the Talmud applies the second reading to the case of David's sexual transgression with Bathsheba, we may assume that the same approach is applied to the deviant wife. According to this, only the merit of Torah study could influence death. This power of Torah comes into action over a person's life, even when he/she has committed transgressions, including sexual transgressions. This is despite Scriptures, which say explicitly that the transgression of fornication separates God from a person, and therefore, exposes him to inevitable calamity. According to the Talmud, this was the mistake of Doeg and Ahitophel. When they pursued David who deviated (sexually) with a deviant wife (Bathsheba),[363] they were mistakenly convinced that David would have no refuge from death. However, they did not know that: "a transgression extinguishes a commandment, but a transgression does not extinguish Torah." The Torah has a special status, which is not similar to the status of commandments. This status derives from its divine essence, which cannot be extinguished by the individual's actions, and at some stage it assumes an independent existence, detached from its current bearer (the learner/person). Thus, be the sins as severe as many waters, this fire entity of Torah is not easily quenched.

We conclude, therefore, that the approach reflected in the initial discussion of the Talmud not only agrees with the Rabbis' general approach to the concept of Torah study, but, specifically, with its metaphors, alluding to the "fire conception" of Torah. Hence, it is extremely unfortunate that, on the contrary, this Talmudic discussion (indeed, based on the printed edition of the Talmud) inspired readers[364] to link it to R. Eliezer in the subsequent Talmudic discussion. Both discussions were interpreted in political terms, as reflecting opposition to Torah study as a whole for women. In this atmosphere the character of Beruria is not only drained of the Torah conception of the Rabbis who, according to this approach, could not bear the idea "that women would be considered candidates for the study of Torah,"[365] but specifically of that of R. Eliezer who, in his dictum, strongly denounced this possibility. However, we will read the following Talmudic discussion about R. Eliezer as detached from the initial discussion about merit, and as referring to the sexual topic. On this basis we hope to view the character of Beruria as compatible not only with R. Eliezer's method of sexuality, as reflected in his dictum, but also with the general Talmudic approach, reflected in the Talmudic interpretation of this issue.

Discussion 2: Sex, Transgression, and Teaching

Ben Azzai

As already hinted, the missing (Talmudic) discussion on which Boyarin builds his conspiracy theory regarding the Talmud's intentions is found in a manuscript from the beginning of the thirteen century, which preserved ancient Sephardi variants of the Talmud.[366] After quoting Ben Azzai from the Mishna (B*): "One is obligated to teach his daughter Torah, so that if she has to drink (the bitter water) she may know that the merit suspends," the Talmud continues:

> Why all this? (*vekhol kakh lama*)—So as not to discredit ("speaking ill of") the water[367]

By its existence, the "missing" discussion not only denies the conspiracy theory, but also through its content, which presents the Talmudic reading of Ben Azzai's opinion in a different light than this theory would have it. Boyarin understands the Talmudic approach as reacting to the threat of Ben Azzai's tolerance in empowering women. Hence the Talmud itself reverts to the other extreme and does not allow "even such an equivocal suggestion of empowerment."[368] However, the Talmudic approach reflected in the missing text contradicts this explanation. When the Talmud wonders: "Why all this?", it relates to Ben Azzai as an extremist or at least as requiring an irregular action. From the answer: "So as not to discredit the water" we understand that the extreme action, which the Talmud is querying, is not the empowerment of the woman, but rather the empowering of the water. Thus, Ben Azzai's instruction to teach the daughter Torah, according to the Talmud, shows great aggression against the woman, because of the price she might possibly pay for the sake of the water. Thus, the critical tone implied in the Talmudic question: "why all this" is not silenced by the answer: "so as not to discredit the water." The Talmudic criticism of Ben Azzai's opinion seems to be connected to the following Talmudic view and discussion of R. Eliezer's opinion in which, undoubtedly, this criticism is anchored, and, in a retrospective reading, sheds a slightly different light on Ben Azzai's opinion.

R. Eliezer

> R. Eliezer says: Whoever teaches his daughter Torah is teaching her *tiflut*—sex). *Tiflut*—Has it crossed your mind? Rather read it as if he teaches her *tiflut* (BT *Sota* 21b)

This is another example where the medieval commentary invades the Talmudic page. In the printed edition the Talmud's question focuses on the word: "*tiflut* (sex)—Has it crossed your mind?" [to read *tiflut* literally] which means as Rashi explains: "Does he (R. Eliezer) call Torah sex?"[369] According to this reading, the Talmudic query was referring to matters of respect and therefore asks how R. Eliezer dared to call the Torah sex, and worse than that, forbidden sex (adultery).

The solution of the Talmud: "rather read it *as if* he teaches her *tiflut*" is explained by Rashi: "as if—that she (the woman) understood from the Torah how to be cunning, and thus do her things (adultery) secretly."[370] The term: "Torah"— to which Rashi assumes the Talmud refers in its broader sense—was not used by R. Eliezer as a synonym for sex–*tiflut*. According to this reading, this phrase reflects R. Eliezer's opinion of the woman's relation to Torah, which leads the woman herself to adultery.

However, in a manuscript of the Talmud we find that the Talmudic focus was on another word, and consequently the opinion of R. Eliezer was understood completely differently. Instead of "*tiflut*—Has it crossed your mind? Rather, read it as if he teaches her," the manuscript reads "teaches her—Has it crossed your mind?"[371] Rather, read it as if he teaches her." Thus, the Talmudic emphasis is on the verb: "teaches," since after all one who teaches his daughter Torah, whatever that may be, does not tell her literally: "go commit adultery"—whatever implications this may have. According to this reading, the solution suggested by the Talmud to read "as if teaches" instead of (actually) "teaches" solves the technical problem, but still leaves the strong language of R. Eliezer in its place. Accordingly, R. Eliezer must be relating to the indirect action as to the action itself,[372] and this analogy is possible only when assuming that the Talmud refers to "Torah" in the sense of a specific law, in this case the law concerning the nature of the bitter water. Hence, one who teaches his daughter that law is exposing her specifically to the weakness of the water. Thus, he is actually as one who is telling her: do not worry, if you commit a sexual transgression, the punishment will not come soon. On this basis, the Talmud asks what is R. Eliezer's reasoning? Why does he think that exposing the daughter to this knowledge bears within it the message of adultery? Is it not an innocent teaching, pure knowledge? The answer the Talmud gives to this question is not based primarily on woman's nature as post-Talmudic commentators interpreted,[373] but is rather a general philosophy of the nature of knowledge.

The Talmud brings a *midrash* to a verse from Proverbs, which is assumed by the Talmud to be the conceptual basis for R. Eliezer's opinion:[374]

I am wisdom, I dwell with cunning (*orma*) (Prov. 8:12)
[Was interpreted as]: Since wisdom has entered one (*adam*), subtlety[375] (*armimut*)[376] has entered him.[377] (BT *Sota* 21b)

First, we see that this *midrash* is replying to the Talmudic logic as we interpreted it previously. "Since wisdom has entered one" is the very process of teaching, and on this point the midrashic interpretation concentrates. Although the Rabbis generally consider "wisdom" as "Torah" in its specific term,[378] it seems that this *midrash* refers to its general sense as knowledge. Hence, when wisdom is infused into a person, subtlety is simultaneously infused with it—subtlety does not exist separately in the learner, but comes as part of the very nature of the teaching process.

Let us return to the Talmudic question on R. Eliezer: why does he think that teaching the law of the nature of the water is the same as teaching sex? The answer according to the *midrash* is that Wisdom is not a frozen entity. Although it offers a specific knowledge, at the same time it also presents itself as seeing beyond itself, i.e., seeing various possibilities of knowledge which are not overt in this teaching but exist in its implications. This shrewdness accompanies the teaching process. It is inevitable that, along with the obligation to teach the daughter the law that merit postpones punishment, flows the knowledge of the weakness of the water and its implications for encouraging sexual sins.

Within the realm of R. Eliezer's conception, we can understand the Talmud's criticism of Ben Azzai: "why all this." Why is Ben Azzai obligating such an extreme action that will put any person to such risk, i.e., the risk of being in such a hazardous a position of being tempted to sin? According to this understanding of the Talmudic criticism, the answer the Talmud gives: "So as not to discredit the water" does not necessarily follow the logic of this criticism which is, as said, according to R. Eliezer's opinion. Thus, "So as not to discredit the water" does not simply mean that the Talmud thinks that Ben Azzai prefers preserving the name of the water to the daughter's risk. The Talmud thinks rather that Ben Azzai disputes the claim of risk. Hence, says the Talmud, "discrediting the water," according to Ben Azzai, does not mean merely that she will disrespectfully say that the water is ineffective; rather discrediting or crediting the water implies the removal/keeping of the warning effect. Thus, according to the Talmud, Ben Azzai thinks that it is important not to discredit the water for the daughter's own sake. This teaching—Torah or law of the water—will prevent her from sinning. It was as a response to this position that the Talmud interpreted the position of R. Eliezer in the *mishna*. According to him, the teaching of this specific segment of Torah is not an admonition against sexual transgression, but, on the contrary, teaches sexual transgression. The reason is that this teaching does not only empower the water, but rather through the rear door, exposes its weakness; hence, this teaching will not prevent one from sinning, but rather encourage one to do so.

R. Joshua

In the context of the subject of sexual behavior, the Talmud proceeds to interpret the third opinion brought in the *mishna*. However, we first present the reading of the post-Talmudic rabbis, whose interpretation of this opinion derives from the same understanding of the "feminine" as does their interpretation of the two preceding opinions (Ben Azzai, R. Eliezer):

> R. Joshua says: a woman prefers one *kab* of sex (*tiflut*)[379] to nine *kabs* of sexual withdrawal (*perishut*). He used to say a foolish pietist (*hasid*),

a cunning evil person, a celibate woman (*perusha*), and smiting (*makot*) of withdrawn persons (*perushin*), those are the destroyers of the world. (Mishna *Sota* 3:4)

Rashi explains:

> She (the woman) prefers to be nourished with little food, while her sex would be accessible to her by intercourse, to nine *kab*s of sexual withdrawal—meaning, to withdraw from *tiflut*—sex. Hence, it is not good that she will study Torah. (Rashi, BT *Sota* 21b)

Tosafot of Evreux,[380] who usually quote Rashi's commentary, add:[381]

> He (R. Joshua) was disputing with Ben Azzai who said that a man is obligated to teach his daughter Torah and R. Joshua says that she prefers having little food while her sexual activity is available by cohabiting with her husband, . . . hence it is not good that she will study Torah.[382]

Meiri, their contemporary, writes:

> This goes to say that she prefers having little food while her husband cohabits[383] with her, to having much food and vast plenty, while her husband withdraws from her. And the meaning implied by this, is that the main purpose of a woman is nothing but working for her husband until he will love her and will cohabit with her, thus she does not bear the burden of Torah study. And I tend to explain that she prefers that her husband will be an ignoramus, and that he will know little affording only the essential needs, while he cohabits with her, to having nine *kab*s, namely vast of wisdom, while he (her husband) will withdraw from her for his wisdom.
>
> As Zipporah said:[384] Happy are these men, and Woe for their wives, and one of the Rabbis said figuratively that women choose Woe for them,[385] and happy are their wives.[386] Hence, how could a woman burden herself with Torah study? Is not her husband's Torah burden difficult enough for her?[387]

Thus, according to the post-Talmudic rabbis, R. Joshua relates to Ben Azzai and R. Eliezer by disputing the former and supporting the latter. Unlike Ben Azzai, whom he assumed to be in favor of women's studying Torah, R. Joshua thinks it is not good for them to study, since all their interests and strength are devoted to sex–*tiflut*. Hence, it seems as if he is identified with R. Eliezer, who is supposed to be against women's study because they study *tiflut* from Torah. Furthermore, as R. Joshua considers *tiflut* to be the main inclination of women,[388] he is more extreme than R. Eliezer in preventing them from learning Torah.[389]

However, neither R. Joshua's saying in the *mishna*, nor its Talmudic interpretation mentions women's study. The subject is purely sexuality and through this, it relates to the previous discussion on Ben Azzai and R. Eliezer, which we also interpreted as within the same subject of sexuality.

Only one letter and one word does the Talmud add when rephrasing R. Joshua's dictum (in the *mishna*) in order to understand its meaning: "a woman prefers one *kab* [and] *tiflut* with him [*imo*]"[390] (BT *Sota* 21b). This "correction" that the Talmud adds to the *mishna's* words, seems to draw the usage of the term *tiflut* away from the connotation of adultery, to the arena of sexual relation between husband and wife, where *tiflut* means sex in its intimate relations.[391] Hence, a woman prefers that her husband bring her less income,[392] but be with her,[393] than that he will be separate from home, bringing more income, but will withdraw from intimacy with her.

According to this Talmudic reading, the third opinion (of R. Joshua in the *mishna*), is indeed linked to the previous dispute (Ben Azzai-R. Eliezer in the *mishna*), by supporting R. Eliezer's opinion, not as regards women's Torah study in general (as post-Talmudic rabbis understood his opinion), but rather as regards the sexual conception on which R. Eliezer based his rejection of the teaching of Torah, i.e., specifically the law of the bitter water. If R. Eliezer thinks that this knowledge will encourage deviation by the daughter, just as any person taught such knowledge might be enticed to deviation, he apparently assumes that women, like men, have a basic sexual desire. This raises the hypothesis that Ben Azzai strongly disagrees: women, unlike men have no natural sexual desires and would naturally tend to be celibate. Therefore, contrary to R. Eliezer's fears, they will not be compelled by this teaching into adultery. On the contrary, this teaching about the water will serve as a threat against deviation, rather than as an encouragement of adultery. The first part of R. Joshua's dictum is placed in confrontation with this sexual conception. The woman is able to forgo financial comforts to have her husband with her, and not the other way round. This means that sexual desire—*tiflut* in its general and natural sense, not only exists in women, but is, rather, preferable, and this is not considered negatively, as understood by the post-Talmudic rabbis,[394] but positively, as indicated in the rest of R. Joshua's dictum (in the *mishna*), which condemns, in principle, the withdrawal of men and women from sex.

Let us now see how the Talmud reads this condemnation:

"A foolish pietist," the Talmud (BT *Sota* 21b) interprets as a man who sees a woman drowning in the sea and says: it is immoral (*lav orah ara*) to look at her (naked)[395] and to save her." "A celibate woman:" the Talmud reads (BT *Sota* 23a) this phrase in comparison to another obscure phrase found in a similar *baraita:* a *tsalianit*[396] virgin.[397] The latter means apparently a devotee, whose piety manifests in unceasing prayers or fasts. [398] This explanation of the Talmud, rather than interpreting the phrase that appears in the *mishna*, actually draws its meaning from a possibly anti-feminine reading. Namely, one should not read this dictum of R. Joshua as misogyny i.e., hatred towards women's piety—prayers and similar activities.[399] Rather, one should read it in connection with the foolish pietist and the subsequent example listed in the *mishna* of "blows (*makot*) of withdrawn persons (*perushin*)." In regard to the latter, the Talmud (23b) brings examples of men who,[400] like the women in the case of the withdrawn virgin,[401] demonstratively affected a total withdrawal from sex, which eventually was found to be hypocritical.[402] Since they were pretending to do something which is actually unnatural to human nature, those people do not build the world with their piety, rather, as the end of the dictum in the *mishna* says, destroy it.[403]

Thus, this *mishna* in tractate *Sota* itself, and as read by the Talmud, expresses a strong condemnation of abstinence, which destroys the world. This approach toward sexuality is integrated very well within R. Eliezer's familiar opinion in the Babylonian Talmudic *baraita* (BT *Yebamot*), which differs from Ben Azzai's there:

E*
> It was taught: R. Eliezer says: whoever does not engage in procreation is as if he sheds blood for it is said: Whoso sheddeth man's blood by man shall his blood be shed. And you, be ye fruitful and multiply. (Gen. 9:6–7)

F*
> R. Akiba[404] says as if he has diminished the Divine Image, since it is said: For in the image of God made He Man. And you, be ye fruitful and multiply. (Gen. 9:6–7)

G*
> Ben Azzai said: As though he sheds blood and diminishes the Divine Image. They said to him: Some interpret well and perform well, you interpret well, but do not perform well. He answered: what can I do that my soul desires Torah, the world could exist by others.

> Our Rabbis taught . . . Abba Hanan said in the name of R. Eliezer: (whoever does not engage in procreation) deserves the penalty of death. (BT *Yebamot* 63b 64a)[405]

First, as usual, Ben Azzai is not disputing, but interpreting his Rabbi, R. Akiba.[406] Moreover, the explanation Ben Azzai offers for R. Akiba's opinion presents R. Akiba himself as not disputing with R. Eliezer, but supplementing him or explaining his opinion. Thus, Ben Azzai says that whoever does not procreate is like a murderer of human beings and like a murderer of God. This conclusion derives from his *midrash*, which he expounds on the verse (in Genesis) used by R. Eliezer and R. Akiba, and combines them. Since Scripture says: why does a murderer deserve a death penalty? "For in the image of God madeth he man" (Gen. 9:6)—for when one spills blood he is murdering God's image.[407] Thus, according to this *midrash* of Ben Azzai, R. Eliezer's conception of sexuality does not only see its vitality to the existence of the world, but also to the human image itself. The commandment of "And you, be ye fruitful and multiply" was not understood in the sense of "filling the earth" (Gen. 9:1) as the purpose or result of sexuality. Rather it means "teem over the earth and multiply there" (ibid., 7)—referring to the very action of sexuality, which was conceived as contrary to murdering of "Earth" (human being) and "Heaven" (God). Hence, R. Eliezer's words: "whoever does not engage in procreation" (E*) do not appear to mean the same as Ben Azzai's: whoever does not bring children in to the world. R. Eliezer means rather: whoever does not engage in sexual relations, and is not involved in this desire, which reflects life as opposed to death, creation as opposed to destruction.

This is not the conception of Ben Azzai (G*), although hermeneutically he presents a brilliant interpretation of Scripture's approach to the vitality of this desire. However, as he himself does not feel sexual desire, he understands sexuality as a duty that is externally incumbent on Man, but is not naturally part of his own human image. Thus, if he withdraws from sex he possibly becomes a passive murderer according to Scripture, by not increasing and filling the earth and by avoiding bringing more life in the image of God to the world. He does not feel as R. Eliezer put it, that he is withdrawing from the very action of life, and thus losing his own human image.

Returning to the Talmudic reading of R. Joshua's opinion (*Sota* 21b–23b) we find the same conception, which views sexual desire as rooted very deeply in the human being, and very strongly condemns sexual abstinence as a pretence and hypocrisy. Looking back from this contact point of R. Joshua to the previous Talmudic discussion on the dispute between Ben Azzai and R. Eliezer (21b), the Talmudic approach is reflected somewhat differently. The Talmud asked of Ben Azzai: "why all this?" and answered: "So as not to discredit the water." This answer means that Ben Azzai, who makes teaching the law of the bitter water obligatory, does not think that it will tempt the woman, just as it would not tempt anyone else. This is because he thinks that sexual desire is not very active in human beings, or at least, not to such an extent that it might be aroused by innocent language. Namely, the sexual desire will not be provoked when there is no intention to awaken it. Therefore, this teaching of the law of bitter water will serve, *comme il faut*, as a warning against sin. It is this conception that R. Eliezer disputes, according to the Talmudic reading. "Since wisdom has entered one (*adam*), subtlety has entered him." Sexual desire is a very strong and live element in human beings—*adam*—women as well as men. Hence, though one should be very much involved in its positive manifestations in intimate sex, one should as well be strongly aware of its negative ones in adultery and other deviations,[408] and this principle is applied to all facets of life. Even language and consciousness are part of this sexual conception. Thus, together with the involvement of wisdom through language and consciousness, the sexual potential of a person is prepared to receive stimulation.

Hence, if one teaches the law of the bitter water, he is teaching the law of its weakness. This then provokes the natural sexual desire in its prohibited application.

Our reading of the Talmudic text concludes that the Talmudic approach is indeed governed by R. Eliezer's conception; governed—not, however, by misogyny as understood by many post-Talmudic and modern readers, but rather by sexuality. Seen this way, there is no conflict between R. Eliezer and Beruria. On the contrary, such a reading of R. Eliezer's dictum leads us directly to her method, which was also very strict on the issue of sexuality. It is implausible that Beruria, who did not maintain silence on one extra innocent word which could be interpreted sexually, would have agreed with Ben Azzai's verdict. She could not accept his demand to teach one's daughter the single law of postponing death in case of a sexual transgression, and she would fear that such teaching would carry connotations that were overly seductive. Neither would she have agreed with Ben Azzai's basic assumption, that sexual desire is not so active in human beings as not to be provoked by language or cognitive hints. Otherwise, her over-reaction to R. Jose is inexplicable.

As previously explained, the severity in the sexual conception of R. Eliezer, as well as of Beruria, derives from their theological conception, i.e., "the fire conception," which requires a total union with Torah and takes a severe view of any lapse in that intimacy caused by transgression. This linkage between R. Eliezer and Beruria leads us to another section in tractate *Avoda Zara*, where we read of the family roots of the conceptual linkage between Beruria and R. Eliezer through the man identified by the Talmud as her father: R. Ḥananya ben Teradion.

Notes

264. Actually, only from the fourteenth century onwards do we find references to this story (cf. R. Jacob ben Moshe Halevi from Mölln [Maharil, Germany 14th c.] in his Responsa, *Shut Maharil* 199, ed. I. Satz [Jerusalem: Machon Yerushalayim, 1980], 315–6. However, it is unclear how many Rabbis in that century were aware of it, see more above p. 72). This fact may explain why this story has not affected the scholarly image of Beruria in the traditional approach, unlike the modern scholarly one, and thus has not prevented the traditional rabbis from continuing to quote Beruria's rulings in other texts, using them as a basis for their halakhic ruling. However, tracing this phenomenon is beyond the scope of this study.

265. My translation.

266. Another folk story of the same kind, in circulation at the time of the Geonim (see Hirschberg below n. 277, p. 72), which also made its way to the important Talmudic commentators (and in some Talmud editions made its way to the Talmudic page itself) is brought in Tosafot, BT *Kid.* 80b, in the name of R. Ḥananel (Lewin brings this story in his *Otzar haGeonim, Perush Rabenu Ḥananel*, BT *Kid.* 80b, 50). The story, which is known in world folklore as "the widow from Ephesus," relates the story of a woman who was seduced on her husband's grave by a guard, who was guarding a hanged man whose body was stolen, and the woman offered to take her husband out of his grave instead. Tosafot bring this story as a possible meaning for the Talmudic dispute as to whether one (male or female) has sexual desire at a time of mourning. The Sages say one has, and Aba Saul says one has not. The Talmud then says: "as in the case of that woman that once happened that she took him out," which was understood as an example for the opinion of the Sages. However, Tosafot (as well as Rashi) raise serious doubts in regard to the Talmudic version, and suggest "corrections" in which the Talmudic words do not refer to the Sages, but rather refer to Aba Saul. Accordingly, Tosafot bring another possible tale to illustrate the Talmud's words (which Rashi also brings), which seems to be another folk story, about a woman who refused to stop mourning her son until she lost all her children and finally died herself. (In *Ma'ase-Buch*, trans. M. Gaster [Philadelphia: Jewish Publication Society of America, 1934], 1:193ff., these two tales are brought in order to show that "women are fickle—but not all of them.") The Talmudic version suggested by Tosafot is now supported by MSS testimonies to BT *Kid.* (See MS Vatican 111. The Venice edition reads

instead of "she took him out" "she was taken out." In the Spanish edition, the story of Tosafot in an Aramaic version was included in the Talmudic text.) However, see below (n. 269) Schwarzbaum (*Mishle Shualim*, 398, 411ff.) who, as in the case of "the Beruria incident," relates to this Geonic tale as the true content of the Talmudic innuendo (see also Schwarzbaum's speculation about the Christian Censors (*Mishle Shualim*, 410, n. 21).

267. For this definition of the late midrashic collections, see A. Shenhar, "The Figure of Rabbi Meir and Its Literary Characterization in the Legends," in *Studies in Judaism*, ed. J. Bahat et al (Haifa: University of Haifa Press, 1976), 263. The problematic terminology in regard to what should be called Midrash and what should not, which seems to have remained unchanged since Zunz (*Vorträge*), is apparently a result of neglect of the field of the Late Midrash.

268. About this phenomenon, see Zunz, *Vorträge*, 157.

269. H. Schwarzbaum, however, regards this late story as the true folkloric meaning of the Talmudic words: "the Beruria incident." Therefore, according to him, the Talmud referred to it in a mere hint, since it was a well-known story, which "needed no re-telling" (Schwarzbaum, *The Mishle Shualim [fox fable] of Rabbi Berechiah haNakdan* [Kiron: Institute For Jewish and Arab Folklore Research,1979], 411–3, n. 21). Later on, Schwarzbaum ("Female Fickleness in Jewish Folklore," in *Jewish Folklore Between East and West, Collected Papers*, ed. E. Yasiff [Be'er-Sheva: Ben Gurion University of the Negev Press, 1989], 177–80; *id.* "International Folklore Motifs in Joseph Ibn Zabara's 'Sefer Shashu'im,'" in *Between East and West*, 372–4, n. 38) found parallels to the late story of "the Beruria incident" in an ancient Greek folk story about the silent philosopher Secundus "who is known to be in existence by the end of the second century CE, and in the languages of the Near East . . . before the sixth century" (B.E. Perry, "The Origin of the Book of Sindbad," *Fabula* 3 [1960]: 85). However, this comparison does not necessarily place the late story as a Talmudic innuendo to an ancient folklore motif, since the Greek story had great influence in medieval times (Schwarzbaum, "Female Fickleness," 181), and there are adaptations in Arabic literature (Perry, "Origin," 88). Moreover, Schwarzbaum has not proved the exclusive connection of the late story to the Greek one, since the folkloristic motif of testing the truth of misogynist sayings exists in medieval pseudo-midrashic pieces borrowed from Arabic literature (see "Solomon/Arab king," in Schwarzbaum, "Female Fickleness," 180, *id.* "International Folklore," 369–73). Also, the Greek saying seems to claim that women are prostitutes, and could be bought with money for sexual intercourse (see Perry, "Origin," 86, and W. Hansen, *Ariadne's Thread, A Guide for International Tales Found in Classical Literature*, [Ithaca and London: Cornell University Press, 2002], 285: "every women was a whore"). Therefore, the Greek story does not emphasize the difficulties of tempting the mother, but rather indicates that she "accepted fifty gold pieces in payment" (Perry, "Origin," 86), while in the late story, the point is the sexual temptation, and the consequent difficulty in succeeding in this temptation. In addition, Schwarzbaum's claim ("Female Fickleness," 179; Boyarin, "Diachronic," 8;

Hansen, *Ariadne's Thread*, 287) that the test was applied to the finest woman is not in the Greek story, other than that she was the mother, neither does it appear in the late story, except for its insertion in the commentary which refers to the Talmudic scholarly figure. It is also possible that the choice of mother/wife for the test in the folk story, was not due to their exceptional virtues, but rather to their being accessible to be tested. The version of G. Ibn Yiḥya, *Sefer Sholshelet hakabala* (Jerusalem: Hadorot Harishonim Vekorotam, 1962), 71: "[women, their mind is light upon them] and it was written in her (Beruria's) book: with the exception of Beruria," is not another version of the late story recorded in the sixteenth century (see Schwarzbaum *Mishle Shualim*, 411, Hansen, *Ariadne's Thread*, 284). It is more an adaptation of, or commentary on the late story of Beruria, to which the other changes in Ibn Yiḥya's story testify. And lastly, in the Greek story the mother strangled herself out of mortification, while in the late story the reason for the strangling is lacking, and the reason for the shame refers to Rabbi Meir, and not to his wife (as wrongly read by Schwarzbaum, "Female Fickleness," 177, 180, and Hansen, *Ariadne's Thread*, 286. Boyarin "Diachronic," 8, applies the style of the late Beruria story to the Greek tale). Thus, it seems more plausible to look for motif parallels of the late medieval story of Beruria among its contemporaries in the Arabic, Near Eastern, or European medieval literature (which developed the motif of women's fickleness and chastity, with or without the Secundus influence), than to look in the ancient literature, and anchor the late story in the Talmudic one. Cf. Hansen, *Ariadne's Thread*, 286: "The composition was highly esteemed in the Near East and in medieval Europe, certainly more than it was in antiquity itself."

270. The word *beih* ("in him") is written without vowels: *be* and was read by the translations as *bee*, which means: it is debasing for me, instead of "it is debasing for him" (see Sokoloff, *Dictionary*, s.v. *zll*, 414). This made room for speculations about Beruria's egotism (see Moonikandem, "Beruria and Rabbi Meir," 48).

271. Regarding this Talmudic term and its attribution to the late stratum of the Talmud, see A. Weiss, *The Talmud in its development* (New York: P. Feldheim, 1954), 21ff. D. Weiss Halivni, *Sources and Traditions, Seder Moed, Rosh Hashana* (Jerusalem: Jewish Theological Seminar of America, 1975), 389, n. 3, suggests that the Talmudic term *Ika de'amrei* reflects two different versions.

272. See our reconstruction of Rashi's commentary below n. 276, which hypothesizes that originally Rashi had a commentary only on the first *Ika de'amrei*.

273. Ilan, *Integrating women*, 190–1, also suggests an alternative explanation to 'the Beruria incident' unlike Rashi. She suggests that the story about the sister was originally about Beruria herself, but attributed to her sister out of respect for Beruria. Although this hypothetical identification between the sister/daughter, as it was presented in the text of BT *AZ*, could in a way, have fitted Beruria's figure as presented in other texts, there are still quite a few disharmonies between the two (see analysis below chap. 5). In addition, Ilan's

hypothesis diverges from the version of the Talmudic text, for which she provides only non-philological and non-Talmudic backing.

274. Actually, there are four issues. I refer to the first of the last two.

275. See Hoshen, "Fire," 268ff. about the function of Elijah's appearance in "the fire conception."

276. At the end of "the Beruria incident" in Rashi (BT AZ 18b) there is a comment: "and R. Meir fled because of the shame" (*ve'arak* R. Meir *mehamat kisufa)*. This comment, naturally, refers to the story brought just before, i.e., the shame of R. Meir was due to the strangling of his wife, or because of what he had caused her to do. However, the words: "because of the shame" (*mehamat kisufa*) seem to be the only genuine part of Rashi's commentary. Originally, "because of the shame" was placed in Rashi before the story of "the Beruria incident." Otherwise, Rashi's commentary as we have it in our editions of the Talmud, would be trivial. In the printed version, Rashi comments on the Talmud's words: *Ika de'amrei mehai maáse* ("some say: it was because of that incident")—"because of this incident he fled," which basically repeat the Talmudic words, with an obvious comment: "he fled." But if we are right that originally this commentary, "because (*mishum*) of this incident he fled" had a continuation, "because (*mehamat*) of the shame," it is meaningful. Rashi's commentary explains the first *Ika de'amre* as referring to the incident of R. Meir and the prostitute, which according to this commentary was the reason for R. Meir's flight because of the shame. Also, compared with MS Parma of Rashi's commentary (BT AZ) there is a change in the word: "because" (*mehamat/mishum*). This gives the impression of an external involvement, which removed the beginning of Rashi's original commentary and inserted a new tale about Beruria, and then attached the rest of Rashi's original commentary to the end of this new tale of Beruria. More about this below nn. 294, 313.

277. *Ḥibur Yafe MehaYeshua*, ed. J. W Hirschberg (Jerusalem: Mosad Harav Kook, 1970). See Hirschberg, 39–40, for the attribution of this source to R. Nisim.

278. Ibid., 29–30.

279. R. Nisim does not mention the other possibility of the *Ika de'amrei*, of eating Gentile cooking.

280. See Schwarzbaum ("International Folklore," 412ff. "Female Fickleness," 187ff.) about these two aspects of the modern folkloric motif: an unchaste and a virtuous woman, that he finds also in the Talmud. Since he regards the late story about Beruria as a genuine Talmudic reference, he sees the late story as one part of the Talmudic story in which the story about Beruria's sister forms another part. See also, Boyarin, "Diachronic," 14, *id. Carnal Israel*, 191, and above, p. 76, although from the literary-cultural aspect.

281. The story about R. Meir and R. Judah the butcher (or cook—*tabah*) appears in "*Midrash Aseret haDibrot*" (10th c.), *Beit Hamidrash*, ed. A. Jellinek (Jerusalem: Bamberger and Wahrmann,1987), 1:81–2. See also another version

of this story: "A Tale about R. Meir," *Batei Midrashot*, ed. A. J. Wertheimer (Jerusalem: Mosad Harav Kook,1950), 1:184–6.

282. This was the bad woman of Judah, the story commences with the good one who died.

283. See Zunz, *Vorträge*, 66, on the late style of that Midrash, and Albeck, n. 102 *ad loc.*, about terms like: "the head of the Babylonian *yeshiva* (academy)," etc. See also Wertheimer, *Batei Midrashot*, 184, n. 1.

284. In the *Ḥibur*, R. Nisim brings another version of this story called: "R. Meir and the perfidious woman." The story is not included in the series about good and bad women (although it seems to belong to the bad women series), but it is brought separately towards the end (*Ḥibur*, 68), and with great changes. Hirschberg, *Ḥibur*, 72–3, unlike Zunz, *Vorträge* 66, thinks that R. Nisim had another source (one of the known tales), which is different from *Midrash Aseret haDibrot*.

285. First, there is no conspicuous title term: "A tale about one of the scholars named R. Meir," or "the head of the *yeshiva* (academy)" as we find in the other parallels. Second, in chap. 23 R. Nisim obviously talks about three *tannaim*: R. Meir, R. Judah, and R. Jose, and seems to refer to the same sages in chap. 25 and the following. In addition, R. Nisim does not attach to this story any moral (also in regard to R. Meir), and its prologue emphasizes that it happened when R. Meir was in the land of Israel—as if ending by distinguishing this story from the previous one in chap. 23, which occurred outside the Land of Israel. Thus, it is plausible that R. Nisim saw it as another tale about R. Meir the *tanna*.

286. See Hirschberg, *Ḥibur*, 29–30.

287. Ibid., 34–7.

288. Also, it must be noted that this story is absent from folkloric literature of the end of 12th c. Ibn Zabara in his *Sefer Shashuim* (*The Book of Delight*, ed. I. Davidson [New York: Jewish Theological Seminary of America, 1913]), and the French R. Berechiah haNakdan in his *Mishle Shualim* (*Fox Fables*, ed. A. M Haberman [Jerusalem: Schocken, 1946]) do not include this story, although it would serve their folkloric purpose perfectly. Thus, they seem to be unaware of this. This is not the case of another tale, which appears in Tosafot BT *Kid.* (see above n. 266) and which both (Davidson, *Shashuim* 2, 314–45, n. 35, Schwarzbaum, *Shualim* 80, 88) referred to. Schwarzbaum (*Shualim*, 411; *id.* "Female Fickleness," 177) sees these two stories as referring to the same folkloristic motifs.

289. R. Simḥah ben Samuel of Vitry, *Mahzor Vitry* 129, ed. S. Horowitz, (Nürnberg: Bolka, 1923), 559.

290. See Maimon in the introduction to his edition of *YTA*, 20.

291. Ibid. See also Y. Levin-Katz, "Between Lilit and Beruria," *Mabua* 28 (1996): 92, n. 35. However, see Boyarin, "Diachronic," 15, n. 13, *id. Carnal Israel*, 192–3 who erroneously reads *YTA*'s term: "the Beruria incident" as referring also to Beruria's *midrash* in BT *Eru.* 54a, and proposes a very far-fetched hypothesis, while this term in *YTA* refers only to the Talmudic incident

in BT *AZ* of Beruria, who sent R. Meir, etc. At any rate, it is worth mentioning that in contemporary Rabbinic literature, we find that the term "the Beruria incident" refers also to her midrashic texts (e.g. R. Obadiah Yosef, *loc. cit.* 4).

292. R. Jonah ben Abraham Girondi, *"Sefer Hayirah,"* in *Ḥayei Olam* (Germany: Ashkenaz,1947), 32.

293. R. Zemah Duran, *Sefer Magen Avot*, above n. 256.

294. Philologically, it is currently impossible to prove this from the MSS, since the only complete MS for Rashi's commentary to BT *AZ* is MS Parma 3155, of the fifteenth century, while the few other existing MSS fragments do not refer to the relevant Talmudic page (BT *AZ* 18b). On the other hand, from the linguistic style it seems that there is enough material for Rashi's researchers to investigate its authenticity. See for instance the usage of the Talmudic phrase: *nashim da'atan kalah/kalot aleihen* (women, their mind is light upon them). In Rashi we find the addition of the word: [*nashim da'atan kalot*] *hen*, and the mixing with Aramaic: *alaihu* instead of the Hebrew: *aleihen*.

295. The accuracy of the editions of Rashi's commentary on the Talmud is a well-known issue. See J. Fraenkel, *Rashi's Methodology in his Exegesis of the Babylonian Talmud* (Jerusalem: The Magnes Press, 1975).

296. This is not to say that Rashi, as well as the Geonim, could not have maintained such an attitude towards women. We only say that this particularly story was not known to them. We disagree with A. Grossman, "Rashi's Teachings Concerning Woman," *Zion* 70, no. 2 (2005): 171–3, who concludes that Rashi had a written or oral tradition for such an interpretation, as he had for the story in BT *Kid.* 80b (see above n. 266), in the light of the Talmudic context that could not be interpreted otherwise. Thus, according to Grossman, these interpretations should be read as exceptions, which do not reflect Rashi's general feminist reading. However, see the MSS testimonies (above n. 266) regarding the philology which Grossman is basing himself on.

297. See Schwarzbaum, above n. 269, Boyarin, *Carnal Israel*,190.

298. See Introduction, where we noted that the cultural syndrome which distinguished the Talmudic culture from the post-Talmudic was based on the hermeneutic one.

299. Actually, the suicide element from the Talmudic perspective is raised in the extended text of "the Beruria incident" in BT *AZ* 18a (see below chap. 5). It refers to the father of Beruria, R. Ḥananya ben Teradion, who prefers to suffer (like the other Tannaim) rather than commit suicide in any way.

300. One should not cause anyone to commit a transgression, all the more so to seduce him to do so. Thus, it seems as though R. Meir and the student in this story transgressed the prohibition: "You shall not . . . put a stumbling block before the blind" (Lev. 19:14), see also Maimonides, the *Book of Commandments*, 299. Also the suicide they caused the wife to commit (whether she is considered an ordinary woman or a scholar) seems to be a transgression of a Torah prohibition, see above n. 299.

301. See for instance the story about R. Meir and his wife in *Midrash Mishle*, 31 (ed. B. L. Visotzky [New York: The Jewish Theological Seminary of

America, 1990], 191ff.), which has no connection to the Talmudic couple. In this story we have the same dichotomy between the Rabbi's world (which does not seem to be the tannaitic one) and the uneducated woman, although this time she is described as virtuous.

302. See above p. 48.

303. Compare with the feministic reading, which did encumber this saying from *Avot* with feministic content (Adler above n. 251, Sarah, "Beruria: A Suitable Case," 20, Moonikandem, "Beruria and Rabbi Meir," 45).

304. See Rashi BT *Kid.* 80b, BT *AZ* 25a (one should not be with two women alone).

305. This meaning of the term: *de'ah kalah* seems to have been in use from the time of the Geonim on, see Tosafot, BT *Zvahim*, 31b, s.v. *kol hapesulin*; BT *Hulin*, 2a, s.v. *hakol shohatin*, in the name of *hilkhot Erez Israel*, *Tanhuma*, *Vayera*, 22, Rashi BT *San.* 107b.

306. See for instance, Soncino translation for BT *AZ op cit.*, Schwarzbaum, *Shualim*, 396, n. 21 31, *id.* "Female Fickleness," sub-chapter and throughout the paper. Schwarzbaum's failure to discriminate made him latch on to the Talmudic term for the treasure of world folklore (of women's fickleness). He applied the same approach to the motifs of the test in the late story and in the Talmudic text ("Female Fickleness," 177, 179, *id.* "International Folklore," n. 38. See also, Boyarin, "Diachronic," 15; *id. Carnal Israel*, 192) which he combined in the bank of international folklore (of women's chastity tests), which actually does not have the same function (see analysis above n. 269). These problems cast a shadow on the relevancy of the folkloristic studies to the Talmudic studies.

307. See BT *Sab.* 33b, in the story of R. Simon ben Yohai when fleeing from the Romans.

308. See also n. 9 of H. Freedman, in Soncino translation, BT *Sab.* ibid.

309. BT *Kid.* 80b.

310. It is presented in the beginning of the Talmud's discussion on the *mishna*, where the Talmud asks why (apparently, why two women should not be alone with one man, and not vice versa). The answer is: a *tanna de'bei Eliyahu* quotation which seems not to stand by itself, but as a reference ("since") to the *mishna*, or to another part of a whole saying, which has not been quoted. The Talmudic discussion which follows *tanna de'bei Eliyahu* relates to a the general question of man and woman being alone, and thus logically should have preceded this particular question raised under the title of *tanna de'bei Eliyahu*. These problems and others raise questions about the editing of the Talmudic *sugia*.

311. Which is obviously based on this version of BT *Kid.* 80b and not on that of BT *Sab.* 33b (see the plural pattern: *kalot* instead of the singular one: *kalah*).

312. Later on, we will refer to this issue in another context of tannaitic discussion.

313. Actually, the story in Rashi itself does not mention Beruria or R. Meir. They are merely implied by the function this story has as a commentary relating to these figures. Regarding the mention of R. Meir at the end of the story, see above n. 276. Thus, originally the late story could have been told about many other figures. The lack of the names of the figures, expected in any written story, maybe alludes to an oral origin of the late story. On this phenomenon in Geonic times, see Hirschberg, *Hibur*, 72.

314. For this, see Ilan, *Integrating women*, who in spite of her decisive rejection of tying the late Beruria to the Talmudic one, associates both figures with the same political epistemology, i.e., the male reaction, although in two contradictory ways (see above p. 25) to the anomaly of women skilled in Torah.

315. See Maharil, *Shut*, who learns from this story that the law of teaching women Torah in the time of the Tannaim was according to R. Eliezer who opposed it (according to the post-Talmudic view) and not, as one might think, according to Ben Azzai who favored it. R. Joseph Azulai (Jerusalem 18th c.) *Sefer Tov Ain* 4, (Jerusalem: E. Weinberger, 1961), suggests by this story the reason for Maimonides' exceptional ruling in accordance with R. Eliezer (Maimonides, *MT, Laws Concerning the Study of the Torah*, 1:13), and its quiet acceptance by his commentator (R. Joseph Karo, *Kesef Mishne, MT ad loc.*) Accordingly, he hypothesizes that the law of teaching women in the time of the Tannaim was originally according to Ben Azzai, and that after "the Beruria incident" they ruled exceptionally according to R. Eliezer.

316. Concerning the place of Torah and the relation to women see Adler ("Virgin in the Brothel," 104) and Boyarin (*Carnal Israel*, 189ff.), who compare the late story with Talmudic texts on a cultural sisterhood basis. Both (Adler, 31 and Boyarin, 193) also take into account another Geonic story about R. Meir's wife, which consummates the Talmudic cultural "acknowledgment/denial of women's autonomy and intellectual achievement."

317. Obviously, the traditional reading identified the late Beruria with the Talmudic one (see above n. 315). See also Schwarzbaum (see above n. 266). However, other modern readers, despite their awareness of the chronological stratum of the late story, did not see the immanent gap between the late figure(s) and the Talmudic one(s) (of Beruria or others). See Moonikandem ("Beruria and Rabbi Meir," 59), Adler ("Virgin in the Brothel," 103ff.), Boyarin (*Carnal Israel*, 191ff., see above p. 76).

318. Boyarin, 193, 195.

319. About obscurity as the very theological nature of the Talmudic texts (tannaitic and amoraic), see Hoshen ("On The Quality of the Rabbinic Text").

320. In the printed editions the explanation of the Talmud: "as if" was included in the Mishnaic variant. However, see Meiri (BT *Sota ad loc.*), who rejects this version, also see BT *Sota* ibid., MS Oxford 2675, and MS Vatican 110.

321. About the etymology and meaning of the term: *tiflut* see below.

322. See R. Nisim (*Hibur*, 36), Rashi and Tosafot, BT *Sota* 21b, Maimonides (*MT, Laws Concerning the Study of the Torah*, 1:13). Most, if not

all, of those who came after Maimonides followed his reading on this generalization (Meiri on *Sota*, Maharil, *Shut*, 193, 199, *Tur*, *Shulḥan Arukh*, *Yoreh De'ah* 246).

323. Boyarin, *Carnal Israel*, 188–9.

324. Ibid. 189.

325. We refer here to the Babylonian Talmud, since we maintain that JT (*Sota* 3:4;18:4;19:1) does not relate directly to the subject of the dispute. In the beginning, JT's discussion relates only to the implication of Ben Azzai's opinion which contrasts with that of R. Elazar ben Azaria. The latter said (JT *Ḥag.* 1:1, 75:4) that it is totally voluntary for women to come to hear the reading of Torah once in seven years (Deut. 31:12). This means that in contrast to Ben Azzai, who obligates the woman to study the law of the bitter water, according to R. Elazar ben Azaria they have no obligation whatsoever to study Torah, not even one law. Also, the story about R. Eliezer, which JT presents immediately after this, without any explicit linkage to the *mishna*, actually does not refer to it. The story tells of R. Eliezer, who refuses to answer a *matrona* (see Jastrow, *Dictionary* 769: "lady mostly used of Roman woman of quality"), who asked him a question referring to the three kinds of death mentioned in regard to the worshippers of the golden calf. "He answered: there is no wisdom for a woman but in the spindle, as it was written in Exodus (35:25) . . . his son Hyrcanus said to him: for not telling her one thing of Torah you have lost me a yearly allowance of three hundreds *kor* of *maser* (tithe). He said to him: Torah words should be burnt rather than be given to women. When she left, his students said to him, you rejected her (in answering this question) but what are you responding to us?" That *midrash,* which was meant to be the real response (even though JT brings it in the name of some late tradition, not R. Eliezer), raises the suspicion that the reason for JT's planting of the whole story of R. Eliezer and the *matrona* in tractate *Sota* was not its reference to his saying in the *mishna*, but rather that *midrash*. The *midrash* is talking about the death of the sinners of the golden calf, which occurred in the same way as the death of the deviant. However, R. Eliezer's answer to the *matrona*, and also his provocative answer to his son, should be read like other stories made in the same formula (e.g. JT *San.* 1:2, 19:2; *Pesikta deRav Kahana* 4:7, ed. B. Mandelbaum [New York: The Jewish Theological Seminary of America, 1987], 1:74) intended to dismiss the gentile's questions regarding Torah with a flimsy answer. All the more so is this true of R. Eliezer, who seems not to believe in such discourses and accordingly evades giving a real answer to the gentile matron (see below n. 435). In BT *Yoma* 66b, the story is about a wise woman (not a *matrona*); the dialogue with the son is lacking; and the answer of R. Eliezer to the woman is part of a series of evasive answers given by R. Eliezer to various questions he was asked. According to the Talmud, "His evasion was due not to his desire to divert them with words [counter-questions], but because he never said anything that he had not heard from his teacher." However, our reading of JT is in contrast to post-talmudists (see Tosafot BT *Sota ad loc.*, Meiri), as well as to modern readers who tried to learn from it the general approach of the Jerusalem Talmud towards

the subject of Women's Torah study. See S. Friedman, "The Study of Torah for Contemporary Woman," in *Women in the Sources of Judaism* (Jerusalem, 1983), 55–6, Boyarin, *Carnal Israel*, 172ff.

326. See also above p. 22, for our rejection of Goodblatt's historical differentiation between Beruria and the daughter of R. Ḥananya ben Teradion.

327. According to every translation (Soncino, ArtScroll, Neusner, *The Talmud of the Land of Israel, Sotah,* [Chicago, The University of Chicago, 1984], 91–2) except Boyarin (see above p. 82).

328. About the term: *tiflut*, see *Aruch Completum*, s.vv. *tafel, tfl*, which means: tastelessness—physically senses and morally, and was borrowed for transgression and lechery. Jastrow, *Dictionary*, 1687, adds: "frivolity, trivialness." This explanation does not suit the meaning of the word used in the second part of the *mishna*, and indeed, see Meiri, *Sota*, who explained *tiflut* spelled with the ninth Hebrew letter (*tet*) as well as with the last Hebrew letter (*tav*), in terms of union and conjunction (cf. *Aruch Completum*, s.vv. *tafal, tfl*, the same hypothesis in regard to the Hebrew word: *tefilin* (phylacteries). Similarly, Bartenura (Mishna, *Sota ad loc.*) explains *tiflut*: "the coitus of lying with men." Unlike most of the translations, ArtScroll translated *tiflut* as: physical intimacy, see also, Neusner, *Talmud of the Land*, 192: "sexual satisfaction." Hence, we suggest that the Sages' term for "sex" is: *tiflut*, which sometimes has negative connotations, as in the first part of the *mishna* (see also, BT *Meg.* 12b), and sometimes has a neutral meaning, such as in the next part of the *mishna* (see above D*, and also, Midrash *BR* 70:11, ed. J. Theodor and Ch. Albeck [Jerusalem: Warhmann, 1965], 2:811). There is room for further investigation of the development of the meaning of this term in the Late Midrash, see Midrash *Seder Eliyahu Rabba* 14, ed. M. Friedmann (Jerusalem: Wahrmann, 1969) 62ff. and its parallels in regard to the additional meanings brought by Jastrow.

329. We divided the *mishna* into four asterixed parts, to which we will refer in the future.

330. Above p. 81, we will see that the Talmudic discussion of the first part of the *mishna*, which diverted to the subject of Torah study might also influence this generalization.

331. For the term: "Torah" as referring also to specific laws, see also Leviticus 6:2, 7, 18, etc. More about the usage of the term: "Torah" in the various periods of the sages, see Urbach, *Sages*, 286–93.

332. See also the opening of Mishna *Sota*: *hamekane* (one who jealous), which means one who warns (*hamazhir*). Rashi (BT *Sota ad loc.*) explains that the *mishna* (in that case R. Eliezer) uses the style of *hamekane*, because he is following "the biblical style" (see Numbers 5:14).

333. Cf. Friedman, "The Study of Torah," 54: "apparently it is clear what R. Eliezer intends to say by the concept Torah" (= in its broad meaning).

334. See BT *Sota* 18b, JT *Sota* 2:5, 18:2, which understood *Torat hakenaot* as referring to the bitter water.

335. About this phrase of the discrediting of the water (which we translated here more literally, according to the Hebrew) see above p. 87, the version of MS Oxford 2675 of BT *Sota*, and the commentary on the Mishna (2:5) *Tiferet Israel* 18.

336. Boyarin, "Diachronic," 11.

337. Usually in the Talmud, if there is a citation from the *mishna* it is followed by a discussion, otherwise there is no citation. Cf. the distorted version of MS. Vatican 110 of BT *Sota*, which seems to derive from this unusual form: "Ben Azzai ... teaches her *tiflut*."

338. The Tosafot (12th c.) BT *Sota* 21b had this incomplete version and thus, in order to complete it, they added (*ad loc.*) the material which they found in JT.

339. This verb, used by Boyarin, apparently under the influence of the Talmudic discussion, is misleading. The verb used must be: "postpone" or such like. For more about it, see below n. 343.

340. Boyarin, *Carnal Israel*, 175.

341. Ibid., 177.

342. The advantage of Torah, which could save people from sinning.

343. Etymologically it means "hang" and from that was borrowed the meaning "postpone," and further "abeyance," and so translated in all published translations of the Talmud (cf. Mishna *Yoma* 8:8).

344. See the Soncino translation to BT *Sota* 21a.

345. See Steinsaltz's explanation in his edition to BT ibid.

346. See Boyarin, *Carnal Israel*, 175.

347. Ibid., 80.

348. Ibid., 195–6, see Boyarin's conclusion about Torah studying for women as a loss of control.

349. See Rashi above p. 83.

350. *Code, Book Four: The Book of Women*, trans. Klein, 358.

351. My translation.

352. In the introduction to this volume of Meiri, A. Lis comments that Meiri brings many variants of the Talmud. At any rate, Maimonides' and Meiri's variants seem to reject the Ashkenazi ones, see Rashi, above p. 82 s.v. "It is certainly (*le'olam*) the merit of the Torah."

353. See also *MT, Laws Concerning the Study of the Torah*, 1:13, when talking about a woman's reward for Torah study, he does take into consideration the ranking of obligation. Thus, he rules that the woman has a reward but unlike one who is commanded. Anyway, in the case of postponing death he does not articulate it in terms of reward, apparently because he interprets our Talmudic text as detached from that sphere.

354. See Prov. 6:22: "When you walk it will guide you, when you lie down it will watch over you, when you wake up it will converse with you."

355. E.g., Torah always protects, while commandments protect only when one is involved with them (see BT *Sota* 21a)

356. The *baraita* gives a parable of one who walks in the dark, using a torch (a limited light—commandment), and eventually day breaks (unlimited light—Torah), see also Prov. 6:21.

357. See above in chapter 3, and below in chapter 5, the applications of the engulfing feature of Torah in the "fire conception," in the characters of R. Eliezer, Beruria, and R. Ḥananya ben Teradion.

358. Maybe the *baraita* reads the parable of "many waters" as referring to sins according to Ps. 69:3,16, which reads "flood" as "troubles" and "wicked people."

359. Obviously, this phrase belongs to the parable of water and fire.

360. There is a dispute how to write the Hebrew word: *shalhevet-Yah*, as one or two words (see Rashi, Eben Ezrah). In addition, whether *Yah* refers to God or is a kind of suffix, or although it is God's name, it is a term of exaggeration, as in the phrase: "God's mountains" (Ps. 36:7).

361. See above p. 12.

362. Paradoxically this approach is brought under the name of R. Joseph, who took the opposite opinion in the first reading of the *baraita*. See the question and the dissatisfied answer of Rashi, s.v. *be'idna*, and Tosafot, s.v. *vehen*.

363. Of course, Bathsheba was not a "deviant wife" in strict halakhic terms, but an adulteress.

364. For traditional readers, see e.g. Meiri, below n. 387, p. 45. For modern readers, see e.g. Friedman, above n. 325, pp. 54–5, Boyarin, *Carnal Israel*, 174–6.

365. Boyarin, *op. cit.* 177.

366. MS Oxford 2675. For a description, see *The Babylonian Talmud, with Variant Reading, Tractate Sota* (Jerusalem: Institute for The Complete Israeli Talmud, 1977), 1:28.

367. In another place in our Talmudic tractate (BT *Sota* 32b) we find the same structure: a Mishnaic quotation, then the question: "Why all this," and the answer: "so as not to discredit." However, see *Institute for Talmud* (BT *Sota*, 300, n. 366), who hypothesize that this Oxford version is an additional interpretation which was inserted into the Talmudic page. They base their hypothesis on Meiri (BT *Sota, ad loc.*) who justifies Ben Azzai by the fear of discrediting the bitter water. Indeed, it seems quite the opposite. Meiri, whose commentary structure integrates quotation and explanation bit-by-bit, puts "the discrediting" as a quotation, and not as an explanation. Hence, Meiri, who lived at the time in which Oxford MS was written, and who preserved Sephardic traditions (the same as this MS), apparently had the same Talmudic version.

368. Boyarin, *Carnal Israel*, 170.

369. The quotation from the Talmud in Rashi is: "(He) teaches her sex—Has it crossed your mind?" However, the same is with Meiri, who apparently had the Talmudic version of MS Oxford (see above n. 367), but explained it according to Rashi, focusing on the word: "sex," with its analogy to "Torah."

370. My translation. Rashi, apparently, based himself on the Geonim, see also the version and explanation of R. Nisim Gaon (below n. 373).

371. See MS Oxford 2675. Rashi's version is: "Teaches her *tiflut*—Has it crossed," etc. However, he explains it as if he had: *Tiflut*—Has it crossed, etc. Meiri, *ad loc.* had the manuscript version but explains it in the same way as Rashi.

372. Below p. 116, we will develop this principle of R. Eliezer as it appears in Tosefta, and BT *AZ*.

373. See R. Nisim, *Ḥibur*, 36, Rashi and Meiri on BT *Sota* 21b.

374. In other MSS it is brought in the name of a Talmudic sage called R. Elazar, see Talmudic variants.

375. See Jastrow, 1120, s.v. *armumit*—shrewdness, apparently following BT *Nida* 55b. I think it has the same meaning here too, not especially cunning in terms of cheating, as Rashi (*ad loc.*) understood. Rashi probably thought of the Hebrew biblical word *orma*. However, the parallel *armumit* in the language of the Sages also has the natural meaning of shrewdness and subtlety.

376. This is the version of MS Oxford, in other versions: *armumit*.

377. The printed edition is: "with him" (*imo*), but if this word refers to wisdom it must be the female pattern (*ima*), and if it refers to the person, it must be "him" (*bo*) as the version of the MS.

378. See the other *midrash*, which the Talmud brings to this verse, BT *Sota* 21b.

379. This is the version of the *mishna* MS Kaufmann A50, and the same in MS Oxford 267 of the Talmud. In the printed edition, the version followed the Talmudic interpretation: *kab and tiflut*, see J. N. Epstein, *Introduction to the Mishnaic Text* (Jerusalem, Tel Aviv: The Magnes Press and Dvir, 1964), 2:670, who claims that the Mishnaic version was the original version of the Talmud also.

380. In the rabbinical literature, this name refers to the commentary on the Talmud attributed to three brothers who lived in Evreux, Normandy, in the first half of the 13th c. See E. E. Urbach, *The Tosaphists: Their History, Writings and Methods* (Jerusalem: Mosad Bialik, 1968), 1:395, see also Halevi-Lifshitz, below n. 381.

381. See J. Halevi-Lifshitz (below n. 382), in his introduction to his edition to *Tosafot Evreux*, p. 15.

382. *Tosafot of Evreux and Rules of Tosafot, on tractate Sota*, ed. J. Halevi-Lifshitz (Jerusalem: Harry Fischel Institute, 1929), 55 (my translation). This commentary appears on the Talmudic page BT *Sota* 21b under the title of Tosafot of Sens, see Halevi-Lifshitz, *Tosafot of Evreux* 12ff.

383. As mentioned, Meiri writes the verb of *tiflut* with the ninth Hebrew letter *tet* (*mitapel*).

384. Moses' wife, according to the Midrash (*Sifre To Numbers* 99, ed. J. Neusner, [Atlanta, Scholars Press, 1986], 116), "Miriam and Aaron spoke against Moses their brother (Num. 12:1) because he withdrew sexually from his wife, and how did they know that? When Eldad and Medad received prophecy,

Zipporah said: 'Woe to the wives of these men.'" In Midrash *Sifre Zutta* (12:1, ed. H.S. Horovits, [Lipsiae, Gustav Fock, 1919], 247), Miriam says: "happy are they," and Zipporah responds to this.

385. For men, since they do not receive prophecy or wisdom.

386. Since their husbands will cohabit with them.

387. Menahem son of Salomon (Meiri), *Beit Habehira (tractate Sota)* (Jerusalem: The Institute of the Complete Israeli Talmud, 1967), 46 (my translation).

388. See J. N. Epstein, *Introduction*, who regards this extreme opinion of R. Joshua as contradicting R. Eliezer who, according to Epstein, only thinks that Torah will teach women *tiflut,* but that women in themselves are not such sexual creatures.

389. See Tife'eret Israel on Mishna *Sota* 3:4, Tosafot Sens, *ad loc.*

390. See Epstein, *Introduction*, for the view that the plain sense of the *mishna* is not the Talmudic interpretation. However, his alternative explanation is illogical. What is the point of one *kab* of adultery vis a vis nine *kab*s of abstinence, regarding R. Eliezer's saying? In addition, Epstein's claim that Rashi, Tosafot and Aruch did not have the version: *imo* in their Talmud, is unclear, at least regarding the first two. Cf. Rashi BT *Ket.* 62b, s.v. *kab* and *tiflut*. Cf. also Tosafot BT *Sota* 21b, in the name of R. Ḥananel, regarding BT *Ket.* 62b. See also Tosafot Evreux and Meiri (see above p. 91), and the manuscripts.

391. As said, Meiri and Tosafot Evreux had this Talmudic "correction," but they apparently did not considered it essential.

392. See Rashi and Tosafot BT *Ket.* 62b.

393. See Rashi, *op cit.*: "a woman wants one *kab* and *tiflut*—for her husband to be with her."

394. Who, for some reason did not connect this part of R. Joshua's dictum to the previous dispute between R. Eliezer and Ben Azzai.

395. See Meiri on BT *Sota* 21b that explains that he does not want to look at the *erva (*nakedness*)*, see Steinsaltz edition for BT *op cit.*

396. See JT *Sota* 3:4, 19a: *tsaimanit* from the word: *tsom* (fast), *Aruch Completum*, s.v. *tsel*, Tosafot, BT *Sota* 22b, Jastrow, *Dictionary* 1284.

397. The term "virgin" could simply refer to a young unmarried woman or also to her sexual state.

398. See JT *Sota* 3:4, 19a, this maiden lost her virginity because of the prayers and fasts, and Tosafot BT *Sota* 22b, add that she is actually a prostitute but pretends to be pious to cover it. It is not far-fetched to assume that this phrase refers also to some sort of religious nun, who dedicates herself to piety as opposed to married life, but this needs further investigation.

399. See BT *Sota* 22b, which refutes this misogynistic reading by the dictum of R. Johanan who had learnt piety from a virgin and a widow. See also Meiri, BT *ad loc*.

400. See (BT *Sota* 22b) the Talmudic explanation for: "blows (*makot*) of withdrawn persons" from a parallel *baraita*, which has a sexual connotation.

The example of "a *shikhmi* withdrawn person—one who behaves like Shekhem" (cf. Gen. 34). The other example, which supposes to fit the "blows of withdrawn persons" is that of "one who lets blood against the walls" (BT ibid.) Rashi *ad loc.*, explains: that this man is closing his eyes so as not to look at women, and thus knocks his head against the wall and bleeds. Also, the connotation that the name "*Perushin*" (withdrawn persons) has to the "Pharisees" (the sect of the Second Temple period represented by the Sages) is associated in the Talmud (*Sota op cit.*) with a sexual situation. Thus the Talmud is talking about one who behaved like Zimri (who was involved in sex with a Midianite girl, see Num. 25:6,14), but expecting a reward like Phineas (who killed them for their sexual action, Num. 25:7–8).

401. See the examples of a parallel *baraita* (BT *Sota* 22a), which include women and a minor male. In JT (*Sota* 3:4, 19:1), the later was connected to lewdness.

402. The term and the concept of hypocrisy are mentioned in the Talmud there regarding the "blows of the withdrawn persons" and plays on the double meaning of "withdrawal"—*perushin* and "Pharisees."

403. The phrase *mevalei olam* refers to human nature in relation to the world more than to a moral or religious state, is obvious from the contradictory phrase *meyashvei olam*—settle the world, which appears there (BT *Sota* 22a). See also, MS Kaufmann, Mishna *Sota* 3:4, *mekhalei olam*.

404. This is the version BT *Yeb.* of MS. Oxford 367, MS Munich 141, Rome 114, and Pizaro edition (1509), in the printed edition, and MS Munich 95 it is "Jacob"—a frequent change. The Tosefta quotes "R. Akiba" but in a very different way from the Talmud (see below n. 405).

405. BT *Yeb.* MS Oxford 367. In Tosefta *Yeb.* 8:6 (MS Vienna, Lieberman edition, 26, MS Erfurt, Zuckermandel edition, 250, n. 4) the version is: (E)lazar ben Azaria. However, both versions of the *baraita* in Tosefta seem to have problems with the tradition of the disputants, which left traces also in the various traditions of that *baraita* in BT. Notwithstanding, in BT, R. Eliezer is still appearing in both *baraitot* (except in MS Munich 141, which reads in the second *baraita*: "El(i)azar ben Jacob," and in MS Munich 95 which reads in the first *baraita*: "Elazar." However, note that both manuscripts (141, 95) read: "Eliezer" in the third *baraita* (brought under the title of "our Rabbis taught"), which maintains the same extreme opinion towards procreation, brought in the first and second *baraitot*). In general, it seems that the tradition of the first *baraita* in BT is more coherent in relation to its internal parts, and in comparison to the opinions of the Sages out of it. Although, some corrected the BT version and attributed this saying to R. Elazar (see M. Higger, *Ozar ha-baraithoth*, vol. 3 [New York: Debe Rabanan, 1940], 257, according to MS Munich 95), compare Gilat (*R. Eliezer Ben Hyrcanus*, 445) who relates to this saying as part of R. Eliezer's conception.

406. See his saying in *Sifra on Leviticus, Nedavah* 2, vol. 2, ed. L. Finkelstein (New York: Jewish Theological Seminary, 1983), 17–8: "Ben Azzai

says: I am not disputing my Rabbi but adding to his words," and Ben Azzai there, indeed, explains and extends R. Akiba's short words.

407. See the version of Tosefta, *Yeb.* 8:7, which directly attributed to R. Akiba the saying: "whoever spills blood cancels the image."

408. About these two poles in R. Eliezer's conception of sexuality see Hoshen, "Fire," 132ff; *id.* "Sexual Relations." Regarding R. Eliezer's severe conception of sexual deviations, see Gilat, *R. Eliezer Ben Hyrcanus,* 417ff.

Chapter Five

The Talmudic Story of Beruria in Context

Moving to tractate *Avoda Zara*, we enter the other textual arena in which modern and traditional scholars have examined the relationships between Beruria and R. Eliezer, and between the post-Talmudic Beruria and the Talmudic text and culture.

Previously, we presented this Talmudic text (10* BT *Avoda Zara* 18a), which narrates the story of Beruria, sending R. Meir to release her sister from the brothel. We identified this story as "the Beruria incident" mentioned at the end of this long Talmudic text, in contrast to post-Talmudic commentary, which ascribed "the Beruria incident" elsewhere. We have found this attribution to be alien to the Talmudic culture and irrelevant to this particular text.

On re-reading the beginning of the Talmudic story about Beruria, we see that the Talmud posits it in a context that inserts the character from "the Beruria incident" deeply in Talmudic text and culture. Furthermore, in this text of *Avoda Zara*, the Talmud reinforces our portrait of Beruria as drawn from the other Talmudic sources, which links her to R. Eliezer's method. The Talmud also reveals the roots of this linkage through the character of her father, R. Hananya ben Teradion, who has been introduced here in *Avoda Zara*, although not explicitly, as a "disciple" of "the fire conception" and of R. Eliezer.[409]

In a series of *baraitot* in *Avoda Zara* (17b), the Talmud unfolds the story in which R. Hananya ben Teradion, Beruria's father, was arrested and executed by the Romans, probably at the time of Hadrian's edicts (135 CE).[410] Going further back in the Talmudic *sugia* (16b), we find that the latter is connected with a *baraita* about R. Eliezer which probably refers to the time of the reign of Trajan (109 CE).[411] Although three decades separate the historical situations reflected in the two *baraitot*, as R. Eliezer was dead at the time of R. Hananya's death, the *baraitot*, which are themselves third century sources, transmit both cases in the same literary formula.[412] The *baraita* about R. Eliezer begins: "The Rabbis taught: when R. Eliezer was caught (arrested) by/for[413] *minut*."[414] This is the same formula with which the *baraita* about R. Hananya begins: "The Rabbis taught: when R. Elazar ben Parta[415] and R. Hananya ben Teradion was (were)[416] caught (arrested) by/for *minut*."[417] By presenting these two *baraitot* consecutively, the Talmud expresses its view that the *baraitot* share a conceptual meaning, which is, as we shall see, "the fire conception." This conception is expressed also in the rest of the *baraitot* attached by the Talmud to the story about R. Hananya's trial. Hence, although the *baraitot* about R. Hananya are populated by other characters—his colleague R. Elazar ben Parta, his wife and his daughter who was sent to the brothel—they are presented in the Talmud through the figure and the theological conception of R. Hananya, which strikes us as bearing all the signs (external and substantial) of R. Eliezer's "fire conception."

We do not agree with the feminist reading of *Avoda Zara*, which suggests that the Talmud created a few figures to confirm R. Eliezer's view of "the feminine." That is to say that the proper woman (the daughter of R. Hananya in the *baraita*) is the uneducated woman, while the educated one (Beruria as at hinted in the Talmud and as presented in post-Talmudic commentary) is intrinsically wanton.[418] Firstly, we have already demonstrated that this understanding of R. Eliezer's opinion, as attributed to his saying in tractate *Sota*, has no Talmudic basis, and is purely post-Talmudic. Secondly, the speculative connection between the *Avoda Zara* text, including its post-Talmudic commentary, and R. Eliezer's saying in tractate *Sota*, ignores the very fact that the Talmud in *Avoda Zara* uses a *baraita* referring to R. Eliezer as the context to the texts (presented later) about R. Hananya ben Teradion and his daughters. Nonetheless, a close reading of that contextual *baraita* in tractate *Avoda Zara* indeed reveals a position held in common with R. Eliezer's saying in tractate *Sota*, not according to the post-Talmudic interpretation of misogyny, but rather within that of sexuality. However, as stated, in tractate *Avoda Zara*, the Talmud presents R. Eliezer's sexual doctrine in its relation to his theological "fire conception," the principles of which are embodied, as we shall see presently, in the figures of R. Hananya ben Teradion and Beruria.

R. Eliezer ben Hyrcanus

Our Rabbis taught: When R. Eliezer was caught (*nitpas*[419] arrested) by/for[420] (*le*)*minut*, they brought him up to the tribune to be judged. Said the hegemon to him: Does an old man like you occupy himself with those idle things? He replied, I acknowledge the Judge as right. The hegemon thought that he referred to him—but he did not say (so)[421]—Rather, he really referred to his Father in Heaven—and said, Because thou hast acknowledged me as right, I pardon: thou art acquitted. When he came home, his disciples called on him to console him, but he would accept no consolation. Said R. Akiba to him, Rabbi, wilt thou permit me to say one thing of what thou hast taught me? He replied, Say it. Rabbi, maybe a *minut* matter came across you and this thing pleased you, and for it thou wast caught for/by *minut*? He exclaimed: Akiba thou hast reminded me. Once, I was walking in the upper-market of Sepphoris. I was found by[422] one of the disciples of Jesus of Nazareth, and Jacob of Kefar-Sekaniah by name, who said to me: It is written in your Torah, Thou shalt not bring the hire of a harlot . . . into the house of the Lord thy God (Deut. 23:9). May such money be applied to the erection of a retiring place (i.e., toilet) for the High Priest? To which I made no reply. Said he to me that his Rabbi Jesus has taught him so: Thus was I taught: For of the hire of a harlot hath she gathered them and unto the hire of a harlot shall they return. they came from a place of filth, let them go to a place of filth (Micah 1:7), and this thing pleased me, and that is why I was caught for/by *minut*, for thereby I transgressed on what has been written in the Torah: Remove thy way far from her (Prov. 5:8)—which refers to *minut* as well as to the Authority, (*rashut*)[423] and come not nigh to the door of her house (Prov. 5:8)—which refers to a harlot. (BT *Avoda Zara* 16b 17a)[424]

This *baraita* and its parallel in Tosefta *Ḥulin* (2:24) have drawn some researchers to hypothesize that R. Eliezer, though "by no means a Christian,"[425] at least "appeared to be friendly toward Christianity and its leaders."[426] However, the text itself describes the grief of R. Eliezer at that accusation (presumably, it was that)[427] because of which he went to extremes in his refusal to be consoled, and the efforts his colleagues made to console him. These descriptions would be irrelevant if the Roman accusation contained even a grain of truth as regards R. Eliezer's present life or in his past.[428] Indeed, one could argue that all these happenings are covering up the very fact that R. Eliezer was a Christian.[429] However, this argument goes against the text, against the dynamics of the Sages in general,[430] and against the tannaitic and amoraic context of this text.[431]

According to our approach, although the Roman accusation is the historical background of this tale, it is actually, as in other texts of the Sages, employed as an incidental pattern for the conceptual fabric reflected in the text,[432] which in this case is R. Eliezer's "fire conception." In a parallel of this *baraita* in Tosefta, the ending says:

> For R. Eliezer teaches: One should always flee from ugliness and from whatever is similar to ugliness. (Tosefta *Hulin*, 2:24)[433]

When applying this conclusion to the whole *tosefta*, it means that even getting close to the prostitute or the theological prostitute, i.e., *minut* (idolatry), is considered by R. Eliezer with the same severity as sinning with the prostitute or idol-worshiping. The same principle is reflected in the strong language of R. Eliezer's saying in BT *Sota*: "one who teaches his daughter Torah (the law of the bitter water) is teaching her *tiflut*—sex—adultery."[434]

Indeed, this is the conceptual principle presented in the preceding *tosefta* (23), for which the following *tosefta* (24) about R. Eliezer serves as an example. The *tosefta* (23) presents the strict prohibition of any contact with *minim* who are idolaters[435] of any sort, including Christian Jews.[436] It prohibits either behaving similarly to *minim*—although the action itself is permitted from the halakhic point of view[437]—or having any indirect benefit from their being *minim*: commercial dealings with them, teaching of their children, or being healed by them. Although all of these Rabbinical restrictions are intended "to make a fence" around the biblical prohibition of idolatry, it seems that they were conceived by Tosefta as a transgression as severe as a transgression of Torah.[438] Or, at least, they were seen in the light of R. Eliezer's warning to be very careful of the Rabbis' laws:

> Beware of their glowing coal, least thou be burnt, for their bite is the bite of a fox, and their sting is the sting of a scorpion, and their hiss is a hiss of a serpent, and all their utterances are like coals of fire. (Mishna *Avot* 2:10)[439]

Tosefta brings two examples: The first, tells about Ben Dama who was bitten by a real snake. He wanted to transgress the Rabbis' prohibition of healing by a *min*—an idolater, in this case a Christian Jew. He claimed that he could bring a proof (from Scripture)[440] for the fact that it is permitted. However, he died before being healed, and was praised by R. Ishmael:

> Happy are you, Ben Dama, that you have not broken through (violated) the decrees[441] of the Rabbis, since everyone who breaks through the Rabbis' fence, a calamity comes upon him, as it was said: one who breaks through the fence is bitten by the snake. (Ecc. 10:8) (Tosefta *Hulin* 2:23)

This tannaitic story already raised questions at the time of Amoraim. Both Talmuds[442] wondered: "after all, he was bitten by a snake." Their answer distinguishes between calamity in this world and that in the next world, or between the real snake of nature and the metaphorical snake of the Rabbis. The problem of this story deepens when the Talmuds ask about the proof that Ben Dama wanted to bring before he died. The Talmuds conclude that it was the verse from Leviticus (18:5): "'you shall observe my decrees and my laws, which man shall carry out and by which he shall live' which implies that one should live by the Torah laws and not die by them."[443] Hence, according to Ben Dama,[444] if one's life is in danger he could transgress the Torah law of idolatry and live, while according to R. Ishmael this was not the case, and on the contrary, in the case of healing by the *minim* one should die and not transgress the Torah prohibition of idolatry.[445]

But is healing by *minim* a Torah or rabbinic prohibition? Thus it seems that although the Tosefta presents this story of Ben Dama as an example of the Rabbis' prohibition of idolatry, it attributes to this transgression the severity of a Torah prohibition, which brings in its wake a severe punishment. This is why Ben Dama, although he did not really sin, actually died from the snakebite. Accordingly, the first example in the Tosefta reflects R. Eliezer's principle, which regards the phrase: "similar to ugliness" as strictly as "ugliness itself." Hence, the terms that Tosefta uses for describing punishment derive from the metaphorical terms of "the fire conception" used by R. Eliezer. Thus a minor transgression of a Rabbinic prohibition, such as healing by a *min*, even if only physical healing and to avoid death,[446] requires a severe punishment, symbolized by the snake and the burning.[447]

The next example brought by the Tosefta regarding R. Eliezer's principle is R. Eliezer himself, who transgressed Rabbinic prohibition and took the strict view of seeing Rabbinic prohibition as transgressing a Torah prohibition, which according to his method deserves a severe punishment.

The opening of this story in both versions (Tosefta, BT) already takes R. Eliezer to the scene of the prostitute: "Once, I was walking in the upper-market of Sepphoris." This walking in the market gives the impression of coming very near to the house of the prostitute who apparently was loitering about and looking for prey to seduce. In this case, the "prostitute" was one of the *minim*, and indeed, R Eliezer was caught[448] by him. "I was found by[449] one of the disciples of Jesus from Nazareth, Jacob of Kefar-Sekaniah by name." According to the BT version, R. Eliezer did not consent to the *min's* attempts to converse with him on Torah matters:

> It is written in your Torah, Thou shalt not bring the hire of a harlot ... into the house of the Lord thy God (Deut. 23:9). May such money be applied to the erection of a retiring place for the High Priest? To which I made no reply. (BT *Avoda Zara* 17a)

However, this silence, which may reflect R. Eliezer's refusal to make any contact with the *min*,[450] is not enough, since according to R. Eliezer: "One should always flee from ugliness and from whatever is similar to ugliness." The question asked by the *min*, which was actually some sort of *midrash*, was perhaps not the "ugliness" (prostitution—*minut*—idolatry) itself, since it was construed as a Torah matter.[451] It was however, certainly similar to the ugliness, since it came from a *min*, whose intention, according to R. Eliezer, is usually idolatry, and here had also obviously inserted these thoughts of *minut* into his *midrash*.[452] Hence, according to R. Eliezer's method, coming so close to the prostitute, and enjoying the "similar to ugliness," albeit unintentionally, deserves the same extreme penalty as enjoying the ugliness itself, i.e., a transgression of the Torah prohibition of idolatry-*minut*. That is what he said about himself: "and that is why I was caught for/by *minut*, for thereby I transgressed what has been written in the Torah: Remove thy way far from her" (Prov. 5:8) (Tosefta, *Hulin*, 2:23).

In this light, we should read R. Eliezer's reaction to the accusation of the judge who was apparently a pagan Roman:

> I acknowledge the Judge as right. The hegemon thought that he referred to him—though he really referred to his Father in Heaven. (BT *Avoda Zara* 16b)

Some scholars have explained this response as evasive,[453] due to their assumption that R. Eliezer wanted to answer the pagan judge, and thus concluded that he did not want to deny the accusation.[454] However, according to the context in Tosefta, this reaction may be read differently.

On the one hand it totally ignores the Roman judgment,[455] which was considered *minut*,[456] and on the other hand it acknowledges the Heavenly judgment, i.e., acknowledges that being caught by /for *minut*, which could result in no less than death, is a punishment for a sin which deserves the death penalty. As Rashi explains: "I acknowledge the Judge. Indeed, He judged me faithfully and thus gave me this trouble, since I transgressed against Him." Applying this explanation to the *baraita* (in Tosefta and BT) means that R. Eliezer justified the death penalty he had almost undergone, as if to say: "He! God—the Heavenly Judge—did very well by me by punishing me." R. Eliezer assumed that by disregarding the Rabbis' warning against coming close to the harlot/idolatry, or in his words, by not running away from the "similar to ugliness," he was considered by the Heavenly Judge as being with the ugliness itself as an idolater, as a *min*. For this reason, he was caught by *minut* (the Roman government), or also accused of *minut* (Christian or other), for the Heavenly Judge found him guilty of the sin of *minut* (idolatry), and thus he was liable to the death penalty.

This acknowledgment by R. Eliezer does not reflect a passive justification of divine punishment, but derives from his "fire conception" that maintains that Divinity and its word—Torah, require a complete union from the individual. As we explained previously, "the fire principle" of the complete union with Torah is a reflection of the positive relations with divinity. This is expressed in the joy feature of fire, which in turn refers to the situation of Sinai.[457] Thus, any transgression against either Torah itself, or against the Rabbis' warning, will cause the bursting out of the burning feature of the fire, which symbolizes the gap between Torah—God and Man. Hence, the severe penalty, which at first glance appears disproportionate to the sin itself, is actually very appropriate to the extreme requirement of "the fire conception" for a complete union with Torah. Accordingly, R. Eliezer's acknowledgement of the heavenly judgment is a recognition of the ideal relationship with Torah and divinity, were it not for the sin which interrupts this ideal.[458]

R. Ḥananya ben Teradion

Within this conceptual framework, after the *baraita* about R. Eliezer, the Talmud presents the *baraitot* about R. Ḥananya ben Teradion—Beruria's father:[459]

> Our Rabbis taught: When R. Elazar ben Parta and R. Hananya ben Teradion were caught (by) for *minut*[460]... R. Hananya said to him (R. Elazar) Happy art thou, who hast been caught on five charges, but wilt be rescued; woe is me who, though having been caught on one charge, will not be rescued; for thou hast occupied thyself with [the study of] the Torah as well as with acts of benevolence, whereas I occupied myself with Torah alone. (BT *Avoda Zara* 17b)

As we have stated, the initial formula: "when ... R. Hananya was caught (by) for *minut*" is similar to that of R. Eliezer's *baraita*. Although there is no explicit reference to Christianity as in the latter case, researchers have already noted that the descriptions of R. Hananya's death in the other *baraitot* are similar to those of the deaths of the Christians at times of persecutions.[461] Accordingly, either R. Hananya was accused like R. Eliezer of *minut*,[462] or else he was accused "by *minut*." Furthermore, as we also said concerning R. Eliezer, the term "*minut*" refers to the pagan sovereignty of the Romans,[463] which also had its impact on their courts with its heathen cults.[464] However, we see that R. Hananya is following R. Eliezer's logic.

> Woe is me who, though having been caught on one charge, will not be rescued; for thou hast occupied thyself with [the study of] the Torah, as well as with acts of benevolence, whereas I occupied myself with Torah alone. This accords with the opinion of R. Huna. For R. Huna said: He who only occupies himself with the study of the Torah is as if he had no God, for it is said: Now for long seasons Israel was without the true God. What is meant by without the true God?—It means that he who only occupies himself with the study of the Torah is as if he had no God. (BT *Avoda Zara* 17b)

First, because R. Hananya acknowledges the justice of his death penalty, he is convinced that it must necessarily occur. Second, he interprets his being "caught (arrested) for/by *minut*" as reflecting a sin that deserves the death penalty, which according to the Talmud is the sin of idolatry. As we saw in regard to R. Eliezer, the sin of being close to the "similar of ugliness"—*minut*—idolatry, in this case: "occupied myself with Torah alone" is interpreted by R. Hananya (according to the Talmudic reading) "as if" being with the ugliness itself: "he had no God." However, as in the case of R. Eliezer, the transgression of coming close to the "simile of ugliness," which was considered strictly "as if" being the ugliness itself, is a very small transgression, quite disproportionate to the severe penalty of death. Nevertheless, both Tannaim considered this penalty as indispensable. Accordingly, the Talmud wonders:

> But did he not occupy himself with acts of benevolence? Surely it has been taught: R. Eliezer ben Jacob says: One should not put his money into a charity-bag, unless it is supervised by a sage such as R. Ḥananya ben Teradion!—He was indeed very trustworthy, but he did not practice charity. (BT *Avoda Zara* 17b)[465]

However, this strained answer does not satisfy the Talmud, and it keeps asking:

> But has it not been taught: He [R. Ḥananya] said to him [R. Jose ben Kisma]: I mistook Purim-money for ordinary charity money, so I distributed [of my own] to the poor!—He did indeed practice charity, but not as much as he might have done. (BT *Avoda Zara* 17b)

The transgression of R. Ḥananya was his confusion of two kinds of charity money, which have different laws.[466] For this small transgression, whether he paid from his own pocket afterwards for this confusion, or not,[467] he was judged as an idolater "caught for *minut*," like one who has no God. Hence, he deserved the worst, a death penalty. Or, more gravely, according to the other *baraita*, this transgression caused him concern about his share in the world to come,[468] namely, not about a temporary punishment, which is merely of this world, but about a total loss.

Commenting on this text, Saul Lieberman has wondered: "where have we heard that due to such a light sin one will not have a part in the next world to come?"[469] Indeed, the problematics of R. Ḥananya's severe conception, which necessitates a major punishment for a minor transgression, and especially this "light" sin of benevolence, could only be explained within R. Eliezer's "fire conception" regarding Divinity and Torah. This conception demands a total union with the overwhelming presence of both these entities in every dimension of reality, as we find in the next source:

> It has been taught, R. Eliezer's[470] disciples asked him: What must one do to be spared the pangs of the Messiah? [He answered,] Let him engage in Torah study and benevolence. (BT *Sanhedrin* 98b)

According to "the fire conception," benevolence reflects the wide circle of reality in which the Torah leaves its imprint on life.[471] Thus, R. Ḥananya's transgression of withdrawing from benevolence and occupying himself with Torah study alone reflects an abstract conception of Torah, which degrades it by reducing its impact on life, and thus ignoring the complete intimacy with God.[472] Thus, we see that "the fire conception" of the Torah's overwhelming presence and the union required with it is vital. Every detour is considered to be a severe deviation ("with no God"), even if it was unintentional, as in the case of R. Eliezer, or if one tries to repair it, like R. Hananya. There is no guarantee that the burning feature—the heavenly judgment—will not burst out from one of the layers of this very structure of the relation with Torah and the Divine.

The acknowledgment of such judgment, which derives from a conception of extreme intimacy between Man and God-Torah, is well expressed in the continuation of R. Hananya's story, which is based on *baraitot* told in the Talmud in its own style:[473]

> When they (the Romans) brought R. Hananya, they asked him, why have you studied Torah? He said to them, exactly as the Lord my God commanded me (BT *Avoda Zara*, 17b)[474]

Following the style of Moses in Deuteronomy: "Behold I have taught you rules and judgment (*hukim* and *mishpatim*) as the Lord my God commanded me" (Deut. 4:5),[475] we are exposed here too in R. Hananya's words to the intimate relation to Torah and its giver—"*my* God." The descriptions of the disproportionate punishment, which is bursting forth, are more readily explained on this conceptual basis of relationship with Torah and Divinity.

> At once, they sentenced him to be burnt, his wife to be slain, and his daughter to be consigned to a brothel. (BT *Avoda Zara* 17b)

Looking at the Talmudic discussion about the nature of the punishment of each member of the family of R. Hananya ben Teradion we find the conception of R. Eliezer[476] as found previously in the *baraita* about R. Eliezer's trial.

> The punishment of being burnt came upon him because he pronounced the Name [of God] in its letters [in its full spelling].[477] (BT *Avoda Zara* 18a)

The involvement with God's name, which probably refers to some sort of esoteric interpretation of Scripture,[478] reflects R. Hananya's great union and enthusiasm with the process of his study: "pronouncing the Name with all its letters." However, the burning at the stake clarifies that this great intimacy with Torah and God's presence would not tolerate the minor transgression, which is considered to be a deviation.[479] The Talmud asks about R. Hananya's transgression:

But how could he do so? Have we not learnt: The following have no portion in the world to come: He who says that Torah is not from heaven, or that the resurrection of the dead is not taught in Torah. Abba Saul says: Also he who pronounces the Name in its full spelling? (ibid.)

From the proximity to other transgressions, it seems that the Talmud understood the sin of pronouncing God's name as an act of denying the transcendental nature of God, like denial of the heavenly nature of Torah, or of the existence of the world beyond this world—the world to come. However, The Talmud does not attribute this severe deviation to R. Hananya's action, and concludes:

He did it in the course of practicing, as we have learnt: Thou shalt not learn to do after the abominations of those nations (Deut. 18:9), but thou mayest learn [about them] in order to understand and to teach. (BT *Avoda Zara* 18a)

It is striking to observe that the same conclusion in regard to R. Hananya was applied by the Talmud elsewhere in regard to R. Eliezer, in the *baraita* which we partly quoted previously, which relates how R. Eliezer was teaching the magic laws of planting and uprooting marrows.[480] The Talmud explains that R. Eliezer did not actually perform the magic, but studied it, in order to understand it and to teach it.[481] But the question is how things became reality when they were intended to be merely abstract, ("teach" and "learn")? Thus, we interpreted[482] R. Eliezer's action as deriving from his "fire conception" of Torah, one of whose features is joy. This symbolizes the learner's enthusiasm during Torah study, which creates a complete union between him and his study. We explained this process also in terms of existentialization of the Halakha-law,[483] that is to say, when the Torah moves from being an abstract object in the learner's intellect to becoming a part of his *existentia*, and hence a reality.[484]

Now, the same interpretation applies here too to the Talmudic conclusion about the Name. R. Hananya did not actually pronounce the Name in its full spelling, but only studied it in order to understand it and to teach it. However, since he was studying by the standards of "the fire conception," his enthusiasm made him become one with his study and this full union with Torah realized it—"he pronounced the Name in its full spelling."

The pressing question is, as the Talmud puts it: "Why then was he punished?" The answer is "Because he was pronouncing the Name in public." This answer takes us back to our first claim, that the minor transgression and deviation from the complete intimacy with Torah obligated R. Ḥananya to be sentenced to the stake. In this case, the consequence of his action could have been the desecration of the Name caused by there being an external observer, i.e., the public,[485] who interrupted the union of R. Ḥananya and the Torah. Thus, according to "the fire conception," the burning feature of Torah bursts out when there are gaps in the complete union between Man and God, although they are caused indirectly and unintentionally.[486]

The Mishna supports our reading of R. Ḥananya's relation to Torah and God, in that spirit of "the fire conception:"

> R. Ḥananya ben Teradion said: [when] two sit together and there are no words of Torah [spoken] between them. Lo, This [constitutes] a session of scorners (*letzim*), As it is said: [Happy is the man who has not walked in the counsel of the wicked (*reshaim*) . . .] Nor sat in the session of scorners (Ps. 1:1). But [when] two sit together and there are words of Torah (spoken) between them, the Divine Presence (*shkhina*) abides among them as it was said: Then they that feared the Lord spoke one with another and the Lord hearkened and heard, and a book of remembrance was written before Him, for them that feared the Lord and that thought upon his Name (Malachi 3:16). I have no [scriptural proof for the presence of God/*shekhina*] except [among] two, whence [is there proof that] even [when there is only] one [person] the Holy One blessed be He appoints unto him a reward?—since it is said: Though he sit and [meditate] in stillness yet he taketh [a reward] unto himself (Lam. 3:28). (Mishna *Avot* 3:2)

Going into the *midrash* of R. Ḥananya (presented in the *mishna*) we find the methodology of the backwards reading applied by Beruria (and R. Eliezer). The verse in Psalms says:

> Happy is the man who has not walked in the counsel of the wicked (*reshaim*), Nor stood in the path of the sinners (*hataim*)], Nor sat in the session of scorners. (Ps. 1:1)

The commentators[487] explain: why does R. Ḥananya says that the lack of Torah leads to the "session of the scorners." Because of the next verse:

> But whose desire (*heftzo*) is in the Torah of the Lord; and in His Torah he meditates day and night. (Ps. 1:2)

Reading the verses forwards, they say: Happy is the man who has not sat in the session of the scorners but in the session of Torah. Reading them backwards, they say as R. Ḥananya's *midrash*: Because the desire of one is in Torah on which he meditates day and night, he has not sat in the session of the scorners, who lack the Torah presence in their surroundings.[488] Thus R. Hananya, like R. Eliezer and Beruria, maintains that Torah fills every part in life. Even an ordinary conversation between two must be of Torah, and even when one is sitting by oneself all, body and soul, must be devoted to Torah "day and night." A small deviation from this overwhelming presence will make one as the wicked and the sinners who are defined by this lack of Torah presence. On the contrary, complete union with Torah will bring one to complete harmony with God. "Then, they that feared the Lord spoke one with another and the Lord hearkened and heard." And He will allow His Divine Presence (*Shekhina*) to rest upon[489] "them that feared the Lord and that thought upon his Name" (Malachi 3:16).

Coming back to R. Hananya's story in the other *baraitot* presented in *Avoda Zara*, we see how the other figures around R. Hananya complete the picture of his theological conception. "The fire conception" is applied harshly, and the demand for a total union with the Torah necessitates the punishment, even if the deviation from that total union is caused by some unintentional omission embedded in some deep level of sub-conscious human behavior.

> His wife was punished by being slain, because she did not prevent him [from doing it]. From this, it was deduced: Any one who has the power to prevent [one from doing transgressions] and does not prevent is punished (caught—*nitpas*)[490] for him. (BT *Avoda Zara* 18a)

The transgression of the wife is not the performance of a forbidden action, but of not preventing a possible consequence of a forbidden action. For this, she was caught by the Romans and was sentenced to death. This means, as R. Eliezer and R. Hananya understood it, that she was actually caught—trapped by the Heavenly Judgment—by a sin, which deserves the death penalty. Once again this disproportionate punishment for the sin is due to "the fire conception" which views the presence of the perfect God as filling all reality, and demands a full union with this Divine perfection. Thus, it does not bear the smallest diversion from it, and bursts out in the burning feature of the heavenly judgment.[491]

The seemingly disproportionately severe punishment of the daughter was also explained because of the [possible] consequences of an apparently regular human action.

> His daughter was consigned to a brothel, for R. Johanan related that once that daughter of his was walking in front of some great men of Rome who remarked: How beautiful are the steps of this maiden! Whereupon she took particular care of her step. (ibid.)

Apparently, "walking in front of some great men of Rome" may give the impression of more than a minor sin. Indeed, Rashi seems to understand it in this spirit, when he explains that after she heard the Romans talking about her, she tried to attract them more. However, from other manuscripts of this Talmudic text[492] it seems that the Romans sat there and she came across them accidentally. In addition, her reaction seems there to be explained differently, namely, that after she heard what they said about her,[493] she actually was careful of her steps and tried to avoid any unintended results. Nonetheless, like R. Ḥananya himself, concerning the charity money, she could not escape the Heavenly Punishment. Therefore, she was caught both by the Romans and by Heavenly Judgment.

This reading is amplified by the following supporting *midrash* which the Talmud brings as an explanation of the daughter's sentencing:

> Which confirms the following words of R. Simeon ben Lakish: What is the meaning of the verse: The iniquity of my heel compasseth me about (Ps. 49:6)?—Sins which one treads under heel in this world compass him about on the Day of Judgment (BT *Avoda Zara* 18a)

The deviation is made by a small transgression which one treads under his heel. This means, transgressions, which are not considered sins, e.g., the unintended consequences of one's actions. For such a minor deviation she was considered a harlot—hence, the Heavenly Judgment burst out, and she was punished by being sent to a brothel.

The severity towards sexual deviation, as is implied by the story of the daughter of R. Ḥananya, is fully in keeping with the latter's sexual conception, which adheres to that of R. Eliezer, who said in the Mishna:

> On the Day of Atonement it is forbidden to . . . wash, and the king and the bride may wash their faces. (Mishna *Yoma* 8:1)

The Talmud asks "According to whom is our *mishna*?" and answers:

> According to R. Ḥananya ben Teradion. For it was taught: [Even] the king and the bride may not wash their faces. R. Ḥananya ben Teradion said in the name of R. Eliezer: The king and the bride may wash their

faces. . . . Why [may] a bride [wash her face]?—Lest she become unattractive to her husband (BT *Yoma* 78b)

According to the Talmudic explanation, R. Ḥananya adopted R. Eliezer's opinion, which considers the intimacy between husband and wife so important, that it should be kept even on the Day of Atonement, and determines the laws of this Holy Day. As mentioned above, R. Eliezer's sexual conception derives from his "fire conception." Just as he requires a total union and intimacy in the relations between human beings and God, likewise he requires total union in the relations between husband and wife.[494] The same attitude applies to a breach of either kind of relations. Hence, the great severity with which both *tannaim* relate to minor transgressions, whether sexual prostitution or theological prostitution *minut*–idolatry.

In the following *baraita* we continue to see how R. Ḥananya's "fire conception" is reflected to us through these three figures:

> As the three of them went out [from the tribunal] they declared their submission to [the Divine] righteous judgment. He quoted: The Rock, His work is perfect; for all his ways are justice (Deut. 32:4) His wife continued: A God of faithfulness and without iniquity, just and right is He, and the daughter quoted: Great in counsel and mighty in work, whose eyes are open upon all the ways of the sons of men, to give everyone according to his ways, and according to the fruit of his doing. (Jer. 32:19). (BT *Avoda Zara* 18a)

Recognizing intimacy and complete union as a basis to the relationship with Torah and divinity leads the three of them, like R. Eliezer, to acknowledge the Heavenly Judgment. These three quotations reflect three aspects of "the fire conception:"[495] the union of Man with the perfect God; the overwhelmingly great punishment when deviating from this presence; and the overwhelming presence of God, which contains two possible relationships: union and thus Joy, or deviation and thus burning.

R. Ḥananya refers to the perfection of God, which demands complete union with God. When reading the verse forward, it says: "the Rock is complete/perfect/united[496] with His work[497]/action"[498]/ creatures[499] (*hazur tamim pa'olo*, Deut. 32:4) However, from the Hebrew, it might be read in reverse: His creatures are wholly united with the Rock. If read in both directions simultaneously, the verse is interpreted conditionally: Since the Rock is complete with his creatures, they should be complete with Him.[500] From this recognition of the perfection of God, and the requirement of his creatures for a total union with Him, comes the acknowledgment of His judgment: "as all His ways are justice."

The wife refers to the non-toleration of any detour from this completeness of God: "A God of faithfulness and without iniquity," which means, as the Talmud elsewhere interpreted this verse: "God punishes the righteous also for a minor transgression."[501]

The daughter refers to the overwhelming presence of this divine nature in all life: "whose eyes are open upon all the ways of the sons of men" (Jer. 32:19). From this recognition, she derives her view of the relationship with God, revealed in the Heavenly Judgment for good and for ill: "to give everyone according to his ways and according to the fruit of his doing." In the context of the daughter's situation, this verse is interpreted with severity, and as referring to the Heavenly Punishment, without questioning its disproportion. When one is caught by the severe overwhelming Divine presence, whose nature is perfect and demands a total union with this perfection, there is no refuge. The only logical thing to do is—following R. Eliezer and R. Ḥananya—look for the sin which trapped (or almost trapped) them within the Heavenly Judgment.

However, this overwhelming feature of God also has a positive aspect, which potentially maintains within it the possibility of intimacy, when there is no sin separating Man from the total union with God. In this case, the overwhelming presence of the divine, who gives "everyone according to his ways and according to the fruit of his doing," (Jer. 32:19) will judge this person as equal to the divine itself. Thus, there will be no "being caught," but rather an intimate state of a total equation between God and Man, in which the fate and the nature of the latter will derive from the former. In "the fire conception," this structure of the intimate relations allows the natural occurrence of the miracle.[502] Although the miracle was not realized in the father's life, the constructive feasibility of the intimate relations was transmitted as a legacy to his daughter.

The very last picture of R. Ḥananya brought in the second *baraita* exposes us simultaneously to contradictory features (intimacy vs. deviation, burning vs. union) of "the fire conception." It is this simultaneity which marks this event with an absurdity.

> They (the Romans) found R. Ḥananya ben Teradion sitting and occupying himself with the Torah, publicly gathering assemblies, and keeping a scroll of the Torah in his bosom. Straightaway they took hold of him, wrapped him in the Scroll of the Torah, placed bundles of branches round him and set them on fire. . . . His daughter exclaimed: Father, that I should see you in this state! He replied: my daughter![503] If

it were I alone being burnt it would have been a thing hard to bear; but now that I am burning together with the Scroll of the Torah, He who will seek (retribution) for this insult of the Torah Scroll, He will seek (retribution also) for my insult.[504] His disciples called out, Rabbi, what seest thou? He answered them: The parchments are being burnt but the letters are soaring on high. Open then thy mouth [said they] so that the fire enter into thee. He replied: Let Him who gave me [my soul] take it away, but no one should injure oneself. (BT *Avoda Zara* 18a)

R. Hananya is occupying himself with Torah with the scroll in his bosom. Later on, the scroll was also wrapped around him. The concept of the overwhelming presence of Torah is made almost physical. When the fire burned them both equally it seems that they became one, as R. Jose ben Kisma said in the beginning of that *baraita*: "It will surprise me if they do not burn both thee and the scroll of the Torah with fire."[505] Unlike the case of R. Eliezer, this oneness with the Torah, as characterized by the fire element, does not produce the joy, or the miracle which manifests this union in its positive feature, as was the case in the fire of Sinai,[506] but this oneness produces the burning—Heavenly Judgment and punishment. As we hear from the continuation of the conversation with R. Jose ben Kisma:

Rabbi, said the other (R. Hananya), How do I stand with regard to the world to come?—Is there any particular act that thou hast done? he (R. Jose ben Kisma) enquired. He (R. Hananya) replied: I once mistook Purim-money for ordinary charity-money, and I distributed (of my own) to the poor. (BT *Avoda Zara* 18a)

R. Hananya recognizes, like R. Eliezer and Beruria,[507] that the harmonic relationship between Man and God, as symbolized in the fire of the revelation at Sinai, does not apply in his case, because of sin which undermines the perfection of the union with God. However, in spite of R. Hananya's awareness of the sin, the intimacy with the Torah and God's presence as an ideal relationship is mirrored in the severity of Heaven's Judgment:

He who will seek (retribution) for this insult of the Torah Scroll, He will seek (retribution also) for my insult . . . Let Him who gave me [my soul] take it away, but no one should injure oneself. (ibid.)

Hence, the fire's blaze melted R. Hananya's body with the Torah's parchments, and melted his soul with the Torah's letters.[508]

Beruria: The Fire Covenant of Father and Daughter

At this point, after the *baraita*, which describes R. Ḥananya's death by burning, wherein he is commanding his "fire legacy" to his daughter, the Talmud inserts the story of "Beruria . . . a daughter of R. Ḥananya ben Teradion" (*AZ* 18a). Above, we understood this story as "the Beruria incident" mentioned in the margin of this Talmudic text (*Avoda Zara* 18b). Indeed, in a second reading, we see that the telling of "the Beruria incident" after the story of the burning of R. Ḥananya ben Teradion presents the daughter's story in the light of its internalization of the "fire principles" embedded in the father's story. Nonetheless, the "fire principles" internalized in the daughter's story are not entirely identical with those found in the father's story; rather, they were internalized as mirror images. This means that instead of presenting the negative aspect of "the fire conception" emerging from the text of the burning father, "the Beruria incident" embodies the positive conceptual potential of that terrifying text.

10*
> Beruria, the wife of R. Meir, was a daughter of R. Ḥananya ben Teradion. Said she (to R. Meir) "It is a disgracing matter that my sister is sitting in a brothel." So he took a *tarkab* of *denarii* and set out. Said he (to himself): If a transgression has not been done to her, a miracle will be done, but if she has transgressed no miracle will be done for her (BT *Avoda Zara* 18a)

Rereading this story in the same conceptual realm within which we read the above *baraitot,* it seems to complete perfectly the portrait we have formed so far of Beruria as one of the adherents of "the fire conception."

In the midst of the flames, the father, who was sentenced to burning, gave his legacy to the daughter: "He who will seek (retribution) for the insult of Torah Scroll, He will seek (retribution also) for my insult." Who was this daughter to whom the "fire legacy" was transmitted? We do not know, since she is not named. However, the Talmud's editing of "the Beruria incident" immediately afterwards, shows that it is indeed the daughter Beruria who internalizes this "fire legacy" and seeks retribution for her sister's insult.

Although Beruria plays a minor part in the story, and her action apparently is limited to the "what," seeking retribution for her sister, we argue that the "how"—the conceptual basis for this "seeking"—is also included in her part. It applies the fire principles of the father's will and is compatible with her conception according to the other Talmudic sources. True, the Talmudic story here forms the "how" through the figure of R. Meir, who goes on her mission. However, in this *sugia* it is not exceptional to embody (literally and not necessarily historically) one conceptual complex in a few figures, as we saw in the material presented by the Talmud prior to this story. This complex presents R. Ḥananya's "fire conception" through the figures of his wife and daughter. Furthermore, according to one of the possible readings (presented in chapter 4), the title "the incident of Beruria" refers to the entire story about Beruria's sending R. Meir, including the role of R. Meir. This means, according to our reading, that the Talmud did not limit the role of Beruria in this story only to the technical action of sending R. Meir, but linked the whole story with its various components to her, and to the principles she embodies.[509]

Reading R. Meir's monologue as revealing the basis for Beruria's "seeking" (retribution for) the insult of her sister, we will find the "fire principle," the same as that of the seeking for her father's insult, i.e., the total union between Man and Torah, from which the equality between the two derives, and thus:

> Now that I am burning together with the Scroll of Torah, He who will seek (retribution) for this insult of the Torah Scroll, He will seek (retribution also) for my insult. (BT *Avoda Zara* 18a)

However, to father and daughter the result of this union should be different. The father demanded retribution alone for Man's insult, while the daughter, Beruria, sought for Man's insult complete salvation too (which expressed itself in the occurrence of the miracle).

R. Meir's monologue expresses not only this "fire conception" of Beruria,[510] but also the reason for the differences between her father and herself. As we see from the monologue, the miracle is conceived not as a *deus-ex machina* or as a supernatural imposition of Heaven,[511] but rather as a manifestation of the intimate relationship between God and his worshipper,[512] where there is no sin. The passive style of the first part: "if a transgression has not been done" almost omits the daughter as part of it. It almost says that if the relationship with God is free of sin, there is nothing interposing between them, and thus the miracle is a natural consequence.[513] The second part attributes more activity to the individual: "If she has transgressed, a miracle will not be done for her." If the daughter, by an active transgression, undermined the intimacy, this transgression itself severs the interrelation with God, hence "no miracle will be done for her."

The understanding of "the Beruria incident" on this conceptual basis seals our very last source about her with "the fire conception" of R. Eliezer. The seeking in "the Beruria incident" for human retribution on the basis of equality with Torah is the realization of the positive aspect of "the fire conception," the joy feature—the harmony with God. "The Beruria incident" is the joyous counter-picture of the horrific end of the burnt father, reflecting a situation where there is no sin, and thus the miracle and salvation must come about.

Above all, "the Beruria incident" brings the figure of Beruria into the fire covenant. The covenant expresses the belief in the possibility of true harmony between Man and God.[514] In spite of God's overwhelming and perfect nature, God's relations with humans are fundamentally positive, symbolized by the joy feature. This is in contrast to the burning feature found in another tannaitic school,[515] which symbolizes the impossibility of such harmonic relations. In "the fire conception" of R. Eliezer, divine punishment—burning—is merely a symptom of gaps in the relationship between Human and God, gaps which are a lack of the idyllic, of faultlessness and intimacy. However, because these gaps are created by sin, they are annulled when there is no sin, and harmony returns naturally to prevail in the relationship between Man and God.

"The Beruria incident," by embodying in mirror images the "fire principles" from R. Ḥananya's story, bestows on Beruria a place as an independent member in "the fire conception" school. Only a true member of this school could translate the terrifying Fire Judgment of the burnt scholar into the possibility of a joyous harmony with God. Only a member of the fire school sees this harmony as the basis of the theological relations.[516] Hence, from the other texts attributed to Beruria in the extensive Talmudic literature, her place in "the fire conception" proves to be of great originality—an originality through which Beruria applies the "fire principles" at every different stratum of the scholar's life.

Final Word

Were R. Ḥananya and Beruria, historically, father and daughter, as the Talmud says? Was "the fire conception" thus transmitted from a father, known to be a member of R. Eliezer's school, to his daughter? Or has this father-daughter relationship been deduced from their both being influenced by R. Eliezer's method?

Although the historical accuracy of the Talmud in this respect has not been successfully challenged,[517] our reading does not pretend to present a clear-cut solution to these historical questions. But, whatever the relationship between R. Hananya and Beruria, there are no reasonable grounds for denying the existence of Beruria the *tannait*. Rather than her figure in the Talmudic literature being a mere literary invention, a feminine token for an educated woman of that or any other time,[518] she is well located as a member of "the fire conception" school of Talmudic culture.

The paradoxical fact that in course of time the figures of R. Eliezer and Beruria were conceived as conceptual enemies is an unsolved riddle, whose answer is to be found somewhere along the strange journey through which History and Culture are traveling.

Notes

409. Indeed, in Mishna *Yoma* (see above p. 126), he is explicitly mentioned as receiving *halakha* from R. Eliezer. See also, A. Hyman, *Toldot Tannaim ve'Amoraim* (Jerusalem: Boys Town Jerusalem Publishers, 1987), 508, that R. Eliezer was the only rabbi mentioned as R. Hananya's rabbi.

410. See S. Lieberman, "On Persecution of the Jewish Religion," in *Salo Wittmayer Baron Jubilee Volume* (Jerusalem: The American Academy for Jewish Research, Hebrew Section, 1974), 3:213, 218; *id. Texts and Studies* (New York: Ktav, 1974), 77, n. 142.

411. R.T. Herford, *Christianity in Talmud and Midrash* (New York: Ktav, 1990), 140–1, Lieberman, *Texts and Studies*, 77.

412. See Lieberman, "Persecution," 230, that the un-historical nature of some sources of the third and fourth century as regards Roman behaviour does not testify against their reliability, since "the tricks of the Roman officials had not changed through the times, and they behaved in the second century as in the fourth century."

413. Regarding this linguistic obscurity in the Hebrew, see below nn. 417, 420.

414. See below n. 420, about the term: *minut* either as Christianity or as general name for idolatry.

415. A contemporary colleague of R. Hananya ben Teradion. Lived in the first third of the second century.

416. In the printed edition, the verb is in the plural: "were caught." In MSS (JTS 15, Munich 95, Paris 1337) the verb appears in the singular "was caught."

417. This is the version of the above MSS, and in Geniza fragment, MS Oxford 10. In the printed edition the words: "by/for *minut*" are missing. For more on this, see below n. 420.

418. See Boyarin, *Carnal Israel*, 191.

419. Boyarin's suggestion (*Dying*, 29) that the Hebrew word: *nitpas* is used here (BT *AZ* 16b) in the intellectual sense, is implausible. First, Boyarin seems to quote the version of Tosefta, which says "caught for *minut* matters," but actually refers (in his explanation) to the version of the Talmud: "caught for/by (*le*) *minut*." Second, the verb: "catch" in regard to the legal Roman arrest is almost a fixed term in tannaitic style (see Tosefta *San.* 8:7, JT *Yeb.* 2:11, 4:1, BT *Yeb.* 61b). Thus, it is more plausible that the term: "caught" (*nitpas*) is taken from the Roman legal interrogation, conducted in a "catching (trapping) method." It took for granted the validity of the crime, and began the interrogation with "catch-questions" which aimed to catch the criminal: "why did you study?" In the case of R. Hananya, Or in the case of R. Eliezer: "an old man like you will occupy himself with these idle things?" See Lieberman, *Texts and Studies*, 34, 22, 25ff. Under this influence of Roman legal usage, the verb and the term: "caught" came in some texts to mean "trapped." See more below nn. 448, 463.

420. In the parallel of that *baraita* in Tosefta *Hulin* 2:24, MS Erfurt, ed. Zuckermandel, 503, and MS Vienna, the version is: "for *minut* matters," See Lieberman (*Texts and studies*, 76), who translated "for *minut*" as Christianity, and comments (ibid., n. 132) that the context which mentions Jesus' name proves the validity of this meaning. However, in the Talmud the word in the *baraita* is: *leminut*, and Rashi (*ad loc.*) explains it as saying that: "R. Eliezer was arrested by *Minim*, who forced him to worship idolatry." This explanation was attacked strongly by Herford (*Christianity*, 140). Following him, Boyarin (*Dying*, 156, n. 37) considered Rashi's explanation so improbable that he speculates that it must express none other than Rashi's "cover up" (of R. Eliezer's Christianity). However, as we shall see above n. 417, the version in all MSS of the Talmud attributed the same formula: "arrested by/for (*le*)*minut*" also to R. Hananya ben Teradion and R. Elazar ben Parta. In this text there is no explicit word regarding Christianity. On the contrary, they are accused *inter alia* of studying Torah. Accordingly, Rashi's commentary is not so improbable, and "*minut*" could be read as referring to the pagan Roman judge, or in general to all Roman authority, or alternatively to all kind of idolaters, from the pagan Romans to the Christian Jews, which seems to be the case of R. Eliezer (more about it see below nn. 423, 437, 463).

421. See Rashi's version.

422. Regarding the changes between the versions: "I was found" and "I found," see below n. 449.

423. See Jastrow, s.v. *rashut* mostly the Roman government in Palestine, Roman officials." In this case refers to the Roman Court and judges.

424. We have mainly quoted the version of MS JTS15.

425. See Herford, *Christianity*, 142.

426. A. Guttmann, "Significance of Miracles for Talmudic Judaism," *HUCA* 20 (1947): 386. See my response to this hypothesis in Hoshen, "Fire,"

91, 123. As against this see Boyarin, *Dying*, 28, 33, that R. Eliezer did not wish to curse Jesus, and that he had "pro-Christian sympathies."

427. According to Rashi, it seems that the accusation of R, Eliezer was the same as that of R. Ḥananya, and thus, "these idle things" refers to Torah study, and not especially to Christianity. However, as we will show later (see above p. 120) in the case of R. Ḥananya, in the eyes of the Romans there was no such difference.

428. This dichotomy between present and past seems to be the odd hypothesis raised by Lieberman (*Texts and Studies*, 78–80).

429. See Boyarin, *Dying*, 156, n. 37.

430. Who are usually unafraid of admitting the worst of the sins (like prostitution, see the context in BT *AZ* 17a). On the contrary, following the principle of "measure for measure," the Sages' dynamics aim intensively to disclose sins, which are conceived as the reasons for all punishments, and even the lighter sins (see BT *AZ* 18a).

431. Boyarin's answer (*Dying*, 32) to these problems is to attribute to the Sages in general and to R. Eliezer specifically the philosophical principles known from theories of Deconstruction and Psychoanalysis, which hold True and False in one hand, in this case denying and recognizing Christianity (idolatry) at the same time. In the same way, Boyarin builds a theory of the "feminine" which he attributes to the Talmudic and midrashic literature, and especially as regards the character of Beruria. According to him, the Talmudic-midrashic literature reflects a "cultural fantasy" that is an "acknowledgement/denial of women's autonomy and intellectual achievements" (*Carnal Israel*, 182, 193). This reading, which presumes to reveal the complexity of the Talmudic world—by basing it on syncretism of heresy and orthodoxy—actually misses it. The Talmudic complexity stands on very different foundations (basically theological and philosophical) than the psychological basis supplied by Psychoanalysis and Deconstruction doctrines. Cf. the feminist readers at the beginning of this book, and Hoshen, "Agnon's Writing," 76ff.

432. About history and philosophical thought in the texts of Sages see Hoshen, "Suffering," 6.

433. This is based on Neusner's translation in his *Tosefta, Qodoshim* (New York: Ktav, 1979), 75; id. *Eliezer ben Hyrcanus: The Tradition and the Man* (Leiden: Brill, 1973), 1:400.

434. See the same strong language attributed to R. Eliezer in tractate *Kala*, 1:3: "they asked R. Eliezer, what is the law of accepting drink from the hand of the bride [literally: what is it to drink from the hand of the bride] while her husband is sitting with her? He said to them: everyone who drinks from the hand of the bride is as if he drinks from the prostitute."

435. This strict approach also seems to fit R. Eliezer's rejection of any social proximity to Gentiles, "since the gentile's usual intention is for idolatry" (Mishna *Ḥulin*, 2:7, BT *Git.* 45b).

436. See Albeck below n. 437, Herford, *Christianity*, 178. About the severity of R. Eliezer regarding idolaters, see Gilat, *R. Eliezer Ben Hyrcanus*,

450ff., who sees it as a reflection of a general hostility of R. Eliezer towards non-Jews.

437. See Tosefta, *Hulin*, 2:19, and Mishna, *Hulin*, 2:9: "one may perform an act of slaughter (so that the blood will flow) into a utensil or into a hole, but not in the market, because he [thereby] carries out (the act in accord with) the rules of *Minim*" (see *Tosefta Qodoshim*, Neusner, 73). See H. Albeck in his commentary on Mishna *Hulin* that *minim* here are sects of idolaters.

438. This seems to be R. Eliezer's general approach, see below chap. 5, for his reaction to his sin. Also, see Gilat, *R. Eliezer Ben Hyrcanus*, 23ff. who attributes to R. Eliezer this severe conception (of relating to the Rabbis prohibitions as Torah prohibitions) in the field of Halakha, and explains it as deriving from R. Eliezer's loyalty to the method of the early Halakha.

439. See above p. 55 and notes *ad loc.*, for the function of this assertion in "the fire conception" of R. Eliezer and Beruria.

440. See the version of the *baraita* in BT *AZ* 27b.

441. See the version in Tosefta *Hulin* 2:23, ed. Zuckermandl: *gezeran* (their decrees) instead of *gederan* (their hedge) and the verb remained: *piratzta* (broke through).

442. See JT *AZ*, 2:2, 40:4, BT *AZ* 27b.

443. Based on the ArtScroll translation.

444. See the discussion in BT *AZ* 27b.

445. Ibid., the Talmud distinguishes as between public and private transgression. See also, Tosafot, *ad loc.*

446. See the Talmud's discussion (*AZ* 27a) that one who is almost dead could be healed by Gentiles, The Talmud's prohibition, derived from the Tosefta story, is limited it to the case of *minut*, since one could be attracted to it.

447. See the same reaction of R. Eliezer (JT *Ber.* 3:5, 6:4, BT *Men.* 32b.), when he sat down on a couch on which a Torah scroll was placed, and "he got up as if bitten by a snake." (*The Jerusalem Talmud, tractate Berakhot*, ed. H.W. Guggenheimer [Berlin: W. de Gruyter, 2000], 319).

448. "Caught" means entrapped (see above n. 419), either by the pagan Romans who trap people by their legal method, or by the idolaters who, like the prostitute, trap people.

449. This is the version in early manuscripts of BT (JTS15, Paris 1337). However, the version in MS Munich 95, the printed edition, and in Tosefta is: "I found." This gives the impression of a "finding" (*meziah*) more than "looking for."

450. This seems to be R. Eliezer's method (see above n. 435). See also his attitudes towards the *matrona* (above n. 325).

451. See Herford, *Christianity*, 145, and n.1, about a possibly non-Christian aspect of this *midrash*.

452. See above n. 435.

453. See Herford, *Christianity*, 142, Lieberman, *Texts and Studies*, 78, Boyarin, *Dying*, 28,

454. Boyarin, *Dying*, 28. Herford, *Christianity*, has another alternative too.

455. See Lieberman, *Texts and Studies*, 79–80, 87–8, that in the Roman's court (especially in times when Christians were persecuted) there was a heathen sacrificial cult.

456. See above p. 115, n. 423, the end of the *baraita* in BT *AZ* 17a, for the proximity between *minut* and authority, which refers to the Roman government. Also, see R. Eliezer in Mishna *Sota* (9:15) who discuss the times of the Messiah: "and the government (*malkhut*) will become *minut*."

457. See above p. 43, Hoshen, "Semiotics," *id*. "Fire in revelation."

458. See also above p. 128.

459. About the proximity of R. Ḥananya to "the fire conception," see "Fire," 265–71.

460. As said (n. 417), this is the version of the manuscripts; the printed edition drops the word: *minut*.

461. See Lieberman, "Persecution," 221.

462. See Herford, *Christianity*, 141 that in the Romans' eyes there was not much difference between Judaism and Christianity. Cf. Lieberman, "Persecution," who does not deduce any religious conclusion from the similarity of R. Ḥananya's death to that of the Christians. However, see above n. 411 for Lieberman's comment concerning the confusion between persecution of Jews and Christians in the 3rd–4th c. sources.

463. See Rashi in BT *Nazir* 52a, s.v. *nitpas lamalkhut* (was caught by the sovereignty).

464. See above n. 455.

465. See MS JTS.15.

466. See Rashi *ad loc.* that Purim charity can not be spent on things other than the Purim meal, unlike ordinary charity.

467. See the versions of the Talmudic text in Rashi *ad loc*.

468. Lieberman ("Persecution," 220) wonders about those who explained that R. Ḥananya was expressing his trust in being eligible for the world to come, rather than concern. Thus he was probably suggesting that he had performed an extraordinary action of merit.

469. Ibid., 220.

470. In the printed edition it is: "Elazar." However, in MSS (Karlsruhe, Reuchlin 2) it is: "Eliezer," see also Rabbinovicz, *Dikdukei Sofrim, ad loc*.

471. See "Fire," 117ff. about the function of "benevolence" in R. Eliezer's fire conception.

472. See "Fire," chap. 1, about the fourth feature of "the fire conception," which is the effect left by the Torah on life and on human being, like the fire that leaves a sign on everyone who deals with it.

473. See Lieberman, "Persecution," 221. However, not all the material about R. Ḥananya in BT *AZ* 17b, 18a, went through a Talmudic literary adaptation. See Lieberman, *op cit.*, 220 on the fact that this does not discredit the Talmud as keeping the tannaitic tradition on which it relied.

474. See a parallel *baraita* of this text in Finkelstein, *Sifre on Deuteronomy*, 307:4, 346.

475. For the intimate sense of the term: "the Lord my God" in connection with biblical figures, and with R. Ḥananya, see "Fire," 241 n. 760, p. 273.

476. See Lieberman, "Persecution," 218–9 who explains all these facts as corresponding to Roman law.

477. "The Name in its letters" could refer to God's name, spelled with four letters that are usually read in its alternate form (Master God etc., see Mishna *Yoma* 6:2), or spelled with forty-two letters (BT *Kid.* 71a, see Rashi below), and which only was whispered by the High Priest on the Day of Atonement.

478. See Rashi *ad loc.* who gives his mystical explanation for this. However, compare R. Ḥananya in the *mishna* above p. 124.

479. See "Fire," 38–99, for the idea that great intimacy with God is dangerous for those who withdraw from this intimacy. This danger is expressed in the burning feature of the fire. See also, Hoshen, "Suffering," for another perspective of these intimate relations with God and their immanent dangers.

480. See BT *San.* 98b, Hoshen "Fire," 109, and above p. 42.

481. This is one way of understanding the Talmud. Another way is to say that he performed magical acts, but not for the sake of Magic. However, this way is not consistent with Scripture; see Hoshen, "Fire," 109.

482. Ibid.

483. Ibid., 108.

484. See also our analysis to JT *Ḥag.* (77:2), "Fire," 39ff. and below n. 506, the same process of enthusiastic studying which transfers the abstract into reality.

485. See Rashi *ad loc.*, who counts as desecration even the process of learning the Name. See Tosafot *ad loc.* that Rashi's version did not include the last Talmudic answer referred to, regarding the public element.

486. See Hoshen, "Fire," chap. 1.

487. See Maimonides and Meiri, in their commentaries on Mishna *Avot* 3:2.

488. See Maimonides, *Commentary, Avot,* 3:2.

489. See *Mishnayoth, Order Nezikin,* trans. P. Blackman (New York: Judaica Press, 1963), 503, n. 12, regarding the meaning of the reward that God will give one who studies Torah.

490. This is the version in BT *AZ*, MS Paris 1337.

491. Note the various examples of this burning feature in "the fire conception" in general, with regard to R. Eliezer, and the character of the biblical and Talmudic Elijahs (See Hoshen, "Fire," throughout).

492. e.g. MS Munich 95.

493. See MS Paris: "immediately after she heard she took particular care of her step".

494. See above pp. 56, 114 and notes.

495. The principles of "the fire conception" were detailed in Hoshen, "Fire." They could also be deduced from the *baraita* of R. Eliezer in BT *AZ* and Tosefta *Ḥulin.*

496. See Nahmanides, Deut. *ad loc.* who explains *tamim* as unchanged.

497. This interpretation of *pa'olo* seems to refer to the whole Creation, which is as God's work.

498. See Finkelstein, *Sifre on Deuteronomy*, 307:4, 344, which interprets *pa'olo* as *pe'ulato* (action). See more below n. 500.

499. See BT *Ber.* 10a, where human beings are called the work of God's hands.

500. *Sifre loc. cit.* seems to refer to this reading: "because His action towards all creatures is perfect, no one brings complaint against Him."

501. BT *Ta'anit* 11a.

502. About the miracle in "the fire conception" as a manifestation of this intimacy of relation between Man and God, see Hoshen, "Fire," 100ff., 266ff.

503. This is the version of MS Paris.

504. See ArtScroll translation.

505. See Lieberman, "Persecution," who explains this assertion historically as a fixed Roman punishment.

506. See JT *Ḥag.* 2:1, 77b. There the Talmud relates the story of R. Eliezer and R. Joshua, who were sitting occupying themselves with Torah Study, and fire fell from Heaven and surrounded them. When their host cried: Rabbis, have you come to burn my house upon me? They answer: Heaven forbid! But we were sitting studying Torah "and the words (of Torah) were as joyful as when they were given at Sinai, and the fire was licking them (the words of Torah) as it licked them at Sinai," as it is written: "and the Mountain was burning with fire up to the heart of heaven" (Deut. 4:11). For analysis of this text, concerning the joy feature of "the fire conception" see, Hoshen, "Fire," 38–53; *id.* "Fire in revelation," *id.* "Semiotics."

507. See above p. 45ff.

508. See MaHarShA in his commentary on BT *AZ* 18a that the letters and the parchments of Torah are like the body and the soul of the human being.

509. For instance, the appearance of Elijah to R. Meir here (BT *AZ* 18b), as one of the reflections of "the fire conception," see "Fire," 268–9, and specifically regarding this text of BT *AZ*.

510. Unlike Moonikandem, "Beruria and Rabbi Meir," 50, who argues that the money solution is Beruria's idea while the religious one is R. Meir's.

511. About the theory of the miracle in "the fire conception," see Hoshen, "Fire," 110ff. 258ff.

512. In regard to those who tried to connect R. Eliezer to Christianity on the basis of the common theory concerning miracles, see Hoshen, "Fire," 93, 125–30, where I show this very difference between "the fire conception" and the New Testament.

513. See R. Eliezer's saying in *Finkelstein, Sifre*, 173:2, 220, regarding sin as preventing revelation. See also "Fire," 119.

514. See above pp. 45ff. 124ff.

515. See R, Akiba's conception, Hoshen, "Suffering."

516. Also in the school of R. Akiba, which we called "the water conception," we might expect a positive translation of such a horrific situation,

but in a very different way. The burning feature—the Divine Judgment, is itself considered positive, while in R. Eliezer's conception, the positive alternative is real and is found outside the burning feature (see Hoshen, "Suffering"). This interpretation supports our claim, that R. Meir in the Talmudic story of "the Beruria incident" is functioning as Beruria's husband, and therefore acting according to "the fire conception's" standards—though he himself was a disciple of R. Akiba, and thus would be expected to act according to "the water conception's" standards.

517. See above p. 22, for the doubts of Goodblatt regarding this genealogy and our response to them.

518. This is, in brief, the differentiation between the various feminist readings of Beruria. See the numerous references in Chaps. 1, 2.

Abbreviations

AJS	Association for Jewish Studies
ADRN	Avot Derabi Natan
AZ	Avoda Zara
Ber	Berakhot
Bik	Bikurim
BM	Baba Metzia
BQ	Baba Kama
BR	Bereshit Rabba
BT	Babylonian Talmud
Eru	Eruvin
Git	Gittin
GRA	R. Eliyahu of Vilna
Hag	Ḥagiga
HD	Ḥasde David
Hor	Horayot
HUCA	Hebrew Union College Annual
JJS	Journal of Jewish Studies
JSOT	Journal for the Study of the Old Testament
JT	Jerusalem Talmud
JTS	Jewish Theological Seminary
Kel	Kelim
Ket	Ketubot
Kid	Kiddushin
Kil	Kilayim
MaHarShA	R. Shmuel Edels
Men	Menaḥot
Meg	Megila
MQ	Mo'ed Qatan
MT	Mishne Torah
Ned	Nedarim
Pes	Pesaḥim
RaBaD	R. Abraham ben David

Bibliography

Adler, R. "The Virgin in the Brothel and other Anomalies: Character and Context in the Legend of Beruriah." *Tikkun* 3, no. 6 (1988): 28–32, 102–5.
Ahdut, E. "The Status of The Jewish Woman in Babylonia in the Talmud Era." PhD diss., The Hebrew University, 1999.
Albeck, H. *Introduction to the Talmud Bavli and Yerushalmi*. Tel Aviv: Dvir, 1987.
Archer, L. J. "Her Price is Beyond Rubies: The Jewish Woman in Graeco-Roman Palestine." *JSOT* supp., 60. Sheffield : JSOT Press, c1990.
Asaf, S. *The Period of the Geonim and their Literature*. Jerusalem: Mosad Harav Kook, 1955.
Ashkenazi, Jehuda ben Yosef. *Mahane Yeuda*. Salonica: M. Nahman, and D. Israelija, 1793.
Atiyah, Y. *Zera Yitzhak*. Livorno: J. Nunis and R. Mildola, 1793–4.
Azulai, J. *Sefer Tov Ain*. Jerusalem: E. Weinberger, 1961.
Bar-Ilan, M. *Some Jewish Women in Antiquity*. Atlanta: Scholars Press, 1998.
Ben Yehuda, E. *A Complete Dictionary, Ancient and Modern Hebrew*. Jerusalem, NY: T. Yosluf, 1959.
Benovitz, M. *BT Berakhot Chapter 1, Talmud Ha-Igud*, edited by S. Friedman. Jerusalem: The Society for the Interpretation of the Talmud, 2006.
Blackman, P. trans. *Mishnayoth, Order Nezikin*. New York: The Judaica Press, 1963.
Boyarin, D. *Carnal Israel, Reading Sex in Talmudic Culture*. Berkeley: University of California Press, 1993.
———. *Dying for God*. Stanford: Stanford University Press, 1999.
———. "The Diachronic As Against the Synchronic in the Tale of Beruria." *Studies in Jewish Folklore* 12–3 (1990): 7–17.
———. *Unheroic Conduct, The Rise of Heterosexuality and the Invention of the Jewish Man*. Berkeley: University of California Press, 1997.
Brody, R. *Readings in Geonic Literature*. Tel Aviv: Hakkibutz Hameuhad, 1998.

———. *The Geonim of Babylonia and the Shaping of the Medieval Jewish Culture*. New Haven: Yale University Press, 1998.
Davidson, I. ed. Ibn Zabara, Joseph, *Sefer Shashuim (The Book of Delight)*. New York: The Jewish Theological Seminary of America, 1914.
Donski, S. ed. *Song of song Rabba*. Jerusalem, Tel Aviv: Dvir, 1980.
Driver, S. R. *Notes on the Hebrew Text and the Topography of the Books of Samuel*. Oxford: Clarendon Press, 1913.
Duran, Z. *Sefer Magen Avot*. Jerusalem: Makhon Haktav, 2003.
Elon, M. *Jewish Law, History, Sources, Principles*. Philadelphia, Jerusalem: The Jewish Publication Society, 1994.
Epstein, J. N. *Introduction to the Mishnaic Text*. Jerusalem, Tel Aviv: The Magnes Press et Dvir, 1964.
———. ed. *Gaonic Commentary on Mishna Taharot, Attributed to R. Hay Gaon*. Jerusalem, Tel Aviv: The Magnes Press, 1982.
———. *Prolegomena ad Litteras Tannaiticas*. Jerusalem, Tel Aviv: The Magnes Press et Dvir, 1957.
Falk, M. "Towards a Feminist Jewish Reconstruction of Monotheism." *Tikkun* 4, no. 4 (1989): 53–6.
Finkelstein, L. ed. *Sifra on Leviticus*, vol. 2. New York: The Jewish Theological Seminary, 1983.
———. *Sifre on Deuteronomy*. New York: The Jewish Theological Seminary of America, 1969.
Fraenkel, J. *Darkei Ha-aggada Vehamidrash*. 2 vols. Givataim: Yad LaTalmud, 1991.
———. *Rashi's Methodology in his Exegesis of the Babylonian Talmud*. Jerusalem: The Magnes Press, 1975.
Frankel, Z. *Hodegetik zur Mischna*. Warsaw, M.L. Calingold, 1923.
Friedman, S. "The Study of Torah for Contemporary Women." In *Women in the Sources of Judaism*. 53–67. Jerusalem: Publisher unknown, 1983.
Friedmann, M. ed. *Seder Eliyahu Rabba*. Jerusalem: Waharmann, 1969.
Gaster, M. trans. *Ma'ase-Buch*. Philadelphia: Jewish Publication Society of America, 1934.
Gerwin, J. "Lucid is God, Beruriah and the Subversion of the Patriarchal Discourse." *Mosaic* 14 (1993): 8–24.
Gilat, Y. D. *R. Eliezer Ben Hyrcanus: A Scholar Outcast*. Ramat Gan: Bar-Ilan University Press, 1984.
———. *The Halakha Its Sources and Development*. Givatim: Yad La-Talmud, 1984.
———. *Studies in the Development of the Halakha*. Ramat Gan: Bar-Ilan University Press, 1992.
Ginzberg, L. *Geonica, Texts and Studies of the Jewish Theological Seminary of America*. 2 vols. New York: The Jewish Theological Seminary of America, 1909.
Goldfeld, A. "Women as Sources of Torah in the Rabbinic Tradition," in *The Jewish Woman, New Perspectives*, edited by E. Koltun, 257–71. New York: Schocken Books, 1976.

Goodblatt, D. "The Beruriah Traditions." *JJS* 26 (1975): 68–85.
Gordis, R. *The Universal Jewish Encyclopedia*, s.v. "Beruriah (Valeria)." New York: The Universal Jewish Encyclopedia, 1940.
Goren, S. "Women are Included in Temporal Commandments." *Mahanaim* 98 (1965): 10–6.
Goshen-Gottstein, A. *The Sinner and the Amnesiac: The Rabbinic Invention of Elisha ben Abuya and Eleazar ben Arach*. Stanford: Stanford University Press, 2000.
Goshen-Gottstein, M. H. *Fragments of Lost Targumim*. Ramat Gan: Bar-Ilan University Press, 1989.
Grossman, A. "Rashi's Teachings Concerning Woman," *Zion* 70, no. 2 (2005): 171–3.
Guggenheimer, H. W. ed. *The Jerusalem Talmud, Tractate Berakhot*. Berlin: W. de Gruyter, 2000.
Guthold, Z. "Legal Status of Women." *Mahanim* 98 (1965): 18–29.
Guttmann, A. "Significance of Miracles for Talmudic Judaism." *HUCA* 20 (1947): 363–406.
Haberman, A. M. ed. Berechiah haNakdan, *Mishle Shualim*. Jerusalem: Schocken, 1946.
Halevi, Jacob ben Moses. *Shut Maharil*, edited by I. Satz. Jerusalem: Machon Yerushalim, 1980.
Halevi-Lifshitz, J. ed. *Tosafot of Evreux and Rules of Tosafot, on Tractate Sota*, Jerusalem: Harry Fischel Institute, 1929.
Hansen, W. *Ariadne's Thread, A Guide for International Tales Found in Classical Literature*. Ithaca and London: Cornell University Press, 2002.
Hardi, Z. Rabin H. *The New Bible Dictionary*. Jerusalem: Keter and Yavneh, 1989.
Harkavy, A. ed. *Studien und Mittheilungen*. Leipzig: G. Haessel, 1880.
Herford, R. T. *Christianity in Talmud and Midrash*. New York: Ktav, 1990.
Higger, M. *Ozar Ha-barithoth*, vol. 3. New York: Debe Rabanan, 1940.
Hirschberg, J. W. ed. *Hibur Yafe MehaYeshua*. Jerusalem: Mosad Harav Kook, 1970.
Horovitz, H. S. ed. *Mechilta d'Rabi Ishmael*. Jerusalem: Shalem, 1998.
Horowitz, S. ed. Simhah ben Samuel of Vitry, *Mahzor Vitry*. Nurnberg: Bolka, 1923.
Hoshen, D. "The Fire Symbol in Talmudic-Aggadic Exegesis." PhD diss., Bar-Ilan University, 1989.
———. "Agnon's Writing: An Additional Tier in the Talmudic-Aggadic Literature." PhD diss., Bar-Ilan University, 2000.
———. "Semiotics as a Religious Question," in *Approaches to Ancient Judaism, New Series*, vol. 5, edited by H. W. Basser and S. Fishbane, 69–77. Atlanta: Scholars Press, 1993.
———. "Suffering and Divinity in R. Akiva's Philosophy." *Da'at* 27 (1991): 5–33.
———. "Elisha ben Abuya, Avoidance and Realization of the Absurd in R. Akiva's Theology." (preprint).

———. "External Structure versus Binary Structure in Sexuality: The Approach of the Rishonim and the Talmudic Sources." *Mo'ed, Annual for Jewish Studies* 15, no. 3 (2005): 63–84.

———. "Fire in Revelation and Torah Study." *Le'ela* 52 (2000): 35–42.

———. "Midrash and Genres," in *Encyclopedia of Midrash, Biblical Interpretation in Formative Judaism*, edited by J. Neusner and A. J. Avery-peck, 121–148. Leiden: Brill, 2005.

———. "On the Quality of the Rabbinic Text, The Opening of the Mishna." in *The Mishnah in Contemporary Perspective*, edited by J. Neusner and A. J. Avery-Peck, vol. 2, 36–80. Leiden: Brill, 2006.

———. "Sexual Relations Between Husband and Wife, The Rishonim Reinterpretation of the Talmudic Sources." *S'vara, A Journal of Philosophy, Law, and Judaism* 3, no. 1 (1993): 39–45.

———. *Agnon: A Saga is (not) a Talmudic Sugia*. Jerusalem: Rubin Mass, 2006.

Hyman, A. *Toldot Tannaim ve'Amoraim*. Jerusalem: Boys Town Jerusalem Publishers, 1987.

Ibn Yḥya, G. *Sefer Sholshelet Hakabala*. Jerusalem: Hadorot Harishonim Vekorotam, 1962.

Ilan, T. *Integrating Women into the Second Temple History*. Tübingen: Mohr Siebeck, 1999.

———. "The Quest for The Historical Beruriah, Rachel and Imma Shalom." *AJS Review* 22, no. 1 (1997): 1–17.

Jastrow, M. *Dictionary of the Talmud*. New York: Pardes, 1950.

Jellinek, A. ed. *Beit Hamidrash*. 6 vols. Jerusalem: Bamberger and Wahrmann,1987.

Kill, J. *Da'at Mikra*. Jerusalem: Mosad Harav Kook, 1981.

Klein, I. trans. *The Code of Maimonides, Book 7: The Book of Agriculture*. New Haven: Yale University Press, 1978.

Koehler, L. *Lexicon in Veteris Testamenti Libros*. Leiden: Brill, 1953.

Lacks, R. *Women and Judaism Myth, History and Struggle*. Garden City, NY: Doubleday, 1980.

Levin-Katz, Y. "Between Lilit and Beruria." *Mabua* 28 (1996): 89–96.

Lewin B. M. ed. *Otzar ha-Geonim*, vol. 4, *Hagiga*. (*Otzar ha-Perushim*). Jerusalem: The Hebrew University Press Association, 1931.

Lieberman, S. *Hayerushalmi Kipshshuto*. New-York and Jerusalem: Jewish Theological Seminary of America, 1995.

———. "On Persecution of the Jewish Religion," in *Salo Wittmayer Baron Jubilee Volume*. Jerusalem: The American Academy for Jewish Research, 1974.

———. *Texts and Studies*. New York: Ktav, 1974.

———. *Tosefeth Rishonim*. Jerusalem: Bamberger and Wahrmann, 1939.

———. *Tosefta Ki-fshutah, Zeraim*. New York: Jewish Theological Seminary of America, 1955.

Maimon, J. L. ed. Judah ben Kalonimus, *Yeḥuse Tannaim Ve'Amoraim*. Jerusalem: Mosad Harav Kook, 1963.

Maimonides. *Commentary on Mishna*. Jerusalem: Mosad Harav Kook, 1963.
———. *Mishne Torah*, traditional edition. Warsaw 1781.
Malter, H. *The Treatise Ta'anit*. New York: American Academy for Jewish Research, 1930.
Mandelbaum, B. ed. *Pesikta deRav Kahana*. New York: The Jewish Theological Seminary of America, 1987.
Medini, E. *Sefer Sede Hemed, Peat HaSadeh*. New York: Avraham Yzhak Friedman, 1966.
Menahem son of Salomon, *Beit Habehira*. Jerusalem: The Institute of the Complete Israeli Talmud, 1967.
Moonikandem, Y. "Beruria and Rabbi Meir—Parallels and Contrasts." *Pathways through Aggada* 2 (1999): 36–63.
Neusner, J. *Eliezer ben Hyrcanus: The Tradition and the Man*. Leiden: Brill, 1973.
———. trans. *The Tosefta, Zeraim, Berakhot*, Hoboken: Ktav, 1986.
———. trans. *Sifra: An Analytical Translation*. Atlanta: Scholars Press, 1998.
———. trans. *Talmud of the Land of Israel*. Chicago: University of Chicago Press, 1996.
———. trans. *The Tosefta, Tohorot*, New York: Ktav, 1977.
———. trans. *Tosefta, Qodoshim*. New York: Ktav, 1979.
Oppenheimer, A. *The Am Ha'aretz, A Study in the Social History of the Jewish People in the Hellenistic-Roman Period*. Leiden: Brill, 1977.
Ozick, S. "Women: Notes Toward Finding the Right Question." *Forum* 35 (1979): 37–60.
Perry, B. E. "The Origin of the Book of Sindbad." *Fabula* 3 (1960): 1-94.
Safrai, S. "The Pious (*Hassidim*) and the Men of Deed." *Zion* 50 (1985): 133–54.
Rokeah, D. "Am ha'aretz, The Pious (*Hasidim*), Jesus and Christians," *Mehqerei Talmud, Talmudic Studies Dedicated to the Memory of Professor Ephraim Urbach*, 876–903. Jerusalem: The Magnes Press, 2005.
Sarah, E. "Beruria: A Suitable Case For Mistreatment . . . or Why We Haven't Got the Sayings of Our Mothers." *European Judaism* 26, no. 12 (1993): 14–23.
Satz, I. ed. *Shut Maharil*. Jerusalem: Machon Yerushalim, 1980.
Schwarzbaum, H. "International Folklore Motifs in Joseph Ibn Zabara's 'Sefer Shashu'im,'" in *Jewish Folklore Between East and West, Collected Papers*, edited by E. Yasiff, 372–4. Be'er-Sheva: Ben Gurion University of the Negev Press, 1989.
———. "Female Fickleness in Jewish Folklore," in *Jewish Folklore Between East and West, Collected Papers*, edited by E. Yasiff, 177–80. Be'er-Sheva: Ben Gurion University of the Negev Press, 1989.
———. *The Mishle Shualim (fox fable) of Rabbi Berechiah ha-nakdan*. Kiron: Institute For Jewish and Arab Folklore Research,1979.
Segal, M. Z. *Torah Neveim Ketubbim*. Tel Aviv, Dvir, 1948.

Shenhar, A. "The Figure of Rabbi Meir and Its Literary Characterization in the Legends," in *Studies in Judaism*, edited by J. Bahat et al. 259–66. Haifa: University of Haifa Press, 1976.

Sokoloff, M. *A Dictionary of Jewish Babylonian Aramaic*. Ramat Gan: Bar-Ilan University Press, 2002.

Talmud Text Databank. CD-ROM, Saul Lieberman Institute for Talmudic Research, Bar-Ilan University.

Tashma, I. M. *Early Franco-German Ritual and Custom*. Jerusalem: The Magnes Press, 1999.

———. *Talmudic Commentary in Europe and North Africa*: Literary History. 3 vols. Jerusalem: The Magnes Press, 1999.

Theodor, J. and Albeck, H. ed. *Midrash Breshit Rabba*. Jerusalem: Warhmann, 1965.

Tregelles, S. P. trans. *Gesenius' Hebrew and Chaldee Lexicon to the Old Testament Scriptures*. Michigan: Wm. B. Erdmans, 1950.

Tov, S. *Characters from the Talmud*. Jerusalem: S. Tov, 1988.

Urbach, E. E. *The Sages, Their Concepts and Beliefs*. Jerusalem: The Magnes Press, 1975.

———. *The Tosaphists: Their History, Writings, and Methods*. Jerusalem: Mosad Bialik, 1968.

Urian. D. "'Our Teachers Break Our Heart': Beruria, Theatre Company of Jerusalem." in *Theatre and Holy Script*, ed. S. Levy, 222–37. Brighton: Sussex Academic Press, 1999,

Uziel, B.Z. *Piske Uziel, Besheélot Hazman*. Jerusalem: Mosad Harav Kook, 1977.

Visotzky, B. L. ed. *Midrash Mishle*. New York: The Jewish Theological Seminary of America, 1990.

Wegner, J. R. "The Image and Status of Women in Classical Rabbinic Judaism," in *Jewish Women Historical Perspective*, edited by J.R. Baskin, 68–93. Detroit: Wayne State University Press, 1991.

Weiss Halivni, D. *Sources and Traditions, Seder Moed, Rosh Hashana*. Jerusalem: Jewish Theological Seminar of America, 1975.

Weiss, A. *The Talmud in its Development*. New York: P. Feldhaim, 1954.

Weiss, J. H. *Zur Geschichte der Judischen Tradition*. Wilna: Romm, 1904.

Wertheimer, A. J. ed. *Bate Midrashot*, 2 vols. Jerusalem: Mosad Harav Kook, 1950.

Yosef, O. *Yabia Omer*. Jerusalem: Porat Yosef, 1974.

Zohar, Z. "The Attitude of Rabbi Yosef Masas Toward Women's Torah Study." *Pe'amim* 82 (1999): 150–62.

Zunz, L. *Die Gottesdiesntlichen Vorträge der Juden Historisch Entwickelt*. Jerusalem: Mosad Bialik, 1974.

Index

A

Adler, R., 5, 25, 27, 29, 64, 67, 102, 103, 143
Aggadist, iii, 38, 48
Ahitophel, 86
Akhnai, 34, 35, 37, 59
Akiba, R., 15, 19, 27, 63, 66, 93, 94, 110, 111, 115, 139, 145
Atiyah, Y., 18, 143
Atonement, 126, 127, 138
Avoda Zara, 18, 26, 57, 66, 67, 68, 69, 70, 71, 76, 77, 96, 98, 99, 101, 102, 108, 113, 114, 115, 118, 120, 121, 122, 123, 125, 126, 127, 129, 130, 131, 134, 135, 136, 137, 138, 139, 141

B

Barren, 42, 48, 49, 50, 64
Ben Dama, 116, 117
Boyarin, D., 5, 27, 28, 29, 57, 76, 79, 80, 82, 83, 87, 97, 99, 100, 101, 102, 103, 104, 105, 106, 107, 134, 135, 136, 143
Brody, R., 5, 7, 8, 143

C

Christian, 4, 17, 24, 48, 63, 68, 97, 115, 116, 119, 120, 133, 134, 135, 136, 137, 139, 145, 147
Covenant, iv, 130

E

Eliezer, R., iv, 2, 22, 26, 29, 31, 34, 35, 36, 37, 38, 39, 40, 41, 42, 43, 45, 46, 48, 49, 51, 52, 53, 54, 55, 56, 57, 59, 60, 61, 62, 63, 64, 65, 66, 68, 75, 76, 77, 78, 79, 80, 81, 87, 88, 89, 90, 91, 92, 93, 94, 95, 103, 104, 105, 107, 108, 109, 110, 111, 113, 114, 115, 116, 117, 118, 119, 120, 121, 122, 123, 124, 125, 126, 127, 128, 129, 132, 133, 134, 135, 136, 137, 138, 139, 140, 144, 147
Elisha, ben Abuya., 14, 19, 24, 145
Ephesus, 96
Epistemology, 4, 18, 21, 73, 103
Epstein, J. N., 58, 59, 108, 109, 144
Existentialism, 35, 38, 55, 62, 123

F

Feminine, v, vi, 18, 21, 23, 24, 25, 26, 29, 32, 39, 48, 54, 58, 59, 60, 61, 67, 74, 101, 114, 135, 140
Fertile, iii, 38, 41, 48, 50
Folklore, 27, 72, 97, 99, 100, 102, 143, 147
Fraenkel, J., 6, 7, 101, 144

G

Galilean, 19, 54, 55, 65, 75
Gamliel, R., 31, 34, 59
gas ru'ah, 41, 42, 45

Genealogy, 14, 22, 25, 26, 27, 72, 77, 140
Gentile, 71, 86, 99, 135, 136
Geonim, 3, 5, 6, 7, 8, 37, 58, 67, 72, 73, 74, 76, 96, 101, 102, 103, 108, 143, 144
Gilat, Y. D., 6, 36, 37, 59, 60, 61, 62, 110, 111, 135, 136, 144
Goodblatt, D., 22, 23, 27, 28, 32, 39, 57, 59, 61, 105, 140, 145
Grossman, A., 101, 145

H

Halakhist, 38, 40
Ḥasde David, 58, 59, 141
Haver, 16, 17, 147
Herford, R. T., 133, 134, 135, 136, 137, 145
Hibur Yafe MehaYeshua, 71, 72, 145
Hirschberg, J. W., 96, 99, 100, 103, 145
History, 5, 6, 17, 26, 27, 28, 64, 77, 108, 131, 132, 133, 139, 144, 146, 147, 148
Hoshen, D., 4, 5, 7, 8, 19, 27, 29, 59, 60, 62, 63, 64, 65, 66, 67, 68, 99, 103, 111, 134, 135, 137, 138, 139, 140, 145

I

Ibn Yḥya, G., 146
Idolatry, 15
Ilan, T., 4, 5, 6, 22, 23, 25, 26, 27, 28, 29, 57, 59, 60, 61, 62, 67, 98, 103, 146
Image, 27, 29, 93, 148
Ishmael, R., 41, 49, 62, 65, 117, 145

J

Joshua, R., iv, 32, 35, 59, 62, 78, 81, 90, 91, 92, 93, 94, 109, 139
Judge, 115, 118, 119, 125, 126, 127, 128, 129, 132, 140

K

Kalonymos, J., 72

L

Lacks, R., 27, 146
Late Midrash, 6, 69, 97, 105
Lieberman, S., 17, 58, 59, 61, 65, 110, 121, 133, 134, 135, 136, 137, 138, 139, 146, 148

M

Maimonides, 8, 11, 12, 15, 16, 17, 18, 19, 58, 59, 65, 67, 83, 84, 101, 103, 106, 138, 146, 147
Malter, H., 28, 147
Mamzer, 9, 11, 12, 14, 80
Meir, R., 15, 21, 22, 24, 26, 27, 28, 33, 34, 39, 43, 52, 55, 57, 62, 69, 70, 71, 72, 73, 97, 98, 99, 100, 101, 102, 103, 113, 130, 131, 139, 140, 147, 148
Meiri, 16, 19, 84, 91, 103, 104, 105, 106, 107, 108, 109, 138
Min, 134, 136
Miracles, 134, 145
Moonikandem, Y., 24, 26, 27, 28, 29, 57, 62, 98, 102, 103, 139, 147
Mountain-palm, 41
Multiple, 42

N

Neusner, J., 7, 17, 18, 19, 57, 58, 60, 61, 105, 108, 135, 136, 146, 147
Nisim, R., 71, 72, 99, 100, 103, 108

O

Oppenheimer, A., 17, 27, 147
Otzar ha-Geonim, 7, 146

P

Perry, B. E., 97, 147
Pharisees, 110
Priest, 9, 11, 12, 14, 15, 16, 19, 86, 115, 118, 138
Purity, 14, 16, 17, 23, 31, 35, 36, 37, 144

R

Repentance, iii, 43, 48
Reward, 81, 84

S

Sarah, E., 5, 60, 64, 102, 147
Schwarzbaum, H., 97, 99, 100, 101, 102, 103, 147
Secundus, 97
Sex, iii, iv, 5, 54, 87, 143, 146
Sin, iii, 19, 43, 126, 145
Sinai, 34, 35, 37, 38, 40, 43, 47, 51, 64, 74, 86, 119, 129, 139
Sota, 23, 63, 76, 77, 78, 80, 81, 82, 83, 84, 86, 88, 89, 91, 92, 93, 94, 103, 104, 105, 106, 107, 108, 109, 110, 114, 116, 137, 145
Standardization of the rules, 36
Status, iii, 9, 16, 27, 28, 29, 143, 145, 148

T

Tashma, I. M., 5, 7, 8, 148

Torah study, 10, 11, 12, 14, 16, 26, 41, 53, 66, 78, 80, 82, 83, 84, 85, 86, 87, 91, 92, 105, 106, 121, 123, 135
Tosafot of Evreux, 91, 108, 145

U

Union, iii, 51, 141
Urbach, E. E., 5, 6, 16, 17, 105, 108, 147, 148

W

Wegner, J. R., 22, 24, 25, 27, 29, 148
Weiss Halivni, D., 6, 7, 98, 148
Wisdom, 89

Y

Yehuse Tannaim ve'Amoraim, 57, 58, 61, 100, 142

Z

Zunz, L., 6, 97, 100, 148

www.ingramcontent.com/pod-product-compliance
Lightning Source LLC
Chambersburg PA
CBHW021409290426
44108CB00010B/446